The Future of Big-City Schools

THE NATIONAL SOCIETY
FOR THE STUDY OF EDUCATION

Series on Contemporary Educational Issues
Kenneth J. Rehage, Series Editor

The 1977 Titles

Early Childhood Education: Issues and Insights, Bernard Spodek and
  Herbert J. Walberg, Editors
*The Future of Big-City Schools: Desegregation Policies and Magnet
  Alternatives,* Daniel U. Levine and Robert J. Havighurst, Editors
Educational Administration: The Developing Decades, Luvern L.
  Cunningham, Walter G. Hack, and Raphael O. Nystrand

The National Society for the Study of Education also publishes Year-
books which are distributed by the University of Chicago Press. Inquiries regarding all publications of the Society, as well as inquiries
about membership in the Society, may be addressed to the Secretary-
Treasurer, 5835 Kimbark Avenue, Chicago, IL 60637. Membership
in the Society is open to any who are interested in promoting the investigation and discussion of educational questions.

The Future of Big-City Schools

Desegregation Policies and Magnet Alternatives

Edited by

DANIEL U. LEVINE
University of Missouri, Kansas City

ROBERT J. HAVIGHURST
University of Chicago

McCutchan Publishing Corporation
2526 Grove Street
Berkeley, California 94704

ISBN 0-8211-1113-2
Library of Congress Catalog Card Number 76-62900

Series Foreword

In the spring of 1976, Daniel U. Levine and Robert J. Havighurst presented the committee for the NSSE Series on Contemporary Educational Issues with a proposal to prepare this volume on the future of big-city schools, with special reference to problems of desegregation and to plans for improvements in instruction, including the establishment of magnet programs. They convinced the committee that such a volume would be an extremely relevant document for 1977 and beyond. They were right. Developments in the past year, including the release in February 1977 of the report of the U.S. Commission on Civil Rights, have brought additional attention to the continuing search for effective solutions to one of the most difficult problems confronting our schools, particularly (but by no means exclusively) those in large cities.

In soliciting contributions to this book, Professors Levine and Havighurst sought to bring together materials on the phenomenon of white flight, on the experience of certain large cities with efforts to deal with problems of desegregation, and on alternative programs, magnet schools, and other efforts to improve instructional programs. The editors, both of whom have had extensive experience with schools in cities where the problem of desegregation is especially acute, have brought to their task the broad perspective each has acquired through such work. The result is a collection of papers that provide a rich background of information relating to the problem of ending the racial isolation of children in the nation's schools.

The National Society for the Study of Education is grateful to Professors Levine and Havighurst, and to the several authors who have contributed chapters to this volume, for their efforts in preparing a work we believe will be very useful in the years immediately ahead.

Kenneth J. Rehage

for the Committee on the Expanded
Publication Program of the
National Society for the Study
of Education

Contributors

John Brandstetter, Principal, Houston Independent School District

Connie Campbell, Research Associate, Center for the Study of Metropolitan Problems in Education, University of Missouri-Kansas City

Charles W. Case, Dean, College of Education, University of Wisconsin-Oshkosh

Robert A. Dentler, Dean, School of Education, Boston University

Eugene E. Eubanks, Assistant Dean, School of Education, University of Missouri-Kansas City

Joseph L. Felix, Administrative Research Branch, School Information System, Cincinnati Public Schools Information Center

John A. Finger, Jr., Professor of Education, Center for Evaluation and Research, Rhode Island College

Virginia K. Griffin, Member, Cincinnati Board of Education

Robert J. Havighurst, Professor of Education and Human Development, University of Chicago

Duane Holm, Director, Metropolitan Area Religious Coalition of Cincinnati

James N. Jacobs, Superintendent of Schools, Cincinnati

Daniel U. Levine, Professor of Education, University of Missouri-Kansas City

Jeanie Keeny Meyer, Research Analyst, Kansas City, Missouri, Police Department

Gary Orfield, Associate Professor of Political Science, University of Illinois-Urbana

Marvin B. Scott, Associate Dean, School of Education, Boston University

Donald R. Waldrip, Educational Consultant, Cincinnati, Ohio

Robert G. Wegmann, Associate Professor of Educational Psychology and Director, Human Sciences Program, University of Houston at Clear Lake City

Contents

Introduction
The Desegregation Controversy in Context

Daniel U. Levine and *Robert J. Havighurst*

This book is not meant to be all things to all readers, but it does examine a number of urban education and related issues in greater depth and breadth than has been done in other well-known sources. The issues examined are not only fundamentally important for urban education; there are several that have recently become prominent in considering the future of big cities as well. Desegregation, for instance, has had an effect on the middle-class population of the city at the same time that it has affected school districts in large cities (the so-called "white flight" controversy). The potential and feasibility of establishing specialized schools to improve educational opportunity and maintain integration (the mushrooming "magnet" and "alternative" school movement) becomes an economic concern of major proportions for city governments. Decisions about the types of desegregation policies that are most desirable in working toward integration affect not only the schools but society in general.

Along with the central themes, peripheral issues are explored. Much of the case study material included was selected in an attempt to enhance understanding of the conclusions reached and to determine which policies and practices might be most desirable and constructive in making decisions about big-city schools in the future. Of course, not all issues dealing with topics of this magnitude can be explored fully in a single volume, and the amount of source material that can be presented is also limited by constraints of space and availability. There has, however, been an effort to include sufficient discussion and background material so that readers can draw on the book not just for understanding but also to develop effective policies and plans for urban and metropolitan school systems in cities beyond those discussed here. In order to make this possible, there has been a conscious attempt to include:

—more detail on the nature and role of big-city magnet and alternative schools than is presently available;

—more detail on specific ways in which colleges and universities can systematically assist in the effort to improve big-city schools;

—an intensive analysis of a major national effort, the Reverend Jesse Jackson's program for improving teaching and learning conditions in big-city schools, which is emerging as one of the most prominent attempts in recent years to improve such schools;

—a more comprehensive set of guidelines for moving toward desegregation in big-city schools and neighborhoods than has yet been readily accessible to educators and interested laymen concerned with reversing trends toward racial and socioeconomic isolation in those schools and neighborhoods.

While preparing this volume, we were acutely aware that it is easy to despair concerning the future of big-city schools. This is particularly true with respect to racial desegregation in the schools. Developments over the past few years have made it clear that, unless other paths are found, there is no reasonable hope for achieving or maintaining mixed student populations in many metropolitan school systems. For example, a ruling by the U.S. Sixth Circuit Court of Appeals in August 1976 signified what might well be considered the "end of the road" for contemporary judicial efforts to promote integration in the public schools. The ruling applied to Detroit, where the court ordered the federal district judge for that area to find a way to desegregate three subregions within the Detroit public school system where enrollment is at least 90 percent black.

The ruling of the court of appeals followed the well-known *Bradley* v. *Milliken* decision of 1974, in which the U.S. District Court ruled that Detroit did not have to merge with fifty-three suburban districts in order to bring about desegregation,[1] and a ruling by District Judge

Robert E. DeMascio, which held that some schools in Detroit would have to remain predominantly black in order to achieve a fairly even distribution by race in other schools since the Detroit school district as a whole had become 75 percent black by 1975.[2] In requiring Judge DeMascio to find or devise a desegregation plan for students in the three subregions that were predominantly black, the appeals judges acknowledged that it would be "extremely difficult, if not impossible" to do this:

We recognize . . . that it would be appropriate for us to supply guidelines to the District Judge as to what he should do . . . . Omission of such guidelines is not based on any failure to consider the problem in depth . . . . It is based upon the conviction . . . that *genuine* constitutional desegregation cannot be accomplished within the school district boundaries of the Detroit School District.[3]

Translated into blunter terms, this means that the appeals judges agreed with Judge DeMascio that further desegregation steps within the Detroit Public Schools probably would be counterproductive because they would tend to encourage withdrawal of white students from schools already well balanced racially and because much of the transportation involved in removing students from schools where the enrollment was more than 90 percent black "would be of black students from predominantly black to other predominantly black schools."[4] This action would, nevertheless, be necessary to meet constitutional guarantees of equal educational opportunity set forth in the Fourteenth Amendment as interpreted by the U.S. Supreme Court.

With this reading of the Constitution, desegregation efforts in many big cities have arrived at a very unpretty pass, or, more accurately, impasse. The courts, as well as the federal and state executive branches of government, have been slow to move toward metropolitan approaches to school desegregation, even though it is clear that desegregation plans limited only to central-city school districts frequently work against the goals they are striving to achieve. New approaches to integration thus are required to escape the present bind, which may satisfy the Constitution but does little or nothing to produce meaningful or lasting integration in many big-city school districts.

Among the most promising of the approaches that might help accomplish this objective are, first, regional or metropolitan remedies for school segregation and, second, magnet school programs to bring about voluntary integration by attracting students of differing social and racial backgrounds. The idea of using regional approaches to work out problems that arise when desegregating schools in large cities recurs throughout this book. Regional remedies are being tried in Louisville, Kentucky, and Wilmington, Delaware, and court cases involving regional remedies were pending as of fall 1976 in Indianapolis, Kansas City, and several other metropolitan areas. The situation that now exists with respect to regional approaches is summarized in Chapter 17.

Magnet school approaches, which receive particular emphasis in Part Two, are the basis for desegregation efforts in a number of big cities, including Dallas, Milwaukee, and St. Louis. In each of these cities, magnet schools are the major components in court-ordered plans to bring about desegregation in the public schools beginning in the 1976–77 academic year. Because magnetization is supposed to attract an integrated student body on a voluntary basis, it is less volatile than "forced" busing. For that reason it is likely that many other cities will try magnet schools in their efforts to desegregate.

Should it become apparent within a few years that magnet schools are not achieving their stated goal of providing desegregated educational opportunities for most students in the public schools, however, there will be renewed legal pressure and more involuntary reassignment and transportation of pupils. The degree to which magnet schools achieve the desired goal depends in part on the perspicacity and wisdom with which educators implement them and recognize and resolve the myriad problems that will arise in both the development and implementation phases. That is why the most important of these problems receive attention in several chapters of this book.

But desegregation will not by itself solve the problem of providing adequate opportunity in schools and other social institutions available to disadvantaged citizens in large cities, particularly those who inhabit predominantly low-income neighborhoods in those cities. Such neighborhoods have deteriorated to the point that merely desegregating schools cannot accomplish much in the way of helping inner-city inhabitants make better use of opportunities available in the schools and other institutions.

In most inner-city schools, for example, achievement levels that are a year or more below the national averages by the time students reach the sixth grade are two or more years below the national averages three years later. Even without taking a position on the validity of nationally standardized achievement tests in reading and other basic skills, it is necessary to point out what this achievement pattern means. In effect, one-fourth to one-half or more of the students in inner-city neighborhoods graduate from or leave public schools without the skills needed to obtain or hold the kind of job that would allow a comfortable and productive life as an adult.

Young people in the inner city, like most people in our society, aspire to live comfortably in an era that not too long ago was characterized as the "Age of Affluence." Ability and motivation to succeed in school and society are seriously damaged, however, amid the conditions that exist in the inner city. Evidence of this, if any is needed, can be found in the high schools of New York and other large cities, where attendance rates are frequently down to 75 percent or less, and they are much lower yet with respect to attendance in class. Such phenomena are now built into the social structure of metropolitan areas to such a degree that there is a permanent "underclass" in the inner-city districts of large metropolitan areas. Charlayne Hunter has reported on the "plight" of black teenagers, which substantially reflects the problems faced by lower-status minority youth in large cities as they seek employment:

These black youth are regarded as part of a secondary labor class, with little chance of moving out of the perpetual state of joblessness or of escaping the vicious cycle of low-paying jobs that lack security or chances of advancement . . . . This is the picture that emerged in interviews with economists, labor analysts, manpower experts, community leaders and black teen-agers themselves . . . .

Contrary to the expectations raised by the Great Society programs of the 60's, which aimed to break the cycle of poverty through training, remediation, and job counseling, the cycle proved resistant.

In fact, as the recession lifts slowly for everyone else, the condition of black teenagers and young adults is steadily deteriorating.[5]

No one knows for sure what can be done to resolve the plight of people who live in the inner city or to reverse trends that have been causing large cities to deteriorate, but it is certain that the attainment of any such goals would require a systematic and comprehensive effort to prevent further deterioration and to redevelop large parts of the city. Developments in recent years indicate that deterioration can be reversed and substantial renewal can be accomplished provided that wise policies are worked out and followed with respect to housing, transportation, education, and other urban functions. Paul R. Porter, who administered the Marshall Plan for the redevelopment of Europe after World War II, recently discussed prospects for the "recovery" of cities in the United States:

> Growth of the metropolis through newcomers has been slowed and will not be resumed on a large scale . . . the inner city, the most vulnerable part of the metropolis, loses population; housing which only the poor will occupy is abandoned; and large residential districts, along with failing industrial districts, slip into ever deeper decay.
>
> What a superb opportunity for cities! . . . To redevelop this land is, of course, an old dream, and during four decades of a federal housing policy fragmentary urban renewal has taken place. But as long as low-income housing was in acute short supply, and as long as there was a strong stream of migration from the countryside, renewal policy (with some exceptions) has been to preserve this land for low-income residents.
>
> The policy, like most buildings on the land, is obsolete. The proper goal should be to transform the decaying districts into new neighborhoods attractive enough to *compete with suburbs* as a place of residence for people who work in the central business district.[6]

Porter proceeds to discuss government finance, land-use planning, housing, transportation, and other urban functions, and to recommend policies that he believes would stimulate successful renewals of large cities in the United States. In addition to making inner-city neighborhoods sufficiently attractive to compete with the suburbs for middle-income population, Porter urges a complementary policy of assisting at least some of the poor living in the inner city "to obtain suitable housing and nearby work opportunities outside large cities";[7] only thus can the central city maintain social and physical solvency within a larger metropolitan area where no government is permanently saddled with a disproportionate share of the problems associated with social and physical disorganization and deterioration.

It would seem that this is an accurate assessment of the underlying problems existing in many cities and metropolitan areas, and of the basic policies that would ultimately lead to the "recovery" of American cities. Certainly central cities cannot function well if they continue to become depositories for large concentrations of poor people. They must retain or attract a substantial middle-income population. The final chapter of this book, in the context of this goal, argues that the central city as a whole must become socioeconomically "mixed" or "balanced." It is because racial integration in schools and neighborhoods appears closely related to socioeconomic integration that the materials selected for this book bear on both goals.

Participants in urban policy making, ranging from government officials to civic leaders to social scientists, stress the need to maintain middle-income population in the central city, and attractive public schools are a key consideration in meeting the need. The Mayor of Kansas City, Missouri, for example, claimed that improvement in the central city school district is the single most critical element in ensuring the future viability of the city,[8] a claim he has backed by working successfully to raise the city sales tax in order to improve funding for the schools. Paul Porter agrees that "probably . . . [no goal] is more important than that the city's schools should be of as high quality as suburban schools"[9] to make the central city competitive with the suburbs, thereby fostering renewal, but he offers virtually no concrete suggestions that would help the public schools fill their key role. In justice to Porter, it must be stated that most major books and articles dealing with the future of large cities are similarly vague regarding school policies. Chapters or sections devoted to an analysis of the public schools typically conclude with such general statements as: "Finance formulas should be changed to provide more funds for central city schools." "Public schools in big cities should be racially integrated." "Improvements should be made in the quality of instruction in inner-city schools." Even in cases where authors provide extensive, concrete recommendations on housing, transportation, and other urban problems, those on education remain noticeably vague.

We do not pretend to have all the answers to all of the problems involving desegregation and instructional improvement in big-city schools, but we have attempted to be as specific as possible in dealing with the problems in the context of larger issues involving the future of large cities and metropolitan areas. The selection of materials in the book has been governed not only by our belief that these materials should provide concrete knowledge of the major issues involving desegregation of big-city schools but also by the conviction that they should enhance understanding of the larger issues in which desegregation is embedded. It is in this sense that we have tried to make a contribution to what we hope will become a serious national discussion of the policies that should be followed in desegregating big-city schools and in otherwise working to make public education a constructive component in efforts to maintain the viability of big cities in the United States.

Notes

1. *Bradley et al.* v. *Milliken et al.*, 94 S. Ct. 1069 (1974).

2. *Bradley et al.* v. *Milliken et al.*, Civil No. 35257 (August 15, 1975).

3. Quoted in Rick Van Sant, "Detroit Ordered to Do More Desegregating," *Cleveland Press*, August 7, 1976, B 2.

4. *Ibid.*

5. Charlayne Hunter, "Black Teen-agers' Jobless Rate Constant Despite U.S. Recovery," *New York Times*, July 11, 1976, 1, 43.

6. Paul R. Porter, *The Recovery of American Cities* (New York: Two Continents, 1976), 14.

7. *Ibid.*, 173.

8. Personal interview, September 27, 1976.

9. Porter, *Recovery of American Cities*, 183.

PART ONE
The "White Flight" Controversy and Its Implications for Big-City Schools

Robert G. Wegmann, in the opening chapter of this volume, presents a systematic review and analysis of a large body of literature on desegregation and resegregation in urban schools and neighborhoods. He also reports on original research contributing to the national debate on the "white flight" issue. Wegmann concludes that white withdrawal and that of the middle class, both connected with desegregated conditions in big-city school districts, are important phenomena that should be considered in planning for the future. He also sets forth a list of tentative conclusions and recommendations for achieving stable and constructive integration in big-city schools and neighborhoods. His analysis and conclusions provide important background material in formulating the policies and recommendations set forth in the final chapter of this book.

In Chapter 2, by Daniel U. Levine and Jeanie Keeny Meyer, there is a summary and assessment of some of the most important materials and arguments dealing with the alleged "flight" of whites from desegregation in public schools. After noting that the issue has been largely settled at least temporarily with acknowledgment that withdrawal poses a threat in big-city districts that have a high percentage of low-status minority students and are surrounded by largely white, middle-status suburbs, the chapter presents original research indicating that such withdrawal has indeed occurred in a large midwestern school district selected for intensive case study.

The final chapter in this part, by Gary Orfield, provides background material dealing with the "white flight" issue in the context of metropolitan development, with particular emphasis on interrelationships between desegregation policies in education and housing. After identifying issues on which further research is most needed and examining the implications of trends in racial migration to suburban areas, Orfield concludes that the desegregation process "works better when it incorporates the racial and economic diversity of the metropolitan area and maintains substantial white majorities in desegregated schools." This theme is echoed in several later chapters where examination of big-city school desegregation problems from differing angles leads to similar conclusions regarding the desirability of working toward desegregation on a metropolitan-wide basis.

1. Desegregation and Resegregation: A Review of the Research on White Flight from Urban Areas

Robert G. Wegmann

A recent summary of research on school desegregation prepared by the National Institute of Education for the Ford administration shows that the flight of whites from American cities is different from city to city, and no one knows which governmental policies might influence or control this phenomenon.[1] Various authors have noted that the social sciences seem to offer little in the way of understanding (or controlling) the problem of resegregation, and there has been no systematic national effort to study the impact of school desegregation over a period of years.[2] In the furor over some recent statements made by James S. Coleman, little attention has been paid to one of the major points of his initial paper, namely, that the federal government has failed to attempt any serious analysis of the massive data that it routinely collects on school racial proportions.[3]

Such an analysis would be a very demanding task. The recent debate between Coleman and his critics has made clear the fact that desegregated schools exist within a multitude of contexts, and each of these contexts influences what does or does not happen in the school.[4] There is an ongoing process of suburbanization, which surely would have occurred even if there were no racial minorities but which disproportionately involves the white population. There has been a ma-

jor downturn in the white birth rate that is now causing, in most
school districts, a loss of white enrollment quite unconnected with desegregation. Longitudinal studies are complicated by the fact that
school attendance areas and school district boundaries change over
time, and comparisons with city census data can be difficult because
many school systems have boundaries that are not coterminus with city
boundaries. Further, there are minority groups other than blacks in
most school systems. Some authors add these other minority students
to the white population when analyzing white flight;[5] others do not.[6]
It is important, therefore, to stress that Reynolds Farley and Alma
Taeuber are quite right when they state that the available data are
poor and the methodology weak in the study of white withdrawal from
desegregated schooling.[7]

The purpose of this chapter is to review research that has been done
on white flight, or, more accurately, on school resegregation — the
phenomenon of white withdrawal (total or partial) from desegregated
public schools. It is important to point out that different researchers
have approached this phenomenon in quite different ways with some
studies stressing factors that are totally ignored in others. The gaps
and inconsistencies in the data thus far available are such that there is
considerable uncertainty not only about the factors contributing to resegregation, but also about the ways in which these factors interact. It
is quite possible that this summary omits or misinterprets major factors, or that further investigation will show some of these factors to be
unimportant.

WITHDRAWAL FROM DESEGREGATED SCHOOLS

Two Initial Distinctions

One of the first things that becomes apparent in the study of school
resegregation is the degree to which issues of race and class are consistently confounded. Blacks and most other minority groups are, of
course, disproportionately poor, and the poor do not do well in school.
Schools where the poor are concentrated are no more attractive to minority parents (especially middle-class minority parents) than they are
to white parents. Gary Orfield notes that some ten thousand black
students in Washington, D.C., are in private schools,[8] and Dennis
Lord reports that the schools of Richmond, Virginia, are now experiencing "black flight" as they become increasingly black and poor and

unattractive to the black middle class.[9] This same phenomenon was noted by Thomas Pettigrew in testimony before the Select Committee on Equal Educational Opportunity of the U.S. Senate.[10] What is often called white flight is actually a class as well as a racial phenomenon.

It is also useful to distinguish between withdrawal and nonentrance. The phrase "white flight" tends to suggest that white students were attending a school, the school was integrated, and then white students found this undesirable and left. Reported drops in white attendance during the "first year" of school desegregation really refer to students who never showed up at all. They did not experience desegregation and find it undesirable; rather, they declined to try the experience in the first place. Some of this decline in white enrollment may consist of students who formerly attended a given school, but chose not to return. Part may also consist of students who, in the absence of school integration, would have moved into a neighborhood, but, because of integration, decided not to make the move.

Studies of racially changing neighborhoods show that, even when there is no abnormal rate of white departure, white entrance into such neighborhoods can, and often does, drop sharply,[11] and such nonentrance can consist disproportionately of families with school-age children. Moving because of dissatisfaction with the schools can be difficult and expensive. It is easier, if one is looking for a house and hears that a desegregation decision is pending or that there are problems at the neighborhood school, to choose a different neighborhood or school district in which to purchase a home.

In addition to nonentrance into the neighborhood served by a particular set of schools (elementary and secondary), there is also the issue of nonentrance into a particular school. Schools are especially susceptible to nonentrance, not only in the sense that there are private and parochial alternatives, but also because of the transitional moves from elementary school to junior high and from junior high to senior high (each school often serving a wider attendance area and having a different reputation and racial composition). As a result, parents and students are repeatedly presented with the necessity of deciding whether or not to enter.

Thus, when one reads Orfield's report that the school system of Inglewood, California, went from about 25 percent black the year before court-ordered integration was put into effect to 35 percent the following September,[12] it is not necessary to assume that all of this loss was caused by white families who either left town or sought other schooling. Some of the loss may well have been due to white families *not* moving in on hearing of impending integration, and thus failing to replace families who, in the normal course of events, would have moved anyway. Some of what seems at first glance to be "anticipatory flight" may, in fact, be "anticipatory nonentrance." Indeed, one of the problems with allowing desegregation suits to drag on unresolved for years is precisely this: over those years the normal proportion of white families may leave the city and an abnormal proportion of white families with children may elect not to move in because they are uncertain whether a desegregation order is coming, as well as anxious about what that would mean. This could be no small factor over time in a population as mobile as that of the United States. According to recent data from the U.S. Bureau of the Census, 38.7 percent of white metropolitan residents were living in a different house in 1974 than the one in which they lived in 1970.[13]

Quality, Safety, and Status

Surprisingly, there seems to be little research available on the motives that lead parents to withdraw their children from desegregated schools. Such discussions as are found center on three areas: parental perceptions of school quality, parental perceptions of student safety in the desegregated school, and parental concerns about social status. In view of the limited data, however, any conclusions about the relative importance of these concerns (or about their actual impact on the decision to withdraw from a desegregated school) must remain tentative.

Neil Sullivan, the superintendent who presided over the desegregation of the Berkeley, California, public schools, describes the main fears of white parents when school desegregation is proposed as fear for their children's safety and fear that educational quality will suffer.[14] Such fears may be exacerbated when students are assigned to schools located in inner-city areas; Lord cites some very high rates of decline in student enrollment under such circumstances.[15]

Concerns about educational quality seem widespread. Orfield cites a national poll showing that a fourth of the public believes that the test scores of white students decline sharply in desegregated schools.[16] Although it is generally *not* the case that such declines in white achievement actually occur, the quality of research in this area leaves much to be desired.[17] Traditional reporting practices in school districts can cause problems. If, for example, lower-achieving minority students from an inner-city area of a major city are mixed with higher-achieving white students from an affluent area, the mean test scores of the formerly high-status school can be expected to go down, even though the more affluent students are doing as well as always and the minority students are doing better than before. Depending on how data are released to the public, quite different impressions can be created.[18]

Many characteristics of inner-city life do militate against success in the bookish atmosphere of the school. Frank Petroni, Ernest Hirsch, and Lillian Petroni describe minority students taking their schoolwork seriously in the face of criticism by fellow students who see preparing for college as "white" behavior.[19] Bioloine Young and Grace Bress cite a *Wall Street Journal* interview indicating that pressure not to study is placed on some minority students by their peers.[20] It would be easy to point out that some white students apply similar pressure on their peers, but it is not that simple. In a 1968 study based on a random sample of 2,625 Baltimore students in grades three to twelve, selected from twenty-six schools, Morris Rosenberg and Roberta Simmons found that school grades seemed to have little impact on the self-esteem of black children, especially those doing poorly in school.[21] Life in the inner-city ghetto generates attitudes, values, and behaviors quite different from those found in more affluent areas. Parents (especially middle-class parents, white or black), who fear these attitudes and have the means to flee them are often inclined to do so lest their children be influenced by them.

The probability that white withdrawal from desegregated schools, when it occurs, need not be attributed to racism per se is strengthened by the fact that the literature shows many white parents voluntarily participating in school integration programs when they were convinced that their children were safe and that the educational quality of the schools was good. In many large cities parochial schools are located in older areas of town, and, although they have a significant minority representation in their student bodies, white, middle-class parents voluntarily pay tuition, and students travel from suburban, outer-city areas to attend them. In Boston, despite the furor over school desegregation, the Trotter School, which is a part of the city's public school system, has operated since the fall of 1969 with an equal ratio of black and white students.[22] The school has a new, expensive plant with modified open classroom instruction, learning centers, and other educational advantages not ordinarily available, and white students are easily recruited. According to press reports, the town of Richardson, a suburb of Dallas, Texas, avoided a court order to desegregate by attracting a sufficient number of whites to a previously all-black school. There is a pupil-teacher ratio of sixteen to one; 80 percent of the faculty have master's degrees; and the extensive curriculum includes arts and crafts, foreign languages, drama, music, gymnastics, and astronomy. More white students applied than could be accommodated. Although open enrollment is usually considered an ineffective tool for large-scale integration, John McAdams has surveyed an impressive list of schools that successfully convinced students to transfer voluntarily when the quality of integrated education was clearly high.[23]

Parental perception of student safety may also be involved in decisions to reject desegregated schooling. Leslie Bobbitt describes the differing perceptions that black and white students bring to the desegregated school.[24] There are often different behavior patterns and ways of handling conflict and hostility. Rumors may fly as latent parental fears are triggered by incidents that would otherwise be ignored. In some cases, of course, inner-city schools in major cities are *not* safe, and physical attacks, shakedowns, and threats do occur. Gretchen Schafft describes the fear of going to the bathroom held by white students in one predominantly black elementary school, and the degree to which white students avoided out-of-school activities.[25] What really seems to be involved in some of these situations is the fact that, although they are desegregated, these schools are not truly integrated. Although black and white students are physically present in the same school, the degree of friendship, understanding, and community is quite low.

Finally, just as some individuals do not wish to live in a neighborhood with members of a group whose social status they view as being beneath their own,[26] some parents who do not have specific concerns about educational quality or safety, as such, may still object to having their children attend school with students from a lower social class. As Micheal Giles, Douglas Gatlin, and Everett Cataldo point out,[27] desegregation often results in not only an influx of black children into the white child's environment, but also an influx of lower-class chil-

dren into a middle-class environment. Among parents with a high income and education, these authors found class prejudice (as opposed
to racial prejudice) significantly related to protest behavior, such as
attending school board meetings, writing letters, or phoning the
school board to protest school desegregation. Another excellent description of how different social classes react to desegregation proposals is provided in Lillian Rubin's account of the polarization of the
Richmond, California, Unified School District.[28] These reactions illustrate again how the whole issue of school resegregation is as much a
matter of class conflict as of racial conflict.

Parental concerns about educational quality, safety, and status may
be present no matter how the desegregated situation comes about.
There is evidence to suggest, however, that the likelihood of a school
resegregating, and the process by which this may occur, will differ
considerably depending on whether the racial balance in the school reflects the neighborhood served by the school or whether some level of
government has intervened to bring about school desegregation quite
apart from the situation in the surrounding neighborhood.

NEIGHBORHOODS AND SCHOOLS IN RACIAL TRANSITION

School desegregation situations may be divided into two broad
classes: those that occur without government intervention and reflect
neighborhood integration in the attendance district served by the
school; and those that occur because either the courts, the local school
board, or the executive branch of the state or federal government has
intervened to desegregate previously segregated schools. It is impossible to study the first type of desegregated (and often resegregating)
schools without also studying the process of racial change within the
school attendance area. To do otherwise would be to study them in a
demographic vacuum, a charge recently leveled against Coleman.[29]

Atlanta, for example, has been judicially cited as having so much
white flight from its public school system that further attempts at integration would be futile.[30] The school system, which originally had a
majority of white students, had changed by 1970 to a majority (69 percent) of black students. The minority population of the city as a
whole, however, was also changing from 38 percent minority in 1960
to 52 percent minority in 1970.[31] Therefore the change in the racial
makeup of Atlanta's schools took place within the context of a general

change in the racial makeup of the entire city. Atlanta, for example, now has a black mayor. Indeed, all of Coleman's findings, as initially presented,[32] must be considered to have occurred within the context of the changing neighborhoods of large central cities. A check by the *New York Times* revealed that there was no court-ordered busing or redistricting in any of the nineteen cities Coleman studied.[33]

This is not to suggest, however, that these changes are not of great significance. According to the U.S. Commission on Civil Rights, enrollment in the hundred largest school districts, which have half of the nation's black pupils, dropped by 280,000 students between 1970 and 1972.[34] Since there was a gain of 146,000 black students during this same period, the data suggest a very considerable loss of white students. Although some of this loss can be attributed to a drop in the white birth rate and other factors, it is clear that a larger proportion of white families with children than of white families without children are likely to live in suburban areas. According to the Bureau of Census, 60.1 percent of the white population of metropolitan areas that is eighteen years of age or over lived in the suburbs in 1974, while 66.6 percent of school-age whites five to seventeen years old were to be found in the suburbs.[35] Again, this need not be totally attributed to problems with schools; suburbanization would no doubt have occurred even if there were no racial minorities in the United States,[36] and suburbs would no doubt have attracted families with school-age children under any conditions. The data suggest, however, that schools are involved.[37]

The most obvious fact about the neighborhood context of school racial proportions is the high degree of residential segregation that characterizes every city in the United States.[38] There are few stable interracial neighborhoods in American cities, and those are generally found only when the black population of the city as a whole is stable (which, owing to natural increase and in-migration, has *not* generally been typical of American cities).[39] Some segregation is due, of course, to differences in income level. Albert Hermalin and Reynolds Farley, however, present rather convincing arguments that economic factors do not account for much of the concentration of blacks in the central city.[40] According to the Census Bureau,[41] blacks constituted only 5 percent of suburban populations in both 1970 and 1974, despite the fact that a majority of metropolitan residents now live in suburbs rather than in the central city. A more reasonable explanation may lie in the division of central cities into black and white housing markets, as Harvey Molotch suggests.[42] This seems to be a structure that is not easily avoided. In a critical review of evidence presented to the court in the Detroit school desegregaton case, Eleanor Wolf cites moving testimony by several black real estate brokers who spoke of the rebuffs, subterfuge, and humiliation they endured in attempting to secure listings in white areas.[43]

Thus, while it is important to understand how the process of school and neighborhood resegregation proceeds, it is necessary to point out one inescapable fact: given constant density, a growing minority population that stays within the central city combined with a white population free to move out of the central city will inevitably produce an increasing number of segregated neighborhoods and segregated schools.[44] As Arthur Stinchcombe, Mary McDill, and Dollie Walker note from studying this phenomenon in Baltimore, the city simply runs out of whites with whom blacks can integrate.[45]

It is on the fringes of the black ghetto that interracial neighborhoods are commonly found.[46] What is striking as one reviews studies of the process of racial transition in these areas is the degree to which white *nonentrance* is much more involved than white flight as such. This is not to deny that some individuals do move from racially changing neighborhoods specifically to avoid an interracial setting. The fundamental pattern, however, seems to be one of blacks moving short distances into racially mixed neighborhoods where whites fail to compete with them for the available housing. In a study of Milwaukee, Harold Rose found that only 4 percent of a sample of Negroes who moved selected new homes more than ten blocks beyond the original ghetto neighborhood.[47] At the same time he found that, when the neighborhood exceeded 30 percent Negro occupancy, the number of new white purchasers of housing fell off sharply. He also cited other data indicating this as a common pattern: neighborhood change, he argued, is less a matter of invasion than of retreat. In a review of the literature on ecological succession, Howard Aldrich also reported no particular rise in the rate of residential mobility in changing neighborhoods.[48] What is important is that no rise is necessary to cause rapid racial transition. Normal mobility, as has been noted, makes a great deal of housing available throughout the metropolitan area. So long as blacks seek to occupy housing on the fringes of the ghetto while whites avoid it, racial change is inevitable. Chester Rapkin and William Grigsby, who studied the Philadelphia area, found this sharp drop in white demand, as did Molotch, who studied the South Shore area of Chicago.[49] Indeed, Molotch found many landlords who did not want black occupants, but there was no other choice because whites were not interested. Such neighborhoods then go through a transition from a white to a black housing market.

Anticipation of Future Racial Change

One key factor in considering the reluctance of whites to purchase homes in racially mixed neighborhoods is the degree to which present racial proportions are projected into the future by potential entrants. It may or may not be significant to discuss the racial balance at which both whites and blacks feel there is "enough" integration,[50] but what is really crucial to most home buyers (and parents enrolling their children in school) is their view of what is likely to happen in the future. The purchase of a home, once again, is a significant commitment. Most parents prefer to leave their children in the same school for a period of years. In any major city with a large minority population, where area after area and school after school has "turned," there is an obvious tendency to assume that a school or area with any degree of minority population will be "next to go," especially if the area is physically close to the ghetto. Wolf reports such a reaction in the Russel Woods area of Detroit after only one or two black families moved in.[51] The white demand for housing dropped markedly. In some situations a drop in white enrollment that occurs before school desegregation actually begins may be caused by the belief that the schools will soon be largely black. Surely the striking white loss in the Inglewood, California, school system has some relation to Inglewood's location. It borders on the Los Angeles ghetto, and there was significant black movement into Inglewood well before court-ordered desegregation began.[52]

In areas where black and white residents are working to maintain an interracial neighborhood, their most difficult struggle is often to attract new white residents.[53] The frequent temptation is to work on more easily obtainable goals, such as increased city services and other neighborhood improvements. As Molotch suggests, however, this can be self-defeating since such actions make the area that much more attractive to prospective black entrants but often fail to alleviate the fears of potential white entrants.[54] Despite years of intense effort, Molotch found that such activities made little impact on the degree of racial change experienced in the South Shore area of Chicago.

The School and Neighborhood Change

The research on just what role schools play in the process of neighborhood change is sketchy but suggestive. A study made in Milwaukee shows that in interracial neighborhoods the proportion of black students in the school is consistently higher than the proportion of black residents in the neighborhood served by the school.[55] And schools, like double beds, enforce a certain intimacy. One can ignore a neighbor down the street;[56] it is harder to ignore someone sitting next to you in the classroom. The school, moreover, is a social institution that serves as the central focal point for much community interaction, just as social relationships formed in school are carried back to the neighborhood.[57]

Parents, students, and schools may or may not be ready for such interaction. To the extent that the school is unprepared and fearful of racial change, it can become a focus of discontent. And the schools are, indeed, often unprepared for, and fearful of, racial change. A study of riots and disruptions in public schools indicates that such disruptions are most likely to occur in a school where the minority population is from 6 percent to 25 percent of the total enrollment and the faculty is not integrated — precisely the situation found in most urban schools as the neighborhoods they serve begin the process of racial transition.[58]

Because of these problems, most studies of changing neighborhoods emphasize that parents with children they intend to enroll in public schools are particularly reluctant to purchase a home in such neighborhoods. Eleanor Wolf and Charles Lebeaux note that the typical middle-class neighborhood undergoing racial change will retain users of parochial schools and older people without children, but not those intending to use the public schools.[59] When Washington, D.C., desegregated its schools, real estate brokers were constantly telephoning the school board to find out which school would serve a given neighborhood.[60] In a study of Baltimore and Atlanta, Charles Clotfelter found that school desegregation led to a decrease in white fami-

lies living in racially mixed neighborhoods. He estimated a loss of
from 2 to 3 percent of whites under fourteen in such areas for every
decrease of 10 percent in the proportion of white students within the
neighborhood school.[61] Chester Rapkin and William Grigsby found
that white purchasers in racially mixed areas in Philadelphia were
disproportionately Catholic, that there were numerous parochial
schools in the area, and that few blacks were Catholic.[62] It seems reasonable to conclude, at least tentatively, that the reluctance of whites
to purchase homes in racially mixed neighborhoods is increased by the
presence of desegregated schools with which potential entrants may
have had no previous experience (and which they may expect will resegregate). Such behavior, of course, acts as a self-fulfilling prophecy.

A number of researchers have noted that the presence of rental
units tends to retard racial transition.[63] For one thing, many rental
units will not admit families with children.[64] Because such policies
keep black (and white) children out of the public schools in these
areas, and bring in whites who are neither affected by what is happening in the schools nor called upon to make the degree of commitment
involved in buying a house, they retard neighborhood racial transition. Clotfelter's study of Atlanta indicated that mere proximity to a
black neighborhood lowered housing prices, but increased the amount
of rent charged tenants.[65] He also found that housing prices fell in
tracts where high schools experience greater desegregation. Thus,
school and neighborhood have a reciprocal relationship, with the
school seemingly more sensitive to racial transition.[66] To consider
what is happening to the racial makeup of the urban school, outside
the context of the racial makeup of its attendance area and the changing racial proportions of the entire school district, is to risk serious
misunderstanding.

It is in this framework that any consideration of the "tipping point"
controversy might most profitably take place. Various authors, including myself, have referred to a point where white departures accelerate or at least become irreversible, leading shortly to a
neighborhood or school becoming all black.[67] Wolf has pointed out
that this concept was accepted without challenge in the Detroit
desegregation case, and references to it can be found in other court
cases.[68] As we shall see, however, while there are occasional surges of
white departure in individual schools in changing neighborhoods, the

more general phenomenon seems to be a relatively constant pattern of black entrance combined with white departure or nonentrance.[69] Schools do not "tip" by themselves. They resegregate because there is a growing black population being steered by a dual housing market to transitional neighborhoods that white buyers are avoiding because they anticipate that the neighborhoods and the schools that serve them will shortly be resegregating. The schools that are desegregated outside the context of the changing neighborhood are, however, an entirely different case, with their own dynamics. These will be explored later in this chapter. Thus it now seems to me that "tipping" is not a particularly useful concept to use in describing the changing racial proportions of schools, whether or not they are neighborhood schools, because it ignores the contexts within which resegregation takes place and tends to imply that there is no such thing as stable integration — which is not true.

How the process of racial transition proceeds in individual schools located in changing neighborhoods can be seen in Table 1-1, which shows the effect on enrollment in eighteen Milwaukee elementary schools. Each of the schools either (a) had between 20 and 80 percent minority enrollment in the fall of 1969 or, (b) although below 20 percent minority enrollment in 1969, had reached at least 30 percent minority enrollment by the fall of 1975 and was predominantly black in its minority composition. The latter requirement led to the omission of four schools that were predominantly Hispanic.[70] The table is arranged so that year-to-year changes in minority and white (other) enrollment are shown for each year, as well as the year-to-year change in total enrollment. Enrollments affected by boundary or grade-level changes are also noted.

An examination of the pattern of change in these eighteen elementary schools reveals occasional surges of white outflow.[71] The overall pattern, however, is one of relatively steady, seemingly inexorable change. Throughout these years, while the white enrollment of the Milwaukee public school system was declining, the black enrollment was growing.[72] Since the system was in no way intervening to bring racial stability to these or any other schools, it was these schools, located generally around the outer edges of the black ghetto, into which the growing black population moved and from which the shrinking white population withdrew.[73]

Table 1-1

Enrollment in eighteen Milwaukee public elementary schools undergoing racial transition, 1968–1975

Clarke St.[a]

Year	Minority No.	%	Change	White No.	%	Change	Total No.	Change
1968	409	52	--	385	48	--	794	--
1969	571	64	162	318	36	-67	889	95
1970	528	71	-43	213	29	-105	741	-148
1971	546	83	18	112	17	-101	658	83
1972	886	87	340	130	13	18	1,016	358
1973	871	93	-15	69	7	-61	940	-76
1974	901	95	30	51	5	-18	952	12
1975	896	96	-5	40	4	-11	936	-16

Clemens

Year	Minority No.	%	Change	White No.	%	Change	Total No.	Change
1968	39	15	--	216	85	--	255	--
1969	41	17	2	200	83	-16	241	-14
1970	32	14	-9	189	86	-11	221	-20
1971	64	30	32	148	70	-41	212	-9
1972	77	36	13	139	64	-9	216	4
1973	122	51	45	116	49	-23	238	22
1974	140	59	18	96	41	-20	236	-2
1975	143	62	3	89	38	-7	232	-4

Congress

Year	Minority No.	%	Change	White No.	%	Change	Total No.	Change
1968	50	8	--	609	92	--	659	--
1969	58	9	8	561	91	-48	619	-40
1970	65	11	7	530	89	-31	595	-24
1971	73	13	8	511	88	-19	584	-11
1972	89	16	16	451	84	-60	540	-44
1973	108	21	19	405	79	-46	513	-27
1974	128	26	20	363	74	-42	491	-22
1975	154	31	26	344	69	-19	498	7

Elm

Year	Minority No.	%	Change	White No.	%	Change	Total No.	Change
1968	369	58	--	262	42	--	631	--
1969	404	71	35	163	29	-99	567	-64
1970	460	71	56	192	29	29	652	85
1971	487	78	27	136	22	-56	623	-29
1972	494	87	7	74	13	-62	568	-55
1973	488	87	-6	76	13	2	564	-4
1974	457	90	-31	50	10	-26	507	-57
1975	443	91	-14	45	9	-5	488	-19

Fratney

Year	Minority No.	%	Change	White No.	%	Change	Total No.	Change
1968	31	6	--	524	94	--	555	--
1969	59	10	28	512	90	-12	571	16
1970	85	15	26	468	85	-44	553	-18
1971	131	24	46	413	76	-55	544	-9
1972	166	32	35	356	68	-57	522	-22
1973	212	38	46	340	62	-16	552	30
1974	287	53	75	256	47	-84	543	-9
1975	240	52	-47	221	48	-35	461	-82

Garden Homes

Year	Minority No.	%	Change	White No.	%	Change	Total No.	Change
1968	405	64	--	229	36	--	634	--
1969	492	78	87	136	22	-93	628	-6
1970	669	85	177	119	15	-17	788	160
1971	634	87	-35	91	13	-28	725	-63
1972	674	95	40	37	5	-54	711	-14
1973	753	98	79	18	2	-19	771	60
1974	767	99	14	9	1	-9	776	5
1975	742	99	-25	8	1	-1	750	-26

Table 1-1 (continued)

Year	Kilbourn Minority No.	%	Change	White No.	%	Change	Total No.	Change	MacDowell Minority No.	%	Change	White No.	%	Change	Total No.	Change	Pierce Minority No.	%	Change	White No.	%	Change	Total No.	Change
1968	158	20	--	649	80	--	807	--	448	75	--	152	25	--	600	--	335	39	--	519	61	--	854	--
1969	144	19	-14	609	81	-40	753	-54	432	70	-16	188	30	36	620	20	387	44	52	495	56	-24	882	28
1970	158	22	14	546	78	-63	704	-49	463	71	31	192	29	4	655	35	402	47	15	454	53	-41	856	-26
1971	146	22	-12	504	78	-42	650	-54	629	78	166	173	22	-19	802	147	460	54	58	396	46	-58	856	0
1972	137	26	-9	399	74	-105	536	-114	612	81	-17	145	19	-28	757	-45	488	58	28	349	42	-47	837	-19
1973	169	33	32	349	67	-50	518	-18	573	85	-39	101	15	-44	674	-83	590	81	102	138	19	-211	728	-109
1974	213	43	44	287	57	-62	500	-18	638	88	65	88	12	-13	726	52	542	75	-48	183	25	45	725	-3
1975	208	45	-5	251	55	-36	459	-41	602	90	-36	69	10	-19	671	-55	479	75	-63	162	25	-21	641	-84

Year	Silver Spring [b] Minority No.	%	Change	White No.	%	Change	Total No.	Change	Story Minority No.	%	Change	White No.	%	Change	Total No.	Change	38th Street Minority No.	%	Change	White No.	%	Change	Total No.	Change
1968	22	8	--	246	92	--	268	--	125	20	--	516	80	--	641	--	34	4	--	831	96	--	865	--
1969	40	14	18	242	86	-4	282	14	122	19	-3	529	81	13	651	10	72	8	38	810	92	-21	882	17
1970	47	16	7	253	84	11	300	18	117	18	-5	517	82	-12	634	-17	87	10	15	814	90	4	901	19
1971	75	23	28	258	77	5	333	33	135	22	18	486	78	-31	621	-13	123	14	36	786	86	-28	909	8
1972	207	44	132	260	56	2	467	134	161	27	26	438	73	-48	599	-22	193	23	70	646	77	-140	839	-70
1973	255	56	48	197	44	-63	452	-15	182	32	21	388	68	-50	570	-29	306	38	113	503	62	-143	809	-30
1974	291	63	36	174	37	-23	465	13	201	36	19	350	64	-38	551	-19	430	54	124	361	46	-142	791	-18
1975	278	68	-13	132	32	-42	410	-55	190	41	-11	270	59	-80	460	-91	546	66	116	282	34	-79	828	37

Table 1-1 (continued)

35th Street / 31st Street / Townsend b

| | 35th Street | | | | | | | | 31st Street | | | | | | | | Townsend b | | | | | | | |
| | Minority | | | White | | | Total | | Minority | | | White | | | Total | | Minority | | | White | | | Total | |
Year	No.	%	Change	No.	%	Change	No.	Change	No.	%	Change	No.	%	Change	No.	Change	No.	%	Change	No.	%	Change	No.	Change
1968	32	7	--	400	93	--	432	--	121	14	--	733	86	--	854	--	74	12	--	549	88	--	623	--
1969	31	8	-1	369	92	-31	400	-32	184	22	63	643	78	-90	827	-27	82	13	9	558	87	9	640	17
1970	34	8	3	393	92	24	427	27	174	24	-10	547	76	-96	721	-106	111	18	29	498	82	-60	609	-31
1971	46	12	12	345	88	-48	391	-36	241	34	67	467	66	-80	708	-13	189	30	78	441	70	-57	630	21
1972	72	20	26	296	80	-49	368	-23	283	43	42	375	57	-92	658	-50	231	44	42	294	56	-147	525	-105
1973	118	30	46	271	70	-25	389	21	359	56	76	278	44	-97	637	-21	310	59	79	214	41	-80	524	-1
1974	135	36	17	242	64	-29	377	-12	427	66	68	220	34	-58	647	10	353	69	43	159	31	-55	512	-12
1975	128	37	-7	219	63	-23	347	-30	413	70	-14	176	30	-44	589	-58	391	76	38	122	24	-37	513	1

24th Street / 27th Street / Wisconsin

| | 24th Street | | | | | | | | 27th Street | | | | | | | | Wisconsin | | | | | | | |
| | Minority | | | White | | | Total | | Minority | | | White | | | Total | | Minority | | | White | | | Total | |
Year	No.	%	Change	No.	%	Change	No.	Change	No.	%	Change	No.	%	Change	No.	Change	No.	%	Change	No.	%	Change	No.	Change
1968	46	8	--	557	92	--	603	--	279	32	--	581	68	--	860	--	236	33	--	482	67	--	718	--
1969	78	12	32	563	88	6	641	38	300	38	21	500	63	-81	800	-60	213	33	-23	437	67	-45	650	-68
1970	71	11	-7	570	89	7	641	0	334	40	34	495	60	-5	829	29	182	31	-31	409	69	-28	591	-59
1971	137	23	66	464	77	-106	601	-40	368	47	34	415	53	-80	783	-46	196	33	14	405	67	-4	601	10
1972	171	32	34	365	68	-99	536	-65	406	53	38	360	47	-55	766	-17	218	39	22	334	61	-71	552	-49
1973	197	41	26	281	59	-84	478	-58	436	58	30	314	42	-46	750	-16	205	43	-13	269	57	-65	474	-78
1974	227	52	30	213	48	-68	440	-38	420	67	-16	211	33	-103	631	-119	260	55	55	217	45	-52	477	3
1975	284	59	57	194	41	-19	478	38	432	70	12	187	30	-24	619	-12	271	52	11	250	48	33	521	44

a An annex to Clark Street School was opened in 1972, changing the attendance pattern.
b Transfers to Silver Spring and to Townsend from outside their attendance areas were halted in 1975 to prevent further racial imbalance.

Understanding changes in the racial composition of secondary schools serving racially mixed attendance areas is somewhat complicated by the fact that open enrollment is extensively used at this level, with many students leaving their home neighborhoods to attend schools more attractive to them.[74] Table 1-2 illustrates the impact of open enrollment. Most elementary children who participate in open enrollment travel only short distances.[75] Thus these moves generally have relatively little racial impact, as Table 1-2 illustrates.

The moves made by secondary students, on the other hand, have strong racial impact. Actually there are two effects, heading in somewhat opposite directions. Minority students leave heavily minority schools and attend more racially balanced schools; white students also leave heavily minority schools in large numbers for schools with a higher proportion of white students.[76] Thus schools like Wright Junior High (located along a convenient bus line) and Riverside High (located east of the black inner city) receive substantial numbers of transfers. In the case of Riverside, there were so many black transfers that the school board froze further transfers, fearing the school would become all black.

Table 1-3 provides information on secondary schools similar to that provided on elementary schools in Table 1-1. Here, too, despite the complications of open enrollment and disproportionate minority dropout in the higher grades, the overall pattern is one of steady white withdrawal (or nonentrance), and partial black replacement. In these schools, as in the system as a whole, the level of downturn in white enrollment is greater than the increase in minority enrollment; hence, total enrollment is generally decreasing.

Social-Class Levels and Neighborhood Change

One additional variable that may be closely related to white flight is the social-class level of the white population in the changing neighborhood. In her study of the Russel Woods section of Detroit, Wolf reports that the moving order of white households was markedly affected by family income, with the more prosperous families moving first. Racial attitudes were irrelevant.[77] According to the Bureau of the Census, whites moving from the central city to suburbs in the same metropolitan area had average incomes of $15,532; whites moving from one part of the city to another had an average income of $12,362.[78] Indeed, it can be observed that the disorders that have

Table 1-2

Number and percentage of student transfers in Milwaukee public schools

Ethnic category	School level	Transfer from schools					Transfer to schools				
		High in minority enrollment		Low in minority enrollment			High in minority enrollment		Low in minority enrollment		
		Number	Percent	Number	Percent	Total	Number	Percent	Number	Percent	Total
Minority	Elementary	1,246	84	243	16	1,489	1,337	76	424	24	1,761
White (other)		415	25	1,239	75	1,654	226	12	1,672	88	1,898
Minority	Junior high	822	86	133	14	955	377	29	912	71	1,289
White (other)		286	34	557	66	843	5	1	821	99	826
Minority	Senior high	1,455	90	166	10	1,621	977	63	598	37	1,595
White (other)		893	32	1,865	68	2,758	100	3	2,820	97	2,920

Source: Adapted from Dwight Rowe, "Educational Outcomes Associated with Ethnic Changes in School Populations," paper presented at the annual meeting of the American Educational Research Association, Washington, D.C., 1975, pages 17-18. Note that the totals of transfers from schools do not match the totals of transfers to schools. The data were taken from computerized records as of March 3, 1975. Because some schools were quicker and more accurate than others in reporting transfers, the data are to some extent incomplete and inconsistent. Schools of high-minority enrollment are defined as those with 50 percent or more minority students. Low-minority enrollment is defined as less than 50 percent minority students. Perhaps as many as seven hundred of the secondary transfers were to Milwaukee Trade and Technical School, a special, nondistrict school with low-minority enrollment. Only open enrollment within the Milwaukee school system is included in these figures. New students from outside the system registering at their district school are not included; nor are students leaving the public school system altogether.

Table 1-3

Enrollment in Milwaukee public junior and senior high schools undergoing racial transition, 1968–1975

Edison Junior High [a]

Year	Minority			White			Total	
	No.	%	Change	No.	%	Change	No.	Change
1968	117	9	--	1,224	91	--	1,341	--
1969	153	11	36	1,198	89	-26	1,351	10
1970	160	10	7	1,379	90	181	1,539	188
1971	189	12	29	1,330	88	-49	1,519	-20
1972	300	22	111	1,049	78	-281	1,349	-170
1973	525	38	225	852	62	-197	1,377	28
1974	560	44	35	715	56	-137	1,275	-102
1975	582	49	22	608	51	-107	1,190	-85

Peckham Junior High [b]

Year	Minority			White			Total	
	No.	%	Change	No.	%	Change	No.	Change
1968	429	38	--	687	62	--	1,116	--
1969	664	54	235	571	46	-116	1,235	-119
1970	830	72	166	324	28	-247	1,154	-81
1971	696	88	-134	92	12	-232	788	-366
1972	776	97	80	23	3	-69	799	11
1973	617	99	-159	8	1	-15	625	-174
1974	724	97	107	22	3	14	746	121
1975	649	98	-75	15	2	-7	664	-82

Wright Junior High

Year	Minority			White			Total	
	No.	%	Change	No.	%	Change	No.	Change
1968	240	21	--	898	79	--	1,138	--
1969	226	21	-14	875	79	-23	1,101	-37
1970	175	17	-51	842	83	-33	1,017	-84
1971	192	18	17	866	82	24	1,058	41
1972	223	21	31	836	79	-30	1,059	1
1973	261	25	38	772	75	-64	1,033	-26
1974	257	27	-4	678	73	-94	935	-98
1975	238	29	-19	570	71	-108	808	-127

Steuben Junior High [a,c]

Year	Minority			White			Total	
	No.	%	Change	No.	%	Change	No.	Change
1968	60	5	--	1,197	95	--	1,257	--
1969	100	7	40	1,249	93	52	1,349	92
1970	105	8	5	1,261	92	12	1,366	17
1971	167	13	62	1,100	87	-161	1,267	-99
1972	185	15	18	1,023	85	-77	1,208	-59
1973	349	33	164	693	67	-330	1,042	-166
1974	389	48	40	424	52	-269	813	-229
1975	352	47	-37	403	53	-21	755	-58

Riverside Senior High [a]

Year	Minority			White			Total	
	No.	%	Change	No.	%	Change	No.	Change
1968	564	30	--	1,302	70	--	1,866	--
1969	649	35	85	1,182	65	-120	1,831	-35
1970	663	39	14	1,046	61	-136	1,709	-122
1971	728	44	65	943	56	-103	1,671	-38
1972	827	51	99	785	49	-158	1,612	-59
1973	917	60	90	613	40	-172	1,530	-82
1974	705	60	-212	464	40	-149	1,169	-361
1975	622	57	-83	467	43	3	1,089	-80

Washington Senior High [a,d]

Year	Minority			White			Total	
	No.	%	Change	No.	%	Change	No.	Change
1968	224	8	--	2,644	92	--	2,868	--
1969	378	14	154	2,379	86	-265	2,757	-111
1970	536	21	158	1,979	79	-400	2,515	-242
1971	903	32	367	1,885	68	-94	2,788	273
1972	1,012	41	109	1,437	59	-448	2,449	-339
1973	1,256	48	244	1,339	52	-98	2,595	146
1974	1,645	56	389	1,294	44	-45	2,939	344
1975	1,695	63	50	1,014	37	-280	2,709	-230

a Transfers to Riverside (1974) and to Steuben, Edison, and Washington (1975) from outside their attendance areas were halted to prevent further racial imbalance.
b The attendance pattern of Peckham was changed in 1974 when Grade 9 was assigned to Washington.
c Grade 9 was assigned to Washington in 1974.
d Washington changed from a three-year school (Grades 10–12) to a four-year school (Grades 9–12) in 1974.

sometimes accompanied court-ordered busing seem to be concentrated in working-class and lower-class areas, perhaps because the people
in these areas, unlike the middle class, cannot easily afford to move.

As a check to see whether the Milwaukee experience was influenced
by white social-class level, the eighteen elementary schools that appear
in Table 1-1 were divided into two groups. One group of nine schools
served attendance areas where mean annual income, based on 1970
census data, was estimated to be below $10,000. The other group of
nine schools served areas where the estimated mean family income was
above $10,000. The average decrease in percentage of white atten-
dance at the poorer schools (1968-1975) was 31.9 percentage points.
In the wealthier areas, it was 46.4 percentage points.[79] Taeuber and
Taeuber found that "invading" blacks are often of higher
socioeconomic status than the white residents they replace, and the
whites leaving tend to be of higher socioeconomic status than those left
behind.[80] Perhaps, then, the wealthier areas of Milwaukee were more
attractive to upwardly mobile blacks seeking better homes and
schools and were also inhabited by whites more able to move if
threatened by racial change in their schools and neighborhoods.

Taken as a whole, the research indicates rather strongly that, so
long as in-migration and natural increase provide a growing minority
population, it is most unlikely that the process of school "desegregation" in changing neighborhoods around the fringes of the inner city
will be anything but a temporary situation between the time when a
school is largely white and a time when it is largely black. Without
government intervention to provide a stable level of integration in the
schools, and simultaneously to provide adequate, safe, and desirable
living opportunities for minority citizens in areas other than those
immediately surrounding the inner city, the process of resegregation
cannot but continue. In some cases, such as Inglewood, this process
has passed the boundary of the central city and is continuing on into
the suburbs.

SCHOOL DESEGREGATION BY GOVERNMENTAL ACTION

The second broad category of school desegregation situation occurs
when either the courts, or the local school board, or the executive
branch of the federal or state government intervenes to bring about
the desegregation of previously segregated schools. In the South, this

has occasionally meant changing from a dual to a unitary, but still neighborhood, school system, particularly in small towns. In most southern towns of any size, however, as in most northern areas, segregated neighborhoods are large enough so that students must be transported if school desegregation is to be accomplished.

White flight may or may not occur in such situations.[81] White Plains, New York, began busing students to desegregate its schools in 1964, and there was a six-year follow-up study in 1970. White students were doing as well or better academically than before integration, black students were doing better, and there had been no white flight.[82] Pasadena, California, on the other hand, recently completed a four-year follow-up study of their experience with school desegregation. There was a significant drop in the achievement levels of students throughout the district, and white enrollment declined precipitously, from 18,000 in 1969 to 11,000 in 1973.[83] While much of this wide variation in the consequences of school desegregation may be attributable to the particular characteristics of individual cities and school districts, as well as to the differences in methods of collecting data and in interpretations of the data, there are some general patterns.

School Racial Proportion and Minority Social Class

A review of the research on white enrollment loss following school desegregation brought about through government intervention suggests that, when it occurs, the two most important factors may be the proportion of minority students involved in desegregation and their social class. Studies dating back to the period immediately after the *Brown* decision in 1954 indicate that resistance to desegregation is closely related to the proportion of black students in the schools.[84] Just as resistance to school desegregation seems to mount as the proportion of black students increases, so apparently does the likelihood of some white withdrawal. James Bosco and Stanley Robin report an additional decline of less than 1 percent in white enrollment after busing began in the Kalamazoo, Michigan, school system, where the enrollment was 18 percent black, but there was an additional decline of 4.7 percent in the white enrollment in the Pontiac, Michigan, school system, where the enrollment was 38 percent black.[85] Clotfelter found a similar relationship between proportion of black students and white flight in Mississippi, with particularly heavy flight from schools where there was a majority of black students.[86] Lord mentions a situation in

Nashville in which the number of whites in one school declined from 560 to 268 when students were bused to an inner-city school that had a black enrollment of 40 percent; the white decline in a similar school was only 15 percent when students were to be bused to a school where the black enrollment was only 20 percent.[87] (One additional factor must, however, be noted: the former students were to be bused throughout the high school years, while the latter were to be bused only for one year.) In a major research project undertaken in Florida by Micheal Giles and others, white withdrawal to private schools increased when the proportion of black students passed a 30 percent "threshold." There was also a close connection to white family income.[88]

The impact on white withdrawal of the proportion of black students may come as much from the difference in social-class level between the black and white students as from the proportion itself. Memphis, Tennessee, and Jackson, Mississippi, for instance, are often cited as particularly striking examples of white withdrawal from desegregated schooling. Farley reports that shortly after the busing order, white enrollment in the public schools of Memphis fell by twenty thousand while the number in private schools rose by fourteen thousand.[89] The *New York Times* reported that Memphis lost 46 percent of its white public school students between 1970 and 1973.[90] Indeed, Thomas Pettigrew and Robert Green argue that Coleman's conclusions on white flight would not have come out as they did were it not for the atypical results from Memphis (and from Atlanta, which has already been discussed).[91] What is striking about white withdrawal from public schools in Memphis is that it occurred in a situation where the black school population was both large (54 percent in 1968) and unusually poor. According to 1970 census data, 35.7 percent of black families in Memphis were below the poverty line, compared with 5.7 percent of nonblack families.[92] Owen Thornberry reported that one estimate showed Memphis ranking second among major cities of the nation in poverty, with 80 percent of this poverty in the black ghetto.[93]

A similar example of a large and markedly poor black population leading to white withdrawal can be found in Jackson. Egerton reported that the Jackson school system, which was 55 percent white before midyear desegregation, lost nine thousand whites and dropped to 40 percent white upon desegregation and to 36 percent white the following year.[94] According to *Time,* half of all white pupils in Jackson now attend private schools.[95] The combination of a high proportion of black students and extreme poverty is as striking in Jackson as it is in Memphis. According to recent census data, 27.3 percent of blacks in Jackson are high school graduates, compared to 77.5 percent of non-blacks and 40.3 percent of the black families are below the poverty line compared to 6.3 percent of nonblack families.[96] The median annual income of black families in Jackson in 1970 was $4,546. Richard Morrill cites Jackson as having the lowest proportion of median black family income to median white family income in the country.[97]

Thus, rightly or wrongly, parents seem to perceive a desegregated school as undesirable if it is both heavily minority and poor. Unless there is strong evidence to the contrary, white or middle-class withdrawal may follow as a result of such perceptions. Conversely, it should not be surprising that no white withdrawal is reported in Howard Ravis's account of a community with a 20 percent black population and lacking extremes of wealth or poverty. Here the school system combined integration with some educational improvements and made a smooth and successful transition to integrated schools.[98]

Social Class of White Students

Just as the social-class level of minority students involved in school integration may be important in determining whether there is racial instability, so may the social-class level of the white students. This may be true partly because of the class prejudices and values already discussed, and also partly because wealthier parents are more able to bear whatever costs might be involved in avoiding desegregated educational settings, whether these be the costs of moving or of private schooling.

Most reports on the use of private schooling deal with the South. A *Time* article has noted that half of the white pupils of Jackson, Mississippi, attend private schools, compared with a sixth of the white children of Charlotte, North Carolina. Private school attendance is also heavy in Memphis.[99] Family income seems to be a key factor in this use of private schooling. Lord, in a study of white flight to private schooling in the Charlotte-Mecklenburg school district, found that income alone explained 54 percent of the variation in the rate of white abandonment of the public schools after integration. He reports that thirteen new private schools have opened there since the 1969 desegregation order.[100] In their careful study of parents who withdrew their children from public schooling in Florida after school desegregation, Everett Cataldo and his associates found that rejection rates for white students assigned to schools with an enrollment that was more than 30 percent black were 4 percent for low-income students, 7 percent for middle-income students, and 17 percent for high-income students.[101] It is important to note that, while such losses may not represent a very high percentage of the public school population (3.6 percent overall), they do deprive the public schools of a disproportionate number of students from the more affluent part of the community.

The data would suggest, then, that several variables may be significantly related to whether or how much white withdrawal might be expected if there is governmental intervention to desegregate formerly segregated public schools. These variables would include the proportion and social-class level of minority students, the social-class level of white students, and the cost and availability of alternative schooling.

A NATIONAL SURVEY

How common is school racial instability nationally? This is a difficult question to answer. Because of boundary changes, grade-level changes, and student assignment changes associated with opening new buildings, only someone fully acquainted with the schools in a given district can really tell if a particular school is actually the "same" school from one year to the next. As a result, most research reports deal with either case studies of the schools in one locality, or national data by district rather than by individual school.

Despite the difficulties involved, however, there is really no way to understand what is happening in a school district without looking at what is happening in individual schools. It is at the level of the individual school that desegregation affects a given youngster, black or white. That is why it seems worth the effort, despite the problems, to attempt a national investigation of school racial stability (and instability).

In 1968 the U.S. Department of Health, Education, and Welfare conducted a survey of the racial proportions in all school districts in the United States with 3,000 or more students, with a sampling of districts with fewer than 3,000 students.[102] This material was published in 1970 and listed, district by district and school by school, the racial breakdowns of an estimated 43.9 percent of the nation's school districts enrolling an estimated 90.8 percent of elementary and secondary school students.[103] The result was a large volume containing some 1,700 pages of fine print. By taking every tenth page (beginning with a page selected by using the first number appearing in a random number table), a sampling of 7,504 schools in 46 states was obtained.[104]

An initial analysis of these schools made it immediately apparent that, at least as of 1968, there were few racially mixed schools to study. My objective was to follow up schools with at least a 30 percent but no more than a 70 percent minority enrollment. Only 535 schools, 7.1 percent of the sampling, met this criterion.

The next step was to consult more recent government data, gathered in the fall of 1972,[105] in order to determine what had happened to the 535 schools over a four-year interval. This was done, although a total of 190 schools could not be followed up for one reason or another. There were 95 schools that were not listed at all in the 1972 report, either because they were in small districts not in the 1972 sample or because they had apparently been either closed or renamed; another 66 schools had changed grades significantly (more than one grade level had been added or deleted, not counting changes at the kindergarten or preschool level); 29 more appeared to be special education schools of one kind or another. These latter almost always draw their students on a district-wide basis.

The remaining 345 schools, which at least appeared to be structurally unchanged from 1968 to 1972, comprised 4.6 percent of the original sampling of 7,504 schools. Of these schools, 190 had a minority enrollment that was predominantly black, 151 had a minority enrollment predominantly Hispanic, and 4 had a minority enrollment predominantly Oriental. Omitting the schools with the Oriental minority,[106] Table 1-4 shows the extent of change in the racial composition of the student population between 1968 and 1972. An examination of the table indicates that schools with predominantly black enrollments were more likely both to have a decrease in minority enrollment (even if small) and to resegregate beyond the 70 percent level than schools where the predominant minority was Hispanic. Many of the former cases, as will be shown, involved governmental action, which appears to be more common in schools where the predominant minority group is black. The latter cases perhaps reflect the tendency of schools with a predominantly black enrollment to resegregate more quickly. Overall,

Table 1-4

Change from 1968 to 1972 in proportion of minority enrollment in selected schools in
relation to predominant minority groups

| Change in proportion of minority enrollment | Predominant minority group | | | | Total number |
| | Black | | Hispanic | | |
	Number	Percent	Number	Percent	
Decrease	65	34.2	24	15.9	89
Increase, but still within 30 percent to 70 percent range	77	40.5	107	70.9	184
Increase, beyond 70 percent range	48	25.3	20	13.2	68
Total	190	100.0	151	100.0	341

schools in which black enrollments increased from 1968 to 1972 had
an average increase of 16.7 percentage points (standard deviation =
14.2). On the other hand, schools where the predominant minority
group was Hispanic and where there was an increase in minority enrollment averaged 10.3 percent change (standard deviation = 7.0)
over the four-year period. Average *decreases* were 7.0 and 8.7 percent
for black and Hispanic schools, respectively. The most common situation in these desegregated schools seems to be one of relatively gradual
but steady resegregation.

Is rapid resegregation more likely in large school systems? When the
data on schools with predominantly black minority enrollments are
broken down by district size, the results are as shown in Table 1-5.
These results suggest that there are large numbers of racially mixed
schools in small school districts, and many of them seem quite stable;
conversely, racially mixed schools in larger districts seem more unstable. These results are consistent with the view that the large and expanding inner-city ghettos in many of these larger school districts are
a major factor in resegregating schools serving the areas bordering the
inner city.

The problem remains, of course, that these data can be only sugges-

Table 1-5

Change from 1968 to 1972 in proportion of minority enrollment in selected schools in relation to school district enrollment

| | School district enrollment | | | | | | |
| | Below 25,000 | | 25,000 to 100,000 | | Above 100,000 | | Total |
Change in proportion of minority enrollment	Number	Percent	Number	Percent	Number	Percent	number
Decrease	46	44.7	16	27.1	3	10.7	65
Increase of 8 percent or less	34	33.0	11	18.6	7	25.0	52
Increase of more than 8 percent	23	22.3	32	54.2	18	64.3	73
Total	103	100.0	59	99.9	28	100.0	190

Note: $X^2 = 27.23$, df = 4, p<.001

tive. Without information from individual school districts, one cannot really be sure what is happening in any of these schools. After reviewing the data, the decision was made to seek further information on the 117 schools in 58 school districts that had 8 percentage points or less of increase in minority enrollment between 1968 and 1972. Letters were written to the superintendents of these districts asking for information on each of the 117 schools. This group was chosen because there is ample evidence in the studies cited earlier to explain racial instability. It is stability that is interesting, and it seemed that a superintendent would be more likely to answer a letter asking for an explanation of how one or more schools was *avoiding* resegregation than one asking why a given school became significantly more segregated, given the possible legal implications of the latter question, no matter how innocently asked.

After a first request for information and a follow-up letter to those who did not initially reply, responses with information about 73 of these schools were received from 40 of the 58 school districts. While the quality and quantity of information provided about each school varied widely, analysis of the responses seemed to indicate that the majority of the schools fell into one of three groups.

The first group consisted of twenty-one schools (in seventeen districts) where the relatively stable racial balance could be explained by some outside event, either initiated by the school system or somehow impinging on the school attendance areas. In sixteen of these schools (thirteen districts) the attendance area was changed, busing was used, or there was some other action by the school system. One of these schools has since been closed. Thirteen of these schools furnished information on their current racial proportions: seven experienced a decrease in minority enrollment between 1972 and 1975, two remained the same, and four increased.

In five additional schools (five districts) some event for which the school district was not responsible explained the drop in minority enrollment between 1968 and 1972. One school served a neighborhood where much of the housing used by blacks was demolished, and the proportion of black students in this school has continued to decrease. Another area experienced a black exodus where existing housing was demolished and new housing was located beyond the school's attendance area. In this instance both black and white populations are dropping, with the proportions remaining stable. The general student population at a third school also declined, with a disproportionate decline in black students, because of industrial expansion. This school will eventually be closed. Finally, there are two schools in districts that are approximately sixty miles from a rapidly expanding southwestern city that are experiencing an influx of new white residents, and the proportion of black students in these schools continues to drop.

The second major group consisted of six elementary schools and a high school located in low socioeconomic areas of five major cities. One of the elementary schools has since closed. The remaining five schools have averaged 12 percentage points of increase in minority enrollment over the 1971–1975 period; the high school increased 4 percentage points. The two most stable elementary schools (2 and 4 percentage points of change) serve attendance areas that include white ethnic neighborhoods very resistant to racial (or ethnic) change. In each of the seven cases both white and minority students are notably poor.

The third group contained eighteen schools (thirteen school districts) located in stable rural areas or small towns. Many of the schools, which appear to be the only ones at a particular grade level in the district, are quite stable. Of the fourteen schools for which 1975 racial data were reported, six increased an average of 4 percentage points in minority enrollment, and eight decreased an average of 9 percentage points. The superintendents mentioned such factors as many younger black families moving to the cities and whites moving in from surrounding areas, a formerly black school district being annexed, and the impact of public housing. One school, because it was small, rural, and isolated from the rest of the district, did not benefit as much as other schools in the district from white movement out of a nearby metropolitan area.

Finally, there were twenty-seven schools (in twelve districts) that did not seem to fit any of the categories. In three of these schools all or a significant part of the student population is in special education programs and comes from throughout the district. Another of the schools serves an upper-middle-class urban renewal area where both black and white residents are well off financially. Despite this fact, the school enrollment has increased from 50 percent minority in 1972 to 65 percent in 1975. The minority enrollments at two schools near a major metropolitan area have remained at approximately 53 percent from 1968 through 1975. In this case the superintendent reports that this is a settled, older area with limited housing available and the number of pupils (black and white) declining steadily. Information provided about the remaining seventeen schools in five major metropolitan areas and four schools in two smaller districts was so sketchy that their situations were difficult to analyze. Nine of these schools are in a district where there is extensive busing to achieve racial balance, but the schools themselves are not involved in the busing; six of the nine show an increase in white enrollment.

Taken as a group, all of these schools illustrate once again the close relationship between racial stability in schools and underlying demographic trends in the school attendance area. Because the situation in the schools can itself influence demographic trends, the direction of causality is difficult to specify. Evidence does at least suggest, however, that such phenomena as white ethnic concentrations resistant to neighborhood change, stable small-town populations, or growing white populations attracted by economic opportunities or attractive living situations provide the natural foundation for stable school integration. This contrasts, of course, with the typical metropolitan situation where a growing black population is being steered by a dual housing market into neighborhoods bordering the inner city, so that neighborhood after neighborhood "turns" from white to black — a sit-

uation so common that it seems to have formed the public image of
the desegregated school as being an essentially unstable phenomenon.
The number of stably integrated schools in small towns and other
more favorable situations seems to have made much less impression on
the public consciousness.

DESEGREGATION AND INTEGRATION

To what extent is the racially mixed school truly integrated? Are the
students merely physically copresent, or are they relating to one another in an environment of mutual understanding and respect? The
relationship of the answers to these questions to white withdrawal has
not, so far as I know, been formally investigated. Yet this aspect of desegregated schooling seems to me to be at the heart of the whole issue.

Anyone who has spent any time in racially mixed schools, especially
high schools, knows that students can be as distant from each other as
if they were on separate planets. Blacks sit in one part of the cafeteria,
and whites in another; the same is true in classrooms, and at assemblies and athletic events. Some social events may even be held separately. Indeed, there is evidence that school desegregation may actually increase feelings of racial identity and separateness.[107] Petroni,
Hirsch, and Petroni conducted extensive interviews with students at a
desegregated high school and found few reports of significant cross-
racial friendship and understanding.[108] And in a study of three
Florida secondary schools immediately after desegregation, Irwin
Silverman and Marvin Shaw found that 95 percent of the communication being carried on as students left the school was white with white or
black with black.[109] Robert Wolf and Rita Simon concluded that,
after seven years of busing in one community, cross-racial friendship
had not substantially increased.[110] When this was pointed out to the
faculty of one of the elementary schools in the study (a school known
for its open, "informal" approach), the faculty unanimously agreed
that nothing had ever been done in the school to enhance the development of interracial understanding, friendship, or communication.

A similar situation (this time where white students were in the
minority) is described by Schafft, who found the white children in a
largely black school avoiding after-school sports, the bathrooms, and
the corridors and using their homes rather than the school as the focus
of their play activities.[111] The attitude of the faculty was expressed by

one of the most competent and well-liked teachers in the school: "If I am to teach, I cannot handle social problems as well."

This seems to be the attitude of American education generally. While a number of studies have investigated interracial attitudes in desegregated schools,[112] the literature is almost devoid of reports about programs that structure the school so that interracial cooperation and understanding are fostered.[113] Yet it should be obvious that schools were never organized with a view to helping people understand each other, and there is no evidence that bringing in students from different racial, class, and neighborhood backgrounds will automatically lead to understanding, appreciation, and friendship.

Perhaps the best analyses of the problems of desegregated versus integrated education are those of Jane Mercer,[114] who has obviously spent much time in racially mixed schools and has done some excellent research on the relationship between interracial friendship, self-esteem, and academic accomplishment. Even though her writings provide excellent descriptions and analyses, however, there is relatively little in them that could serve as a blueprint for the school administrator who is trying to decide what to do tomorrow in order to overcome the racial, class, and cultural gulf that is so frequently a part of racially mixed education.[115] There is a gap here that, in my judgment, may be the key not only to the control of white flight but to the survival of national commitment to school integration.

IN CONCLUSION

The issue of white withdrawal from desegregated schools is an unusually complex one, and the research to date has not been equal to the task of fully explaining all that is involved. Trying to understand this complicated phenomenon is much like trying to put together a giant, confusing jigsaw puzzle with many of the pieces missing. For almost every pattern there seems to be a contrary instance. The research that has been done, like this chapter, contains many gaps in the data presented, many unanswered questions, and many unverified assumptions. The following tentative conclusions do, nonetheless, seem justified.

1. White withdrawal from desegregated schools may or may not occur. Some schools maintain a high level of integration for years, some change slowly, and some resegregate very rapidly. Others

    may experience some white withdrawal followed by stability, or even by white reentrance.

2. Racially mixed schools located in areas bordering the inner city present some markedly different patterns of resegregation from schools located in school districts that have experienced district-wide desegregation. It is important not to extrapolate from the one situation to the other.

3. In situations where there has been no governmental action to bring about desegregation, white withdrawal seems to be linked more than anything else to the underlying demographic consequences of increased minority population growth. This growth takes place primarily in neighborhoods located on the edge of the inner city, as area after area "turns" from white to black. The schools "turn" more quickly than the area generally, and they play a significant role in making this process relatively rapid and generally irreversible. Stable school integration seems to be a necessary, if not sufficient, precondition for stable neighborhood integration.

4. Decisions on where to purchase a home or where to send one's children to school are made, not only on the basis of the present situation, but on estimates of what is likely to happen in the future. The belief that presently integrated schools and neighborhoods will shortly resegregate is a major barrier to attracting whites to integrated settings.

5. Little formal research has been done on the motivations behind white withdrawal from desegregated schooling. Worries about the quality of education, student safety, and social status differences may be among the chief causes. To the extent that this is true it could be expected that, other things being equal, school integration would more likely be stable and successful when combined with programs of educational improvement, in settings where concerns about safety are adequately met, and when programs of which parents can be proud are featured.

6. School desegregation ordinarily creates situations that have the potential for both racial and class conflict. The degree of white withdrawal to be expected when there is governmental intervention to desegregate schools may vary depending on the proportion of minority students who are being assigned to a given school and the social-class gap between minority and white students.

7. White withdrawal from desegregated schooling has widely varying costs in different settings. Moving to a nearby segregated suburb, moving outside a county school district, attending a parochial school, attending a private school, transferring to a segregated public school within the same system, or leaving town are examples of options that may or may not be present in any given situation. Each of these options, if available, will have different costs for different families, just as families will have varying abilities to meet those costs. So long as school desegregation is feared (or experienced) as painful, threatening, or undesirable, it can be expected that the number of families fleeing the desegregated school will be proportionate to the cost of alternatives and the family's ability to pay those costs.

8. Although there is a certain degree of racial mixing in many public schools, there may also be a notable lack of cross-racial friendship, understanding, and acceptance. Most of the superintendents who replied to the request for information on racial relations in the survey reported above answered that the racial situation was "calm," or that there were very few "incidents." Few made any claim that they had attained anything like genuine community; nor was there much indication that extensive efforts were being made toward this end.

AND FOR THE FUTURE

Given the incomplete nature of research on white withdrawal from desegregated schooling, policy implications are perhaps better stated as personal opinion rather than as "proven" by the research that has been reviewed in this chapter. The suggestions below are so offered.

1. There is serious need for a thorough, national study of white flight. Scattered case studies and sketchy national data are not enough. Unless the public schools of this country are going to continue to contribute heavily to the development of two societies, one white and one black with neither understanding nor trusting the other, white withdrawal from desegregated schooling needs to be better understood — and avoided. It is significant that the references cited in this paper are from journals of law, political science, economics, education, geography, sociology, psychology, and urban affairs. Any such study would have to be a significantly interdisciplinary effort.

2. While it may be true that government intervention to desegregate schools has in some instances precipitated white withdrawal, it is equally true that the lack of any positive government intervention in the so-called "changing neighborhoods" surrounding the inner city has been responsible for continuous and continuing resegregation. It would be helpful, in discussing problems of school desegregation in major metropolitan areas, to separate the discussion of what to do about inner-city schools from the special problems of resegregating schools on the fringes of the ghetto. If the steady growth of the ghetto is to be arrested, it must be done in the fringe areas. A comprehensive approach to fostering racially stable and integrated neighborhoods and schools would go far toward removing the present connection in the minds of many Americans between school desegregation and eventual resegregation.

3. Finally, there is a great need to emphasize the quality of school integration, and to develop and communicate practical approaches to overcome cultural and class barriers between the races. The available evidence does not suggest that, if one can just get black and white students into the same school building, the rest will take care of itself. It will not. School integration worthy of the name will only come about as the result of conscious, deliberate effort.

Notes

1. The summary, reported in *Education Daily* for October 20, 1975, was prepared for Daniel P. Moynihan, who was reportedly assisting President Ford in dealing withh school desegregation and busing issues.

2. Gary Orfield, "School Integration and Its Academic Critics," *Civil Rights Digest* 5 (Summer 1973): 2-10; Vagn Hansen, "Desegregation, Resegregation, and the Southern Courts," paper presented at the annual meeting of the Southern Political Science Association, Atlanta, 1972. ERIC: ED 083 349.

3. James S. Coleman, "Recent Trends in School Integration," *Educational Researcher* 4 (July-August 1975): 3-12.

4. See, for example, *id.*, "Busing Backfired," *National Observer*, June 7, 1975, 1, 18; *id.*, "Racial Segregation in the Schools: New Research with New Policy Implications," *Phi Delta Kappan* 57 (October 1975): 75-78; *id.*, "Coleman on Jackson on Coleman," *Educational Researcher* 5 (February 1976): 3-4; *id.*, "A Reply to Green and Pettigrew," *Phi Delta Kappan* 57 (March 1976): 454-455. For some critiques of Coleman's work, see Gregg Jackson, "Reanalysis of Coleman's 'Recent Trends in School Integration,'" *Educational Researcher* 4 (November 1975): 21-25; Robert Green and Thomas Pettigrew, "Urban Desegregation and White Flight: A Response

to Coleman," *Phi Delta Kappan* 57 (February 1976): 399-402; Thomas Pettigrew and Robert Green, "School Desegregation in Large Cities: A Critique of the Coleman 'White Flight' Thesis," *Harvard Educational Review* 46 (February 1976): 1-53.

5. Reynolds Farley, "Racial Integration in the Public Schools, 1967 to 1972: Assessing the Effect of Governmental Policies," *Sociological Focus* 8 (January 1975): 7; *id.* and Alma Taeuber, "Racial Segregation in the Public Schools," *American Journal of Sociology* 79 (January 1974): 890.

6. Coleman, "Recent Trends in School Integration"; Christine Rossell, "School Desegregation and White Flight," *Political Science Quarterly* 90 (Winter 1975-76): 679-680.

7. Farley and Taeuber, "Racial Segregation in the Public Schools."

8. Gary Orfield, "White Flight Research: Its Importance, Perplexities, and Possible Policy Implications," in *Symposium on School Desegregation and White Flight*, ed. *id.* (Washington, D.C.: Center for National Policy Review, 1975), 43-68.

9. J. Dennis Lord, "School Busing and White Abandonment of Public Schools," *Southeastern Geographer* 15 (November 1975): 81-92.

10. U.S. Congress, Senate, Select Committee on Equal Educational Opportunity, Hearings before the Select Committee on Equal Educational Opportunity of the U.S. Senate, 91st Congress, 2d Session, May 13, 1970, 743-801.

11. Harold Rose, "The Development of an Urban Subsystem: The Case of the Negro Ghetto," *Annals of the Association of American Geographers* 60 (March 1970): 1-17; Harvey Molotch, *Managed Integration* (Berkeley: University of California Press, 1972).

12. Orfield, "White Flight Research."

13. U.S. Bureau of the Census, "Social and Economic Characteristics of the Metropolitan and Nonmetropolitan Population: 1974 and 1970," *Current Population Reports*, Series P-23, No. 55 (Washington, D.C.: U.S. Government Printing Office, 1975).

14. Studs Terkel, "Two Superintendents Discuss Integration: Inverview," in *Integrated Education*, ed. Meyer Weinberg (Beverly Hills, Calif.: Glencoe Press, 1968), 29-41.

15. Lord, "School Busing and White Abandonment."

16. Orfield, "School Integration and Its Academic Critics."

17. *Ibid.*; Nancy St. John, *School Desegregation: Outcomes for Children* (New York: John Wiley & Sons, 1975). If declines do occur, however, this may contribute to white withdrawal. See Harold Kurtz, *Educational and Demographic Consequences of Four Years of School Desegregation in the Pasadena Unified School District* (Pasadena, Calif.: Pasadena Unified School District, 1975).

18. For a good example of the intelligent and positive use of evaluation research in the process of effectively integrating a formerly segregated school system, see Maurice Eash and Sue Rasher, "Mandated Desegregation and Improved Achievement: A Longitudinal Study," *Phi Delta Kappan* 58 (January 1977): 394-397.

19. Frank Petroni, Ernest Hirsch, and C. Lillian Petroni, *Two, Four, Six, Eight, When You Gonna Integrate?* (New York: Behavioral Publications, 1970).

20. Bioloine Young and Grace Bress, "A New Educational Decision: Is Detroit the End of the School Bus Line?" *Phi Delta Kappan* 56 (April 1975): 515-520.

21. Morris Rosenberg and Roberta Simmons, *Black and White Self-esteem: The Urban School Child* (Washington, D.C.: American Sociological Association, n.d.).

22. "How They Did It in Boston," *School Management* 15 (May 1971): 11-15.

23. John McAdams, "Can Open Enrollment Work?" *The Public Interest*, No. 37 (Fall 1974): 69-88.

24. Leslie Bobbitt, "Discipline in Desegregated Schools," in *Proceedings of Conference on Development in School Desegregation and the Law*, ed. Charles Moody, Charles Vergon, and John Taylor (Ann Arbor: University of Michigan School of Education, 1972), 184-199. ERIC: ED 074 157.

25. Gretchen Schafft, "Together Yet Separate: Territoriality among White Children in Predominantly Black Classrooms," paper presented at the annual meeting of the American Anthropological Association, San Francisco, 1975; see also *Time*, January 12, 1976, 38.

26. See Avery Guest and James Weed, "Ethnic Residential Segregation: Patterns of Change," *American Journal of Sociology* 81 (March 1976): 1088-1111.

27. Micheal Giles, Douglas Gatlin, and Everett Cataldo, "Racial and Class Prejudice: Their Relative Effects on Protest against School Desegregation," *American Sociological Review* 41 (April 1976): 280-288.

28. Lillian Rubin, *Busing and Backlash* (Berkeley: University of California Press, 1972).

29. Rossell, "School Desegregation and White Flight"; Pettigrew and Green, "School Desegregation in Large Cities."

30. Betsy Levin and Philip Moise, "School Desegregation Litigation in the Seventies and the Use of Social Science Evidence: An Annotated Guide," *Law and Contemporary Problems* 39 (Winter 1975): 50-133; Robert Wegmann, "Neighborhoods and Schools in Racial Transition," *Growth and Change* 6 (July 1975): 3-8.

31. Note that the proportion of minority students in the public schools is *typically* half again as much as the proportion of minority citizens in the general population of central cities, so that a 52 percent minority population in the city and a 69 percent minority population in the school system are not at all unusual. See Farley and Taeuber, "Racial Segregation in the Public Schools"; Wegmann, "Neighborhoods and Schools in Racial Transition."

32. Coleman, "Recent Trends in School Integration."

33. *New York Times*, July 11, 1975, 1, 7.

34. U.S. Commission on Civil Rights, *Twenty Years after Brown: Equality of Educational Opportunity* (Washington, D.C.: the Commission, 1975).

35. U.S. Bureau of the Census, "Social and Economic Characteristics of the Metropolitan and Nonmetropolitan Population." This finding may be stronger than it looks. Whites in the central city are poorer than whites in the suburbs, and the poor have more children. Hence one would expect to find more rather than fewer whites of school age in the central city.

36. See Robert Weaver, "The Suburbanization of America," paper presented to the U.S. Commission on Civil Rights at a consultation on "School Desegregation: The Courts and Suburban Migration," Washington, D.C., 1975.

37. See Jean Milgram, "Integrated Neighborhood and Integrated Education," *Integrated Education* 12 (May-June 1974): 29-30; see also Charles Kaiser, " 'Resegregation' the Urban Challenge," *New York Times*, April 25, 1976, section 8.

38. Karl Taeuber and Alma Taeuber, *Negroes in Cities* (Chicago: Aldine Publishing Co., 1965).

39. For a study of stable interracial neighborhoods, see Norman Bradburn, Seymour Sudman, Galen Gockel, and Joseph Noel, *Side by Side* (Chicago: Quadrangle Books, 1971); see also John Diekhoff, "My Fair Ludlow," *Educational Forum* 33 (March 1969): 281-288.

40. Albert Hermalin and Reynolds Farley, "The Potential for Residential Integration in Cities and Suburbs: Implications for the Busing Controversy," *American Sociological Review* 38 (October 1973): 595-610; see also Raymond Zelder, "Racial Segregation in Urban Housing Markets," *Journal of Regional Science* 10 (April 1970): 93-105; Reynolds Farley, "Residential Segregation and Its Implications for School Integration," *Law and Contemporary Problems* 39 (Winter 1975): 164-193.

41. U.S. Bureau of the Census, "Social and Economic Characteristics of the Metropolitan and Nonmetropolitan Population."

42. Molotch, *Managed Integration*.

43. Eleanor Wolf, "Social Science and the Courts: The Detroit Schools Case," *The Public Interest*, No. 42 (Winter 1976): 102-120. If all this is to be placed in context, it is important to be aware that, even ignoring race, ethnic residential segregation is by no means a thing of the past in the United States. Guest and Weed, who studied ethnic residential segregation in Boston, Cleveland, and Seattle, found that the "old" American groups of predominantly Northern European descent, various "newer" groups of later immigration, and racial minorities are all relatively segregated from each other. Ethnic segregation is at least equal to if not greater than that by occupation, and much greater than that by family or life-cycle status. Nor did ethnic segregation seem to be decreasing much, at least from 1960 to 1970. Much of this ethnic segregation is a matter of relative social status, though not all. These findings are consistent with the view that *group* social status is related to ethnic residential segregation. See Guest and Weed, "Ethnic Residential Segregation."

44. For proposed solutions to the spread of segregated housing patterns, see Anthony Downs, "Residential Segregation: Its Effects on Education," *Civil Rights Digest* 3 (Fall 1970): 2-8; also Myron Ross, "Prices, Segregation, and Racial Harmony," *Journal of Black Studies* 2 (December 1971): 225-243.

45. Arthur Stinchcombe, Mary McDill, and Dollie Walker, "Demography of Organizations," *American Journal of Sociology* 74 (November 1968): 221-229.

46. For an excellent bibliography on racially mixed neighborhoods, see Mark Beach, *Desegregated Housing and Interracial Neighborhoods: A Bibliographic Guide* (Philadelphia: National Neighbors, 1975). A number of scholars have built computer models in an attempt to simulate and predict the patterns of ghetto expansion, with interesting if imperfect results. See Richard Morrill, "The Negro Ghetto: Problems and Alternatives," *Geographical Review* 55 (July 1965): 339-361; Rose, "The Development of an Urban Subsystem"; Harold Rose, "The Spatial Development of Black Residential Subsystems," *Economic Geography* 48 (January 1972): 43-65; see also Charles Barresi, "Neighborhood Patterns of Invasion and Succession," paper presented at the annual meeting of the American Sociological Association, Denver, 1971. ERIC: ED 055 124.

47. Rose, "The Development of an Urban Subsystem."

48. Howard Aldrich, "Ecological Succession in Racially Changing Neighborhoods: A Review of the Literature," *Urban Affairs Quarterly* 10 (March 1975): 327–348.

49. Chester Rapkin and William Grigsby, *The Demand for Housing in Racially Mixed Areas* (Berkeley: University of California Press, 1960); Molotch, *Managed Integration*.

50. See Nathan Glazer, "On 'Opening Up' the Suburbs," *The Public Interest*, No. 37 (Fall 1974): 89–111.

51. Eleanor Wolf, "The Tipping-Point in Racially Changing Neighborhoods," *American Institute of Planners Journal* 29 (August 1963): 217–222; see also Bradburn et al., *Side by Side*.

52. See Kurtz, *Educational and Demographic Consequences*; Orfield, "White Flight Research." Christine Rossell, in a personal communication, also points out that Inglewood is on the flight path of Los Angeles International Airport. For a description of the politics of school desegregation in Inglewood, see Norene Harris, Nathaniel Jackson, and Carl Rydingsword, "Inglewood, California: An Experience in Desegregation," in *The Integration of American Schools*, ed. Norene Harris, Nathaniel Jackson, and Carl Rydingsword (Boston: Allyn and Bacon, 1975), 78–92.

53. See Eleanor Wolf and Charles Lebeaux, "Class and Race in the Changing City," in *Urban Research and Policy Planning*, ed. Leo Schnore and Henry Fagin (Beverly Hills, Calif: Sage Publications, 1967), 99–129; see also Diekhoff, "My Fair Ludlow."

54. Molotch, *Managed Integration*.

55. Wegmann, "Neighborhoods and Schools in Racial Transition."

56. For data on the lack of interracial neighboring despite interracial housing, see Carolyn Zeul and Craig Humphrey, "The Integration of Black Residents in Suburban Neighborhoods: A Reexamination of the Contact Hypothesis," *Social Problems* 18 (Spring 1971): 462–474; see also Laurence Cagle, "Interracial Housing: A Reassessment of the Equal-Status Contact Hypothesis," *Sociology and Social Research* 57 (April 1973): 342–355.

57. Molotch cites a study by Roper who found that most neighboring behavior in middle-class settings was due directly or indirectly to the visiting patterns of young children. See Molotch, *Managed Integration*, 58.

58. Michael Reagan, *Busing: Ground Zero in School Desegregation: A Literature Review with Policy Recommendations* (Syracuse, N.Y.: Policy Institute, Syracuse University Research Corporation, 1972). On the problems of overly rapid racial transition, see also Malcolm Peabody, Jr., "Custom Changing," *Journal of Intergroup Relations* 2 (Summer 1973): 46–58.

59. Wolf and Lebeaux, "Class and Race in the Changing City."

60. Carl Hansen, *Danger in Washington* (West Nyack, N.Y.: Parker Publishing Co., 1968).

61. Charles Clotfelter, "Spatial Rearrangement and the Tiebout Hypothesis: The Case of School Desegregation," *Southern Economic Journal* 42 (October 1975): 263–271.

62. Rapkin and Grigsby, *The Demand for Housing in Racially Mixed Areas*.

63. Wolf and Lebeaux, "Class and Race in the Changing City"; Rapkin and Grigsby, *The Demand for Housing in Racially Mixed Areas*; Bradburn et al., *Side by Side*.

64. A recent survey by *Neighbors*, a newsletter oriented toward interracial living, found, for example, that over 50 percent of the landlords in various sections of the San Francisco area would not rent to applicants with children.

65. Charles Clotfelter, "The Effect of School Desegregation on Housing Prices," *Review of Economics and Statistics* 57 (November 1975): 446–451.

66. See Wegmann, "Neighborhoods and Schools in Racial Transition."

67. See, for example, Morton Grodzins, "Metropolitan Segregation," *Scientific American* 197 (October 1957): 33–41; Hansen, *Danger in Washington*; Wegmann, "Neighborhoods and Schools in Racial Transition"; and [no author], "Note: Merging Urban and Suburban School Systems," *Georgetown Law Journal* 60 (May 1972): 1279–1307. The best conceptual discussion is in Thomas Schelling, *Neighborhood Tipping* (Cambridge, Mass.: Harvard Institute of Economic Research, 1969).

68. Wolf, "Social Science and the Courts"; Levin and Moise, "School Desegregation Litigation in the Seventies."

69. Arthur Stinchcombe, Mary McDill, and Dollie Walker, "Is There a Racial Tipping Point in Changing Schools?" *Journal of Social Issues* 25 (January 1969): 127–136; Wolf, "The Tipping Point in Racially Changing Neighborhoods."

70. The data for 1969–1975 are taken from records kept by the Milwaukee Public School System. The author is a former member of the school board of that city. The data for 1968 are from the U.S. Department of Health, Education, and Welfare. I wish to express my appreciation to members of the Milwaukee Public School staff who helped me obtain this information. A few schools were omitted, although they technically met these criteria: Jackie Robinson (originally Peckham Annex), to which students have been bused from a number of areas and which is now a specialty, nondistrict school; Cass Street Elementary School, which receives a large number of minority students bused in from overcrowded schools outside its district; Jefferson, a nondistrict school for students with reading problems; Pleasant View School for the mentally handicapped; and Gaenslen School for the physically handicapped.

Data on a largely Hispanic school are reported later in this chapter. I have generally set this material aside, preferring to concentrate primarily on white flight from predominantly black schools. The whole issue of the predominantly Hispanic school is an interesting one, but almost no research seems to have been done on this topic.

71. Note Elm and Garden Homes in 1969; Clarke Street in 1970 and 1971; Clemens in 1971; Townsend and Kilbourn in 1972; Silver Spring and Pierce in 1973; Fratney and 27th Street in 1974; and Story in 1975. In reviewing an earlier draft of this chapter, Christine Rossell suggested explicitly mentioning that there were also years in which such movement was markedly absent. Note, for example, 38th Street in 1970 and 1975; Clemens in 1972; Elm and Fratney in 1973; Pierce in 1974; and Wisconsin in 1975.

72. See G. Dwight Rowe, "Educational Outcomes Associated with Ethnic Changes in School Populations," paper presented at the annual meeting of the American Educational Research Association, Washington, D.C., 1975.

73. I made a number of proposals intended to help reduce racial isolation while serving on the school board (1971–1974). With minor exceptions, they were voted down.

74. Wegmann, "Neighborhoods and Schools in Racial Transition."

75. Often a particular home will be physically closer to one school although actually in the attendance zone of another; or a parent may want to avoid his child's crossing a busy street; or a youngster may need to be sent to the next closest school to avoid cer-. tain other children who cause him trouble. None of these changes takes the child any great distance, particularly since elementary attendance areas are so much smaller than those for secondary schools.

76. Gregg Jackson, in reviewing an earlier draft of this chapter, pointed out that Table 1-2 would be clearer if the destinations of students transferring from highand low-minority schools were shown separately. The point is well taken; unfortunately the data in Rowe's paper are not presented in a way that makes this separation possible.

77. Eleanor Wolf, "The Baxter Area: A New Trend in Neighborhood Change?" *Phylon* 26 (Winter 1965): 344–353.

78. U.S. Bureau of the Census, "Social and Economic Characteristics of the Metropolitan and Nonmetropolitan Population."

79. The coefficient of correlation between estimated family income and the number of percentage points increase in minority enrollment is 0.45. Statistical significance at the 0.05 level (two-tailed) requires a correlation coefficient of 0.468. Donald Noel, in reviewing an earlier draft of this chapter, suggested that this finding might be stronger than it appears if the schools serving higher-income neighborhoods had a substantially lower proportion of minority students at the beginning of the period 1968–1975. This is, in fact, the case. In 1968 the high-income schools had an average of 15 percent minority enrollment (an average of 9 percent if the one school with substantial minority enrollment is omitted), compared to an average of 38 percent minority enrollment in the lower-income schools. While one might have expected more rapid white withdrawal from schools already having a substantial black population, the reverse was the case.

80. Taeuber and Taeuber, *Negroes in Cities*.

81. See Rossell, "School Desegregation and White Flight." Note that Rossell argues that white withdrawal, even when it does occur at a rate higher than in the years before desegregation, is largely confined to the year of school desegregation. While there is undoubtedly a trend in this direction, I am not certain whether the data are yet extensive enough to establish this trend firmly. Rossell's article, however, defines the issues exceptionally well.

82. "Notes on Busing and School Integration in White Plains, Pasadena, and Harrisburg." Report of the Western Regional School Desegregation Project, University of California, Riverside, 1971. ERIC: ED 066 542.

83. Kurtz, "Educational and Demographic Consequences." In a personal communication, Kurtz suggested that among the reasons for this exceptionally high rate of white withdrawal might be the traditionally high mobility rates in the Los Angeles area; the presence of over eighty other school districts in Los Angeles County; the overwhelmingly white racial composition of contiguous districts; the presence of a large number of private schools in Pasadena and the surrounding area; the relatively high socioeconomic status of the white population; the high proportion of minority students; and the considerable amount of busing involved in the plan. He also attributes the slowing of white withdrawal at the present time to the policies of the new (and antibusing) school board.

84. See Thomas Pettigrew and M. Richard Cramer, "The Demography of Desegregation," *Journal of Social Issues* 15 (No. 4, 1959): 61-71; Donald Matthews and James Prothro, "Stateways versus Folkways: Critical Factors in Southern Reactions to *Brown* v. *Board of Education*," in *Essays on the American Constitution,* ed. Gottfried Dietze (New York: Prentice-Hall, 1964), 139-156; James Prothro, "Stateways versus Folkways Revisited: An Error in Prediction," *Journal of Politics* 34 (May 1972): 352-364; Charles Bullock and Harrell Rodgers, Jr., "Perceptual Distortion and Policy Implementation: Evaluations of the Effectiveness of School Desegregation Techniques," paper presented at the annual meeting of the Southwest Political Science Association, San Antonio, 1975; Thomas Dye, "Urban School Desegregation," *Urban Affairs Quarterly* 4 (December 1968): 141-165; Farley, "Racial Integration in the Public Schools, 1967 to 1972"; A. B. Cochran and Thomas Uhlman, "Black Populations and School Integration—A Research Note," *Phylon* 34 (March 1973): 43-48; Micheal Giles and Thomas Walker, "Judicial Policy Making and Southern School Segregation," *Journal of Politics* 37 (November 1975): 917-936. The best overall account of the government's attempt to enforce the Civil Rights Act of 1964 with respect to southern schools may be found in Gary Orfield, *The Reconstruction of Southern Education* (New York: John Wiley & Sons, 1969). Many of the above citations discuss the resistance of policy makers to desegregation in areas with substantial black populations. It should be explicitly stated that it is an assumption on my part that the resistance of these policy makers to school desegregation reflects the same fears and attitudes in the white population generally that might lead to white withdrawal following school desegregation. See also Robert Levine, "The Silent Majority: Neither Simple nor Simple-minded," *Public Opinion Quarterly* 35 (Winter 1971-1972): 571-577; John Egerton, *School Desegregation: A Report Card from the South* (Atlanta: Southern Regional Council, 1976).

85. James Bosco and Stanley Robin, "White Flight from Court-Ordered Busing?" *Urban Education* 9 (April 1974): 87-98. Bosco and Robin also believe that this additional decline in white enrollment will not continue.

86. Charles Clotfelter, "School Desegregation, Tipping, and Private School Enrollment," *Journal of Human Resources* 11 (Winter 1976): 28-50. A particularly striking example is given by Craven. In September 1969 there were 2,408 black and 256 white students in one South Carolina school district; after desegregation, only one white student enrolled for the school year 1973-74. See J. Braxton Craven, Jr., "The Impact of Social Science Evidence on the Judge: A Personal Comment," *Law and Contemporary Problems* 39 (Winter 1975): 149-156.

87. Lord, "School Busing and White Abandonment of Public Schools."

88. Micheal Giles, Everett Cataldo, and Douglas Gatlin, "White Flight and Percent Black: The Tipping Point Reexamined," *Social Science Quarterly* 56 (June 1975): 85-92.

89. Farley, "Racial Integration in the Public Schools, 1967 to 1972." For a recent report on the situation in Memphis, see "Public Schools in Memphis: Struggling but with Head Well above Water," *Southern Journal* 4 (Spring 1975): 2-5.

90. *New York Times,* July 11, 1975, 7.

91. Pettigrew and Green, "School Desegregation in Large Cities."

92. U.S. Bureau of the Census, "1970 Census of Population and Housing: Memphis, Tenn.-Ark. SMSA," PHC (1)-127 (Washington, D.C.: U.S. Government Printing Office, 1972).

93. Owen T. Thornberry, "Sociological Factors," in *Memphis in the 70s*, ed. Bergin S. Merrill, Jr. (Memphis: Memphis State University, 1970), 242-257.

94. John Egerton, "Report Card on Southern School Desegregation: Jackson and Nashville," *Saturday Review* 55 (April 1, 1972): 41-42, 47-48.

95. *Time*, December 15, 1975, 54.

96. U.S. Bureau of the Census, "1970 Census of Population and Housing: Jackson, Mississippi SMSA," PHC (1)-94 (Washington, D.C.: U.S. Government Printing Office, 1972).

97. Morrill, "The Negro Ghetto."

98. Howard Ravis, "The School District of Kankakee, Illinois," *School Management* 15 (August 1971): 18-21.

99. "Public Schools in Memphis," *Time*, December 15, 1975. One of the points made in this article is that the private schools that sprang up in Memphis after large-scale court-ordered desegregation are now becoming institutionalized.

100. Lord, "School Busing and White Abandonment of Public Schools."

101. Everett Cataldo, Micheal Giles, Deborah Athos, and Douglas Gatlin, "Desegregation and White Flight," *Integrated Education* 13 (January-February 1975): 3-5; see also Clotfelter, "School Desegregation, Tipping, and Private School Enrollment."

102. U.S. Department of Health, Education, and Welfare, *Directory of Public Elementary and Secondary Schools in Selected Districts: Fall 1968* (Washington, D.C.: U.S. Government Printing Office, 1970).

103. Anyone familiar with school systems knows that such data, no matter how "hard" they may look, should not be taken too seriously. Some schools keep much better records than others; some school employees are reluctant to ask a student his race, if they are not certain of it; some school systems use computerized record keeping of variable accuracy, completeness, and consistency. The HEW report itself mentions how often reports came in with the district total not matching the sum of the individual schools in the district. Attendance changes daily in many large urban school systems, and records of both enrollment and attendance can leave much to be desired. For all of these reasons such figures are at best approximate; hence, I have generally rounded off percentages to the nearest whole number, rather than give an impression of more precision than is really the case.

104. I have used the word "sampling" deliberately since this is clearly not a random sample of schools throughout the country. Vagaries of page layout make it at best a kind of cluster sample of a stratified sample. Given all the other uncertainties about these schools, one must state again that these results are intended to be only suggestive.

105. U.S. Department of Health, Education, and Welfare, *Directory of Public Elementary and Secondary Schools in Selected Districts: Fall 1972* (Washington, D.C.: U.S. Government Printing Office, 1974).

106. A valuable perspective on changing racial ratios in largely black schools might well come from the study of racial and ethnic change in schools generally. In the four schools where the predominant minority group was Oriental, all increased in minority

enrollment between 1968 and 1972, averaging almost 13 percentage points of change per school.

107. See Bobbitt, "Discipline in Desegregated Schools"; David Armor, "The Evidence on Busing," *The Public Interest*, No. 28 (Summer 1972): 90-126; St. John, *School Desegregation*.

108. Petroni, Hirsch, and Petroni, *Two, Four, Six, Eight, When You Gonna Integrate?*

109. Irwin Silverman and Marvin Shaw, "Effects of Sudden, Mass School Desegregation on Interracial Interaction and Attitudes in One Southern City," paper presented at the annual meeting of the Eastern Psychological Association, New York, 1971. ERIC: ED 053 410. See also Leonard Marascuilo and Fred Dagenais, "Identification of Social Groups Based on Social Integration in a Multiracial High School," paper presented at the annual meeting of the American Educational Research Association, Chicago, 1974. ERIC: ED 094 031. An early study of this problem is Morrill Hall and Harold Gentry, "Isolation of Negro Students in Integrated Public Schools," *Journal of Negro Education* 38 (Spring 1969): 156-161.

110. Robert Wolf and Rita Simon, "Does Busing Improve the Racial Interactions of Children?" *Educational Researcher* 4 (January 1975): 5-10; see also Armin Beck, Eliezer Krumbein, and F. D. Erickson, "Strategies for Change: Conditions for School Desegregation," *Phi Delta Kappan* 50 (January 1969): 280-283; and Louise Singleton, Steven Asher, and Florence Alston, "Sociometric Ratings and Social Interaction among Third Grade Children in an Integrated School District," paper presented at the annual meeting of the American Educational Research Association, San Francisco, 1976.

111. Schafft, "Together Yet Separate."

112. In addition to the studies already cited, see Lawrence G. Felice, "Mandatory Busing and Minority Student Achievement: New Evidence and Negative Results," paper presented at the annual meeting of the American Sociological Association, San Francisco, 1975; and Nancy St. John and Ralph Lewis, "Race and the Social Structure of the Elementary Classroom," *Sociology of Education* 48 (Summer 1975): 346-368. Throughout their book, *The Integration of American Schools*, Harris, Jackson, and Rydingsword have a good sense of the difference between mere segregation and real integration.

113. Among the few examples are Elliot Aronson, Nancy Blaney, Jev Sikes, Cookie Stephan, and Matthew Snapp, "The Jigsaw Route to Learning and Liking," *Psychology Today* 8 (February 1975): 43-50; Elizabeth Cohen, Marlaine Lockheed, and Mark Lohman, "The Center for Interracial Cooperation: A Field Experiment," *Sociology of Education* 49 (January 1976): 47-58; David DeVries and Keith Edwards, "Student Teams and Learning Games: Their Effects on Cross-Race and Cross-Sex Interaction," *Journal of Educational Psychology* 66 (October 1974): 741-749; and Walter Stephan and James Kennedy, "An Experimental Study of Interethnic Competition in Segregated Schools," *Journal of School Psychology* 13 (Fall 1975): 234-247.

114. Jane Mercer, "Evaluating Integrated Education," in *School Desegregation, Public Information and the Media*, ed. Charles Moody and Charles Vergon (Ann Arbor: University of Michigan School of Education, 1973), 33-49; Jane Mercer, "Research Findings in School Desegregation," in *Report on the Future of School Desegre-*

gation in the United States, ed. Ogle Duff (Pittsburgh: University of Pittsburgh Consultative Resource Center on School Desegregation and Conflict, 1973), 94–122; Jane Mercer, Marietta Coleman, and Jack Harloe, "Racial/Ethnic Segregation and Desegregation in American Public Education," in *Uses of the Sociology of Education*, Seventy-third Yearbook of the National Society for the Study of Education, Part II, ed. C. Wayne Gordon (Chicago: University of Chicago Press, 1974), 274–329.

115. An excellent overview of what this involves can be found in Gary Orfield, "How to Make Desegregation Work: The Adaptation of Schools to Their Newly-Integrated Student Bodies," *Law and Contemporary Problems* 39 (Spring 1975): 313–340; see also Nate Jackson and Carl Rydingsword, "Desegregated High Schools Need Strong, Innovative Principals: An Interview with David Reiss," in Harris, Jackson, and Rydingsword, *The Integration of American Schools*, 207–214; and Lorenzo Thomas, "Creativity and Stress in Recently Integrated Schools," *Freedomways* 15 (Summer 1975): 221–225.

2. Desegregation and White Enrollment Decline in a Big-City School District

Daniel U. Levine and *Jeanie Keeny Meyer*

THE RESEARCH CONTROVERSY OVER DESEGREGATION

During the past few years a major research controversy has arisen on the issue of whether or not desegregation accelerates the decline in enrollment of whites in central city public school districts. Until 1975 only a small number of studies were reported that dealt with this issue. Micheal Giles, Everett Cataldo, and Douglas Gatlin, for example, concluded that there is no clear "tipping point" or "threshold" at a hypothesized 30 percent minority enrollment level beyond which schools tend to resegregate more rapidly than might happen below this level.[1] Their studies, however, were conducted in Florida, where some county-wide school districts are surrounded by districts also undergoing desegregation. For this reason the conclusions may not be applicable in states outside the South, which generally lack state-wide desegregation efforts that inhibit white flight by shutting off avenues of "escape" from systematic desegregation plans.

In the spring of 1975, James Coleman reported on the preliminary results of a study he and his colleagues conducted using data on the degree to which white and black students attended segregated schools between 1968 and 1973.[2] To focus on the issue of whether segregation in relatively large districts (25,000 or more students) was being perpetuated or increased owing to "segregating responses on the part of whites" to desegregation, Coleman and his colleagues made a separate analysis of the seventy largest central city school districts in the United States. Using regression analysis, they concluded that among the twenty largest districts the increase in the number of whites leaving districts where black students constituted 50 percent of the enrollment and where the increase in black proportion was 5 percent in the preceding two-year period was 19 percent higher than hypothetical estimates for whites leaving districts with no black students.

The release of this preliminary report and the widespread publicity it received precipitated much discussion both in professional publications and the popular press. Professional reactions were mostly critical of the methods Coleman and his colleagues had employed in their study and the conclusions they drew, which critics did not believe substantiated the existence of a white flight phenomenon over and beyond natural changes occurring in urban areas as a result of such causes as the deterioration of housing.

For example, Coleman's conclusions were disputed by Reynolds Farley, who collected data on forty southern and seventy-five northern or western city school districts enrolling 60 percent of the nation's black elementary students and 20 percent of the nation's white elementary students.[3] Utilizing a measure of segregation based on the degree to which the racial composition of school enrollments in these districts was similar or dissimilar to the respective district percentages of black and white population, Farley studied changes in enrollment between 1967 and 1972. He concluded that in neither the South nor the North "is there a significant relationship between school integration and white flight."[4]

After examining patterns in a number of cities that actively implemented integration plans, however, Farley further concluded that his data were

consistent with the hypothesis that whites fear integrated schools with large black enrollments and withdraw their children from public schools prior to integration. They also are consistent with many other hypotheses. Cities with a high proportion black may have particularly unfavorable tax bases, may be losing employment, may be viewed by whites as dangerous, or may have an especially old stock of housing . . . . When public schools are desegregated or when they become predominantly black, some white parents—perhaps many—hasten their move away from the central city. However, whites are moving out of central cities for many reasons.[5]

Gregg Jackson identified several "methodological limitations" in Coleman's approach and then reanalyzed the data and added additional data dealing separately with the nineteen largest school districts and the fifty next largest districts.[6] These analyses suggested "rather different findings and conclusions" from those of Coleman:

First, in the 69 largest school districts the rate of white public school enrollment declines between 1970–72 was generally greater in districts with a higher proportion of blacks. Second, in the 19 largest districts (all in large cities) the declines in white enrollment over this period were also generally higher in districts with greater increases between 1968–1970 in the extent to which the average white pupil had black schoolmates, and this relation holds even after controlling for a number of other factors. Third, in the 19 largest districts, declines in white public school enrollment are *not* consistently related to changes between 1968–1970 in the degree of segregation within the districts . . . . Fourth, in the 50 next largest districts declines in white public school enrollment are not related to either changes in the degree of racial proximity or changes in the degree of desegregation, at least not after controlling for the *district's* proportion of blacks [original italics].[7]

One of the most virulent criticisms of Coleman's methods and conclusions originated with Christine Rossell. After reporting the results of her own analysis of desegregation and enrollment trends in seventy large- and medium-sized northern school districts, she concluded that her study "shows with clear, verifiable data, that there is little or no white flight as a result of school desegregation. . . . Coleman has pulled off one of the great swindles of public policy research."[8] Rossell's data dealt with school racial composition over a ten-year period, 1963–1973. Her methods of data gathering and analysis incorporated several advances over previous studies. They included collection of data directly from persons in the cities in the sample, utilization of longitudinal data covering a longer time span, construction of a useful quantitative measure of the proportion of black and white students reassigned for the purposes of school integration, and statistics for the analysis of time-series trends. In addition, Rossell presented a large amount of raw data so that readers could check her analysis and draw their own conclusions.

As with other studies examining relationships between school integration and decline in white enrollment, Rossell's research still presents a variety of problems. They involve the definition of desegregation, the types of school districts that should be included in a single analysis (for example, central-city districts only or city and suburban districts), and the proper unit for analysis (for example, the individual

school, the school district, the metropolitan area). Such issues are critical because they determine whether one compares entities that may
be very different with respect to the issue in question, as when heavily
minority central-city districts ringed by predominantly white suburban districts are compared with county-level districts adjacent to
districts that already have substantial desegregation. The likelihood of
white withdrawal from the public schools following desegregation is
much greater in the former case than in the latter.

Rossell attempted to minimize such differentials in constituting her
sample but she did not entirely succeed because of the need to maintain a relatively large sample in order to carry out multivariate analysis. In addition, her study takes little account of the possibility that
imminent large-scale desegregation, such as might follow a court
order, may stimulate as much or more white withdrawal before desegregation as after. Her method of time-series analysis may, therefore,
be misleading for cities like San Francisco, where the rate of white
withdrawal increased to 4.1 percent two years before a major desegregation plan was implemented and then fell off to 3 percent after desegregation.

Still another major critique of Coleman's conclusions has been prepared by Robert Green and Thomas Pettigrew, who painstakingly reviewed the development of Coleman's analysis at four points in time.
They concluded that "there has been a confusion between his limited
research and his sweeping views against court-ordered desegregation."
Green and Pettigrew reanalyzed Coleman's data and also introduced
data of their own before reaching the following conclusions concerning the relationship between desegregation and the decline in white
enrollment in the public schools.

1. There has been an enormous, long-term trend of whites leaving the central cities
   for the suburbs and blacks coming into the largest central cities.
2. There is agreement among the studies that there is little or no effect of desegregation on white flight in medium- and smaller-sized cities.
3. There is also agreement that there is little or no effect of desegregation on the
   white flight of students in metropolitan-wide districts.
4. Desegregation required by federal court orders has not had different effects on
   white flight from other desegregation of equal magnitude.
5. The loss of white and black students from large urban school systems is significantly related to the proportion of black students in the systems.
6. Extensive school desegregation in the largest, nonmetropolitan school districts,
   particularly in the South, may hasten white flight of students in the first year of
   the process; but at least part of this effect may be compensated for in later years. [9]

Robert Wegmann has more recently reviewed the research dealing with change in school racial composition following desegregation and has reached tentative conclusions generally in agreement with those of Green and Pettigrew: "White flight may or may not occur . . . . The degree of white flight to be expected when there is governmental intervention to desegregate schools may vary depending on the proportion of minority students who are being assigned to a given school, and the social class gap between the minority and white students."[10] Both these conditions—high proportion of minorities and large gap in social class between minority and white students—tend to be more characteristic of big-city school districts than of small-city or suburban school districts.

In addition, Wegmann also clearly identified a number of additional variables that appear to play a part in determining whether decline in white enrollment accelerates following desegregation. For example, his review of the literature suggested that nonentrance of whites (that is, failure to enroll students in local public schools) often may be more important than withdrawal of currently enrolled children, depending on the type of racial transition and the rate at which that transition is occurring in neighborhood housing. His analysis also suggested that court-ordered desegregation may have different effects on white enrollment than does desegregation attributable to neighborhood change, and that the pace and level of desegregation may affect decisions to withdraw from or not to enroll children in the public schools. These findings indicate that it is often misleading to draw conclusions from samples that do not take account of conditions of buildings or neighborhoods and changes in the composition of school enrollment.

The differences of opinion among researchers studying white withdrawal and school desegregation now have been reduced to a minimum following the most recent reanalysis made by Coleman and his colleagues of their own data. Responding to the criticisms of Jackson and others, Coleman reported that the results of his latest analysis "show that the effect of desegregation on white loss is dramatically different for a city that has largely black schools and largely white suburbs . . . and for a city that has a small proportion of blacks and no sharp racial differences between city and suburbs . . . . The former condition characterizes the larger, older, northern and eastern cities, while the latter more nearly characterizes newer cities in the West, and southern cities with county-wide school districts."[11]

In short, among at least some of the participants in the controversy on desegregation research, there is now explicit agreement that accelerated white withdrawal connected with school desegregation is most likely to occur in large northern districts with a relatively high proportion of minority students surrounded by predominantly white suburban districts.

A major lesson to be learned from the controversy among researchers is that areas with markedly different characteristics should not be lumped together when one is trying to determine whether desegregation accelerates the decrease in enrollment of white students. Among the factors that need to be taken into account are the social class as well as the racial composition of a school district; the nature of differences between a city school district and the school districts in its suburbs; regional differences; and the nature and extent of desegregation actions. It would be useful also to have more case studies of enrollment patterns in individual school districts. Such studies allow for longitudinal analysis of an individual school to determine whether the results obtained by researchers using district-wide data are confirmed by events in individual schools, where the phenomena in question actually occur. The purpose of the study reported in the following pages is to provide such an analysis for the Kansas City (Missouri) Public School District, a relatively large central-city district in the lower Midwest.

A STUDY OF DESEGREGATION AND DECLINE
IN WHITE ENROLLMENT

The Kansas City (Missouri) Public School District is a central-city school district where the percentage of minority students has been increasing for most of the past twenty years. The number of white students declined from 32,412 in 1956 to 21,405 in 1976, while the number of black students increased from 10,076 to 33,001.

Located in a metropolitan area with a population in 1970 of 1,253,916, the district serves only part of Kansas City, which also includes all or part of twelve other school districts. Most of the minority population of the city, however, is included within the Kansas City school district. As of 1972–73, minority students constituted 54 percent of the district's enrollment, as compared with 8 percent minority enrollment in the remainder of the metropolitan area.

Although data on the percentage of minority students inside and outside the district in 1950 and 1960 are not available, it is clear that the Kansas City school district, as compared with surrounding districts, has had a relatively high proportion of minority students throughout this period, during which many of its schools have changed from predominantly white to desegregated to predominantly black. In addition, the median family income in 1970 within the district ($8,803) already was considerably below that of the metropolitan area as a whole ($10,568).

To determine whether the decline in white enrollment in this district was associated with degree and rate of desegregation at the individual school level, data were examined for all seventy-five elementary schools during all or most of the period between 1956 and 1975. It should be noted that nearly all the desegregation that occurred in this district during the period under study was "natural." That is, there was no court-ordered desegregation plan, and only a few schools were briefly desegregated in a limited fashion through busing at various periods in order to relieve overcrowding or to help obtain federal grants available to desegregated school districts. It should also be noted that certain schools experienced an accelerated decline in white enrollment more than once in the period covered by this analysis, as in the case of a school where this decline changed from 10 percent in one four-year period to 20 percent and then 30 percent in the two following four-year periods.

Comparison of Initial Percentage and Subsequent Increase in Percentage of Black Enrollment

It is frequently hypothesized that unsegregated urban schools having a relatively high percentage of minority students (30 to 50 percent) are more likely to become segregated and predominantly black than are schools in which minority students constitute a smaller proportion of the student body. Presumably this could happen because, other things being equal, white parents may tend to withdraw their children more readily from schools that they perceive as likely to become predominantly nonwhite than from schools perceived as having potential for stable integration. This tendency may be particularly evident if members of an incoming minority group are lower in socioeconomic status than students already in a school or if, as probably sometimes happens, some white parents merely assume that these students are likely to be disadvantaged socioeconomically.

In order to discover the relationship between initial percentage of black students and subsequent racial change in elementary schools in the Kansas City school district, changes in percentage of minority students were compared over two-year periods for selected years between 1956 and 1974 for three groups of schools that had varying proportions of black students. At the beginning of each two-year period schools in Group A had 15 to 29 percent minority enrollment; those in Group B, 30 to 45 percent; and those in Group C, 46 to 60 percent.

Table 2-1

Elementary schools in Kansas City, Missouri, grouped according to percentage of black enrollment, 1958-1972, and average percentage of increase in black enrollment during subsequent two-year period

	Number of schools, grouped by percentage of black enrollment				Average percentage of increase by group		
Year	A (15-29%)	B (30-45%)	C (46-60%)	Subsequent period	A	B	C
1958	3	1	1	1958-60	8.3	2.0	38.0
1960	5	3	1	1960-62	16.3	21.0	39.0
1962	7	2	3	1962-64	14.3	3.2	22.5
1964	3	4	2	1964-66	13.7	8.2	21.8
1966	6	2	1	1966-68	5.8	27.1	36.4
1968	6	2	1	1968-70	7.7	14.8	36.4
1970	5	4	1	1970-72	7.7	29.8	29.9
1971	7	4	1	1971-73	13.3	17.1	19.3
1972	4	2	0	1972-74	6.2	30.0	--

The data in Table 2-1 show that schools in Group A had much smaller increases in percentage of black enrollment during subsequent two-year periods than did schools in Groups B and C. Although the numbers of schools in the comparison groups for any period are too small for one to draw firm conclusions, the increase in the number of black students in subsequent two-year periods averaged 10.5 percent for schools in Group A, 18.2 percent for schools in Group B, and 28.2 percent for schools in Group C. These findings suggest that elementary schools in Group A were more likely to remain stably integrated, at least for the following two-year period, than were those in Groups B and C.

It should be said that Group A probably included a higher proportion of schools to which black students were bused in order to relieve overcrowding elsewhere than did schools in the other two groups. Thus the conclusions may be partly attributed to school board policies, to practical limitations on the amount of transportation to the schools in question, and to the likelihood that the racial turnover was not as rapid in the neighborhoods in which these schools are located as in those of Groups B and C. Schools in Group C, on the other hand, were less able to increase substantially in black enrollment in subsequent years than were the ones in Group A. Taken together, these findings appear to confirm the hypothesis that schools reaching a certain threshold in percentage of minority enrollment are more likely to become predominantly minority than schools with a small proportion of minority enrollment. But this threshold probably varies greatly in accordance with such local conditions as perceptions of neighborhood services, previous history of the community, social class mixture in school and community, and quality of educational leadership and programming in local schools. No attempt was made, therefore, to identify a precise tipping point in the Kansas City school district. It appears, however, that once the black enrollment has reached 30 to 60 percent the schools have tended to become almost completely black during subsequent years.

Comparison of Initial and Subsequent Percentage of Increase in Black Enrollment

It is frequently hypothesized that a rapid increase in the percentage of black students enrolled in a school is more likely to stimulate withdrawal among whites than is a more gradual increase. In order to examine this possibility, the percentage of increase in black enrollment for Kansas City elementary schools for various one- and two-year periods between 1956 and 1972 was calculated, and the schools were grouped as follows: Group X included schools in which the black enrollment increased from 1 to 10 percent, and Group Y included schools in which black enrollment increased by more than 10 percent. The percentage of increase in black enrollment in Groups X and Y was then compared for the immediately following two-year period. The results are shown in Table 2-2.

Table 2-2 indicates that schools in Group Y exhibited a much greater increase in percentage of black enrollment during the subsequent two-year periods than did schools in Group X. On seven of the nine comparisons, the increase in the percentage of black enrollment among Group X schools was at least double that among Group Y schools.

Table 2-2

Elementary schools in Kansas City, Missouri, grouped according to percentage of
increase in black enrollment during intitial one- or two-year periods, 1956-1972,
and average percentage of increase in black enrollment during subsequent
two-year periods

Initial period	Number of schools grouped by percentage of increase in black enrollment		Subsequent period	Average percentage of increase by group	
	X (1-10%)	Y (more than 10%)		X	Y
1956-58	8	6	1958-60	9.0	20.8
1958-60	9	6	1960-62	9.6	27.3
1960-62	8	8	1962-64	7.9	17.3
1962-64	11	7	1964-66	9.6	14.1
1964-66	10	8	1966-68	8.9	13.5
1966-68	9	8	1968-70	6.6	18.2
1968-70	13	16	1970-72	5.9	11.1
1970-71	11	6	1971-73	8.8	19.1
1971-72	11	3	1972-74	4.4	11.2

Over the entire period for which data were collected, Group X schools
had an average increase in black enrollment of approximately 8 percent, while the comparable figure for schools in Group Y was 16 percent. Thus, schools experiencing a substantial increase in percentage
of black enrollment in the initial period also had a much larger subsequent increase in percentage of black enrollment and a correspondingly larger decrease in percentage of white enrollment than did
schools in which desegregation occurred less rapidly and precipitously.

Comparison of Levels of Desegregation and Subsequent Racial Composition

The relationship between levels of segregation and subsequent racial composition was examined by identifying four levels of segregation and by determining the number of schools at each level in selected
years. In a designated year, as shown in Table 2-3, black enrollment
was 15 to 29 percent for Group A schools, 30 to 45 percent for Group
B schools, 46 to 60 percent for Group C schools, and 61 to 80 percent for
Group D schools. The percent of black enrollment in each group of schools
was then examined four to six years after the designated year.

Table 2-3

Elementary schools in Kansas City, Missouri, grouped according to percentage of black enrollment in a designated year, compared with average percentage of increase in black enrollment four to six years later

Desig- nated year	Number of schools by group				Compari- son year	Average percentage of black enrollment in comparison year by group			
	A (15-29%)	B (30-45%)	C (46-60%)	D (61-80%)		A	B	C	D
1960	5	3	1	0	1966	54.6	66.7	97.9	- -
1962	5	2	3	0	1966	45.5	40.1	83.9	- -
1964	4	4	2	1	1970	51.2	41.3	92.8	97.5
1966	9	4	2	2	1970	24.3	56.2	57.0	92.8
1968	10	4	1	4	1974	29.8	60.0	97.1	85.5
1970	8	3	1	2	1974	31.9	76.4	95.0	99.9

Table 2-3 also shows that schools at all levels of desegregation in the designated year generally were more segregated four to six years later. Beginning with the comparison in 1966, however, schools in Group A tended to remain stably integrated and on the average did not have a much higher proportion of black students four or six years later. That pattern of change indicates that it may be possible to maintain desegregation in the elementary schools of Kansas City as long as minority students do not constitute much more than 30 percent of the enrollment.

Changes in Number of White Students in Schools with Differing Percentages of Black Enrollment

Another way to examine the possibility that decline in enrollment of white students is associated with level of desegregation is to consider the actual number of these students in schools at differing levels of desegregation and to determine the actual rise or fall in their enrollment. This approach has the advantage of being independent of general changes in enrollment that could obscure the relationship between desegregation and white withdrawal.

This possibility was explored by computing a ratio based on the number of white students in 1974 divided by the number of white students in 1968 for elementary schools in Groups A, B, C, and D. The

Table 2-4

Ratio of white students in 1974 to white students in 1968 for schools in Kansas City, Missouri, grouped according to percentage of black enrollment

Group	Number of schools	Ratio
A (15–29%)	10	0.45
B (30–45%)	4	0.27
C (46–60%)	1	0.03
D (60–80%)	4	0.08

results are shown in Table 2-4. The table shows that the number of white students in 1974 as compared with 1968 was substantially higher (1974–1968 ratio = .45) among the ten schools in Group A than among the nine schools in Groups B, C, and D. This finding suggests that white enrollment declined in the latter schools at a much more rapid rate than was true in Group A schools.

Statistical Correlation between Changes in Racial Composition in Two-Year Periods

Still another way to examine the question of whether increases in black enrollment in one time period are associated with still higher increases in subsequent time periods is to compute the correlation be-

Table 2-5

Correlations between increases in percentage of black enrollment in thirty-three elementary schools in Kansas City, Missouri, for two-year periods between 1956 and 1974

Time periods	r	p	r^a	p
1956–58 with 1958–60	.60	.001	.57	.001
1958–60 with 1960–62	.63	.001	.70	.001
1960–62 with 1962–64	.42	.015	.63	.001
1962–64 with 1964–66	.08	.625	.46	.007
1964–66 with 1966–68	.47	.006	.62	.001
1966–68 with 1968–70	.08	.638	.19	.300
1968–70 with 1970–72	.00	.976	.47	.006
1970–72 with 1972–74	.12	.490	.14	.450

[a] Correlations reported in this column are between scores transformed to logarithms.

Note: r = correlation; p = probability

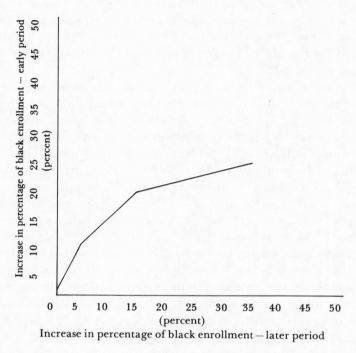

Figure 2-1

Hypothetical plot showing relationship between increase in
percentage of black enrollment in school
during early and later periods

tween changes in racial composition at differing times. Thus, correlation coefficients between increases in percentage of black enrollment were computed for consecutive two-year periods between 1956 and 1974. If the percentage of black enrollment increases during one time period and also during the following time period, the correlation coefficients will be positive and significantly different from zero. Simple correlations between increases in the percentage of black students for the two-year periods are shown in the second column of Table 2-5. Only the thirty-three schools that had at least 2 percent black enrollment in 1964 were included in the study.

The correlation coefficients in the second column of Table 2-5 suggest that increases in percentage of black enrollment in one two-year period generally were associated with increases in the following two-year period. They do not indicate, however, whether increases in earlier periods were associated with still larger increases in later periods. If the latter were the case, the pattern of association when each school is plotted for a set of two-year periods might look something like that shown in Figure 2-1.

This pattern would indicate that: schools experiencing a small increase (less than 10 percent) in the early period also experienced a small increase in the later period; schools that had a moderate increase (between 10 and 20 percent) in the early period tended to increase moderately (5 to 15 percent) in the later period; and schools exhibiting a large increase (20 to 25 percent) in the early period increased markedly (15 to 35 percent) in the later period.

When actual plots for the two-year periods between 1956 and 1974 were inspected, most were found to be somewhat similar to that shown in Figure 2-1. This indicates that a number of schools that increased in percentage of black enrollment during one time period either experienced a sharp rise in the percentage of black enrollment during the following period or continued to increase by approximately the same amount as in the preceding period. In many cases, schools showing a similar increase in both periods were approaching 100 percent black and thus could not increase very rapidly in the later period.

If a curve such as that shown in Figure 2-1 were present in the data discussed here, transforming scores on both variables to logarithms should substantially increase the statistical correlations between them. Correlations between the logged or curvilinear data for the two-year periods are shown in the fourth column of Table 2-5. Several of the correlation coefficients increased dramatically, particularly where they were not already quite high for these kinds of data. Thus the data in Table 2-5 suggest that schools in Kansas City frequently experienced an acceleration in the increase in the percentage of black enrollment once they had already begun to increase in this characteristic during the years 1956 to 1974.

Most of the data from the study described above deal with the percentages of white and black students enrolled. They do not, therefore, directly address the issue of absolute declines in white enrollment accompanying desegregation. The findings are, however, consistent with the conclusion that the decline in white enrollment has tended to accelerate in schools with a relatively high percentage of black students (about 30 percent or above) or with a recent rapid increase in the percentage of black students enrolled. Policy makers should heed these findings. If one of their goals is to avoid accelerating declines in white enrollment that have helped resegregate many big-city schools during the past twenty years, they must be cautious in determining the level and rate of desegregation to be obtained in the near future in these schools.

Notes

1. Micheal W. Giles, Everett F. Cataldo, and Douglas Gatlin, "The Impact of Busing on White Flight," *Social Science Quarterly* 55 (September 1974): 493–501.

2. James S. Coleman, "Recent Trends in School Integration," *Educational Researcher* 4 (July-August): 3–12.

3. Reynolds Farley, "School Integration and White Flight," in *Symposium on School Desegregation and White Flight,* ed. Gary Orfield (Washington, D.C.: Brookings Institution, 1975).

4. *Ibid.*, 6.

5. *Ibid.*, 8.

6. Gregg Jackson, "Reanalysis of Coleman's 'Recent Trends in School Integration,'" *Educational Researcher* 4 (November 1975): 21–26.

7. *Ibid.*, 25.

8. Christine H. Rossell, "The Political and Social Impact of School Desegregation Policy: A Preliminary Report," paper presented at the annual meeting of the American Political Science Association, San Francisco, 1975, 53–54.

9. Robert L. Green and Thomas F. Pettigrew, "Public School Desegregation and White Flight: A Reply to Professor Coleman," paper prepared for the U.S. Civil Rights Commission, Washington, D.C., 1975, 36–38.

10. Robert G. Wegmann, "White Flight: Some Hypotheses," paper presented at the annual meeting of the American Educational Research Association, San Francisco, 1976, 33–34. Chapter 1 of this volume is based on Wegmann's paper.

11. James S. Coleman, "Coleman on Jackson on Coleman," *Educational Researcher* 5 (February 1976): 4.

3. Policy Implications of Research on White Flight in Metropolitan Areas

Gary Orfield

At first glance the problem of research on white flight appears to be relatively simple. The difference between white enrollment before and after school desegregation is attributed to white resistance to desegregation. Statistics related to the change are commonly used by newspaper reporters, local school officials, and opponents of desegregation with little or no recognition that there is a general trend toward declining enrollments both in cities and in many suburbs, that patterns of white out-migration developed long before court-ordered desegregation, or that special local circumstances occur simultaneously with desegregation.

Even when scholarly research attempts to make statistical provision for these trends, other complexities arise. Is school desegregation the sole cause of a decision to move, or does it merely trigger earlier departures by some families almost certain to move anyway? Are there other significant changes in the city or in the metropolitan area at the time that account for an observed change in enrollment and residence patterns? Is accelerated flight a continuing problem produced by desegregation or is it a one-year spurt generated by the tumult of change? Does the statistical model exclude major influences on family choices? Inadequate treatment of any of these issues could produce seriously misleading policy conclusions.

70

Even simple definitions can have enormous implications for the meaning of research findings. Thus, in testing the proposition that whites are fleeing from school desegregation, the researcher must define "desegregation." Different definitions can produce wide variance in the findings.

Most white flight research, including that of James S. Coleman, defines desegregation as any situation where significant numbers of black and white children happen to be in the same school at a particular time. In the absence of a city-wide desegregation plan, most children in such "desegregated" schools will actually be attending school on the periphery of an expanding ghetto, for the neighborhoods are not integrated in any meaningful sense. Rather they are in rapid transition from an all-white to an all-black residential pattern. Looking at enrollment patterns in such schools and observing the rapid shifts in racial statistics, some people conclude that the integration of the school caused its rapid resegregation. Actually, underlying these statistics is a very simple tautological principle: as ghettos expand, the neighborhoods they expand into become increasingly black.

The danger of basing school policy on an inaccurate definition of desegregation can perhaps be demonstrated through the use of a comparable example from the housing field. In 1940 Newark, New Jersey, ranked as the most desegregated big city in the United States. By the 1960s, however, that city had actually experienced an increase in segregation while most other cities were moving in the opposite direction.[1] An analyst could conclude, from this, that residential integration is counterproductive and results in increasing segregation. If the analyst happened to notice that the black and white housing markets in the city had remained highly segregated except along ghetto boundaries, a more reasonable conclusion might be that rapid ghetto expansion produces an increasingly black city.[2] What appeared statistically to be integration was actually only rapid racial transition of neighborhoods. From the first conclusion it would appear that nothing more need be done to integrate housing, while the second conclusion might support a recommendation that would encourage dispersion of the growing black population, thereby producing a more stable pattern of integration.

Evidence that white flight increases after school desegregation must be viewed with considerable caution. Coleman agrees that, if stabilizing the white population is a major long-term policy goal, it is very possible that desegregation over a much broader area, rather than no desegregation at all, is the best procedure.[3] Given the fact that there is no way to prevent further expansion of the ghettos, the spread of segregation in both schools and housing is virtually inevitable in the absence of a powerful policy to alter the normal self-fulfilling prophecies of neighborhood transition.

This brief discussion of some of the complexities of research on white flight does not mean that the question cannot be studied effectively. It does indicate, however, that results of tentative research should be read with great caution.

WHITE FLIGHT AND URBAN CHANGE

Interpreting white flight research requires an implicit or explicit model of the process of racial change in a metropolitan area, particularly a set of assumptions about housing segregation, the nature of the causal relationships between school and housing decisions, and the future population prospects of central cities in the absence of school desegregation. White flight is related not only to school desegregation but also to the underlying demographics of the community, the consequences of dividing a metropolitan area into many separate governments and school districts, the nature of the local housing market, and perhaps even to such elusive qualities as the area's racial climate and the record of the local leadership in handling racial issues. To establish firmly any argument about white flight one needs some kind of general theory of urban racial change to develop testable hypotheses about the factors causing white flight.

Convincing analysis requires treatment of the number of simultaneous changes influencing urban life and public attitudes during the past few years. The range and diversity of factors that might influence the rate of racial transition can be suggested by a simple, noninclusive list of common conditions in cities during the late 1960s and early 1970s:

1. record levels of housing construction, overwhelmingly concentrated in the suburbs;
2. major urban riots;
3. rapid continued movement of urban jobs to suburban facilities;
4. trend toward racial polarization in city politics and the emergence of black political leaders;

5. increasing crime and public fears of violence;
6. more rapid expansion of ghetto boundaries made possible by the federal fair housing law of 1968;
7. increases in strikingly disproportionate taxation in some areas of central cities;
8. decline in the actual level of central city services in some cities;
9. housing subsidy programs of unprecedented magnitude that tended to accelerate racial transition in the city, to create opportunities for lower-income whites in the suburbs, and, sometimes, to end with the elimination of thousands of units from the central-city housing stock; and
10. major financial incentives, in terms of down payment and financing, for young families to purchase new outlying suburban housing.

The basic problem is that most of these major changes all work toward increased suburbanization, and thus their effects can easily be confounded. There are other problems, specifically problems relating to education. Many city schools have deteriorating physical plants, and local newspapers carry reports of steadily declining achievement test scores. Teacher strikes have eroded confidence and sometimes produced substantial enrollment declines. Financial crises have forced rising student-teacher ratios in some cities.

Separating out the influence of various elements is exceedingly difficult but vitally important if one is to draw any valid policy conclusions. It is difficult because the problems interact in shaping family decisions. Whites who left Atlanta in 1973, for instance, decided to do so in an atmosphere affected not only by a modest school integration plan but also in a climate of polarization over the drive of Maynard Jackson to become the South's first big-city black mayor.[4]

A family that leaves Detroit when a school integration plan is implemented would also be aware of the city's income tax, its 1967 riot, the extremely high level of violent crime, cutbacks in the police force, the city's black mayor, the massive abandonment of housing in the city, the recent loss of more than a fifth of the city's job base, and the city's severe current economic crisis.[5] While the school crisis might be the final factor that determines when the family actually moves, the general condition of the city virtually guarantees that the family would have moved eventually and that it would not be replaced by a similar white family. Not only do the various forces work in the same direction, but several are simultaneously intensifying.

Indications that the school issue itself is not a sufficient explanation for white flight can be found on every side. If the changing racial composition of the public schools were the central problem, for example, one could expect a heavy increase in the enrollment of whites in the relatively inexpensive Catholic schools that are heavily concentrated in central cities. Although these schools are real alternatives in areas threatened by racial change, their enrollments have declined sharply in recent years.[6]

WHITE FLIGHT OR JUST FLIGHT?

The assumption that the rapid movement of white families from central cities is a flight merely from racial contact has been substantially undermined by recent evidence that minority groups themselves are beginning to flee the same area very rapidly when they are able to buy suburban housing. Black public school enrollments are stabilizing or declining in a number of central cities, and black middle-class families are increasingly moving to the inner suburbs, that is, to the ring of smaller urban areas immediately surrounding the central city. Even among middle-class black families who retain central-city residence, a substantial number of parents send their children to private schools. The intensity of the blacks' desire to escape central-city conditions is indicated by a survey of black residents in Chicago, in which 54 percent of the participants said they would prefer to live in the suburbs.[7]

The situation in the Washington, D.C., metropolitan area suggests possible future patterns. In the first four years of the 1970s the black population of the city fell by 5 percent. The city's suburbs, on the other hand, experienced an astonishing 61 percent increase in black population in the same brief period. The decline in central-city black population was more than twice as rapid as the out-migration of the city's remaining whites. Almost three-fifths of the total suburban population growth came from new black residents.[8]

More than a third of the black children in the Washington metropolitan area attended suburban schools by 1972, and the number is steadily rising.[9] District of Columbia public school statistics show that, even among the blacks who remain in the city, about ten thousand are using private schools.[10] The city, in other words, is experiencing massive black flight, and its public schools are becoming not simply black institutions but lower-class institutions as well. Elementary school enrollment declined 5.4 percent in the single year between fall 1973 and fall 1974.[11] Obviously these families are not fleeing contacts with blacks; they are responding to both the problems of city life and the attractions of the suburbs.

The schools of California's largest cities indicate the complexity of the issue. The growth in the black enrollment in the Los Angeles area is outside the central city. Although the Mexican-American enrollment has grown rapidly in the nation's second largest school system, the black enrollment has changed little since 1968, and it recently entered a period of significant decline. Although the Chicano student population has expanded 30 percent since 1968, black enrollment has actually dropped 5 percent during the last two school years.[12]

The results are even more confusing in San Francisco, the first big city outside the South to implement an extensive desegregation plan. The San Francisco schools have been experiencing not only white flight but also black flight and even Hispanic flight. From September 1972 to September 1974, San Francisco's black enrollment declined by a ninth, and its Hispanic enrollment fell by a twelfth.[13]

The California statistics could be attributed to black resistance to contact with Mexican-Americans in Los Angeles and to black and Hispanic hostility to San Francisco's growing numbers of Korean and Filipino students.[14] It is, of course, far more plausible to attribute the movement to many of the same long-term factors that shaped white suburbanization.

POLICY RECOMMENDATIONS AND THEIR CONTEXT

Failure to consider the accelerating decline of many large central cities and their diminishing appeal for any family with other options can introduce a conservative bias into the interpretation of policy implications of research findings. If research is focused tightly on the short-term effect of school desegregation on white migration and if future research efforts actually demonstrate such an effect, this could be read as evidence against doing anything. If, however, the focus were to be widened to include the whole array of forces influencing locational decisions over a period of years, the dominant trend that emerges points directly toward a particularly severe form of both racial and social-class isolation in central-city school systems. If the latter diagnosis of the problem is correct, the policy implications are quite different. Assuming that the onset of school integration only highlights and perhaps temporarily accelerates already well-established social trends, one could recommend that major efforts be made to change the structure of incentives and perceptions that shape those trends.

Public discussion of white flight research in recent months has focused on the assertion that school desegregation has greatly intensified out-migration, usually based on newspaper interviews with James Coleman. Several scholars employing more sophisticated analytic techniques than Coleman's have concluded that desegregation plans have no discernible effect, on the average, on the rate of white suburbanization.

Yet, even if one were to concede the validity of Coleman's method of analysis and accept his results completely, his study suggests only that the initiation of desegregation in a city with a 50 percent black enrollment will produce an additional loss of 5.5 percent of the white students. This flight is significantly less than the same school system can expect to lose for other reasons in a normal year. In other words, the results show, at worst, that the desegregation of a big-city system and a 50 percent black enrollment might bring the schools to their final ghetto status about a year sooner than otherwise projected.[15]

Coleman found that this effect is even weaker in northern cities and minimal in cities where the school districts are smaller in enrollment than the twenty-two largest school districts. Further, he provided evidence of additional loss resulting from long-term impact of the desegregation plan after the first year.[16] In other words, in most cities where desegregation issues are still pending, the effect of school integration on population movements is uncertain, probably small or nonexistent, according to available data.

Research that focuses on the possible incremental effect of the initiation of desegregation is, of course, a valid intellectual undertaking. Policy recommendations that are made without any reference to the broader causes of migration should not, however, be taken seriously. If the central cities in the United States are moving rapidly toward the condition prophesied in the report made by the National Advisory Commission of Civil Disorder in 1968, then a policy proposal to lower slightly the rate of out-migration by ignoring unconstitutional school segregation can have only the most marginal importance.

ISSUES NEEDING RESEARCH

Serious recommendations about school desegregation policy should be based on analysis of alternatives that might lessen the incentives for

the departure of the middle class and even provide some encouragement to the return of middle-class white and black families to the central city and its schools. Two policies need extensive research. First,
one could try to determine why many cities experienced little or no loss
after desegregation while others had a massive drop in white enrollment. Closer study of the extreme cases might well suggest procedures
and methods that would avoid this initial loss of enrollment or forms
of federal assistance that would be particularly helpful. Similarly,
there should be close analysis of Atlanta and Memphis, where massive
losses skewed the findings of the Coleman study.

More important, in the long run, there should be serious study of
the value of metropolitan desegregation plans. Such plans are now in
operation in many of the largest school districts in the South. Las
Vegas also has one, and Louisville is implementing one. By eliminating segregation in predominantly white schools throughout entire
metropolitan areas, these plans may diminish the incentives for suburbanization and eventually lower some of the barriers against return
of middle-class families to the central cities and their schools.

The only research available on this issue, a study of Florida school
districts done by Micheal Giles, Everett Cataldo, and Douglas Gatlin
suggests that the metropolitan approach does indeed tend to avoid any
significant transfer out of the public school system. The issue needs
careful comparative research.

WHITE FLIGHT IN SUBURBIA

Although the discussion of white flight has focused on central cities,
the problem may actually become most serious in inner suburbs, as
ghettos spill over city boundaries in a growing number of metropolitan
areas. Because most suburban school districts are small, a relatively
modest number of new black residents often has a significant impact
on a district's enrollment patterns and helps create a self-fulfilling
prophecy of transition to a ghetto school system.

This process is evident in two suburbs — Compton and Inglewood —
adjoining the Watts ghetto in Los Angeles. Both communities went in
relatively short periods of time from predominantly white to almost
completely black enrollments. Inglewood had a desegregation plan.
Compton did not. Yet both went through a brief biracial transition
and then resegregated.[17] They behaved very much like a section of a
big city undergoing racial transition. In fact, they are parts of a huge

metropolitan city. The reason they have gone through the entire process so rapidly and completely, why they are so extremely vulnerable to white ghettoization, is that the entire system is really only a large neighborhood. The school district boundaries isolate the individual small suburb from the diversity of the metropolitan area. The isolated nature of the small school district, superimposed on a process of residential change based on monolithic ghetto expansion, meant that suburban districts once far whiter than the city became far blacker than the city in a brief period of time.

In the 1960s Inglewood, a working-class suburb of almost a hundred thousand people, began receiving black residents, a number of whom had left their homes in Compton after that suburb became part of the Los Angeles ghetto. By 1970, when desegregation was ordered by the court, black students constituted about 25 percent of the school population, and there was a substantially lower proportion of black residents in the suburb. The next year, the proportion of black students rose to 35 percent. Within four school years the system became overwhelmingly black. The court took the rare step of formally releasing the district from its desegregation plan since there were too few whites left to integrate.[18] An analysis of the dynamics of the Inglewood situation emphasized the futility and heavy social cost of attempting to deal with the issue in one individual school district at a time:

> The freedom to leave encourages a high degree of rancor. People are able to take hard-line positions . . . because they are not ultimately dependent on a negotiated settlement . . . . The process is exacerbated by the fact that each individual decision to move out increases the pressures on the remaining residents to move.
> When looked at in this way, the problem of school desegregation takes on metropolitan significance. People may relocate from community to community within the same metropolitan area without affecting their jobs and other important social relations. Relocation outside the metropolitan area is another matter. . . . In short, they have a stake in the metropolitan area that they do not have in a particular suburban community.[19]

Without a cross-district desegregation plan, the inner suburbs near the city ghettos and those suburban communities most willing to practice genuine fair housing tend to become the focal points for black movement and for school resegregation. In the St. Louis metropolitan area, for example, the suburb of University City had been an early leader in housing integration. By 1972, its school enrollment was 55 percent black, with a larger black majority in the lower grades.[20]

The problem will become increasingly evident in the inner suburbs of New York and Newark. Even during the 1960s the inner ring of suburbs was losing 3,000 whites while gaining 9,000 blacks and 2,000 Puerto Ricans in an average year.[21] This problem became substantially more serious in the 1970s. The area was headed toward growing numbers of ghetto suburban school systems.

Where suburban school systems are small and black suburbanization begins in earnest, the only alternative to repetition of the Inglewood experience would be some kind of desegregation plan crossing district lines, preferably with supporting housing policies. The most immediate and dramatic benefits of a metropolitan desegregation plan might well accrue to inner suburbs.

SCHOOL DESEGREGATION AND HOUSING INTEGRATION

The only way truly to avoid the problem of white flight and to accomplish stable school integration, some researchers suggest, is to integrate housing. Once civil rights laws strike down suburban housing discrimination, the argument goes, the schools will be integrated quietly as a natural result of changing residential patterns.

It may well be, however, that this argument can be turned on its head. It is hard to imagine how stable housing integration involving large numbers of blacks could be achieved in any reasonable period of time without an area-wide framework of integrated schools. Unless the normal process of channeling black residents to limited areas breaks down completely, there will be suburban ghettos with their own segregated schools. Once channeling is directed toward a particular area, that area tends to become increasingly black unless new white families continue to move in to replace those who depart in the normal process of rapid residential mobility.

Under the existing system there is virtually no incentive for a white family desiring to avoid segregated ghetto schools to move into a neighborhood with a substantial number of black neighbors. In all probability, based on past experience, the neighborhood school will soon become overwhelmingly black.[22] Even those who would accept integration will very seldom accept this. The logical choice, therefore, is to seek one of the many segregated white areas in the metropolitan community. Without a desegregation plan, in other words, the white family often does not perceive a choice between an integrated and an all-white school—only between an all-white school and one that is almost certain to become virtually all black. The only way one can break into this cycle of expectations is to assure families that the schools will be integrated wherever they move and that they will not become overwhelmingly nonwhite anywhere. This assurance could strengthen a serious campaign for housing integration if federal, state, and local officials ever decided to mount one.

Any stable, large-scale residential integration, extending beyond communities with special institutions and particularly favorable attitudes, probably requires a solution to the problem of segregated schools. This certainly seems true in considering residential integration in the inner-city black neighborhoods. Americans have become so accustomed to thinking of ghetto expansion as an irreversible, inexorable process that there has been little serious thought about the possibility of a significant movement of young white families back into central-city ghetto neighborhoods.

There are several reasons for thinking that such a reverse movement might be possible, at least in certain central cities that remain viable economic and cultural centers. The skyrocketing cost of housing, severe environmental restrictions on building in many suburbs, the increasing costs of supporting the two-car, energy-consuming life-style, as well as trends toward far smaller families and more working wives, are all compatible with a possible central-city revival. Such a reverse migration is now taking place in several parts of Washington, Philadelphia, and some other major cities.[23] Renovated communities have proved particularly attractive to young professionals, the very group that city leaders are most eager to attract and retain. Very few of these new residents, however, use the public schools; residence is largely limited to those without school-age children and those able to afford private schools. Most middle-class families would have to pay a prohibitive price to live in the central city. If the central-city schools were integrated on a level that reflected the population distribution of the entire metropolitan area, at least this cost would be eliminated. The attractions of accessibility, diversity, energy economy, cultural opportunities, and the basically superior quality of older buildings might then permit a significant in-migration. Once such a migration reached a substantial scale, it would diminish the costs of maintaining school integration.

WHITE FLIGHT AND NATIONAL HOUSING POLICY

The phenomenon described as white flight by those studying school desegregation is often seen from another angle as a true triumph of the basic tools of U.S. housing policy during the post-World War II period. Facilitating white suburbanization has been a basic goal — explicit at first and implicit still. Federal policies have helped shape the environment in which every family makes its choice about where to live, and those policies have skewed the choice very heavily in favor of the suburbs. When these policies are superimposed on a dual housing market where blacks are excluded from most new suburban housing, the policies clearly foster white flight.

These policies have taken many forms. Until 1950 the Federal Housing Administration openly favored segregated suburban developments in granting mortgage insurance, insurance commitments that aided in both the initial construction financing and the sale of housing. Until the late 1960s HUD took no significant action against segregation in public housing.[24] Massive new housing subsidy programs created by the housing act in 1968 were often used in ways that resulted in increased segregation.[25] The large tax credit allowed for the purchase of new homes in 1975 unintentionally provides a powerful incentive for movement to the outermost suburbs. These policies have drawn investment to the suburbs, created powerful financial incentives for young families to choose suburban homes, and often intensified and expanded central-city segregation.

One dramatic example of the relationship between federal housing policy and the departure of white families was provided in Detroit in the early 1970s. A program for low-income homeownership was implemented in a way that saddled poor minority families with overpriced and deteriorated housing they could not afford to maintain. For a time the process created an artificially inflated market allowing lower-income white families to sell out and get enough money to leave for the suburbs. A former director of the Detroit FHA office, William Whitbeck, analyzed the results of a disaster that ultimately left the government holding 11,000 vacant unusable houses:

What happened in Detroit is that the white flight from the city was facilitated by the FHA to the nth degree. Not only did the readily available FHA insured mortgages facilitate somebody selling and leaving the city, but of course we insured the other end of the transaction, when he bought a new house out in the suburbs. We greased the skids the whole way. It's no wonder that Detroit lost 190,000 people from 1960 through 1970. The system was like a greased runway.[26]

It would seem that federal housing policies have clearly worked to facilitate housing segregation. The effort has been sustained, powerful, and effective, with no significant attempt to offset the effect by exerting equal effort to retain or return young middle-class families to the central cities. If the problem is to be controlled, there surely must be such an effort.

POLICY IMPLICATIONS

Existing research on white flight and urban desegregation can support only limited policy recommendations. The current research findings suggest that the implementation of a desegregation plan, in itself, would have only a modest impact on racial patterns in most communities where the issue is still open. The very limited experience with city-wide desegregation plans in the North and West, however, means that this conclusion rests on a very modest empirical base. The data suggest that any possible effect of desegregation plans on migration is largely limited to the nation's biggest cities, and that desegregation of many smaller cities can be feasibly undertaken without accelerating white departures.

The available research does suggest that the first year of desegregation is a critical period for deciding to leave the public schools or move to another school district. This problem might be moderated by expansion of the small federal program providing special assistance for the transition, as well as strong leadership supporting compliance with the law.

The research also contains some indications that problems would be significantly diminished by metropolitan desegregation. While the evidence is limited, it strongly supports the argument that the process works better when it incorporates the racial and economic diversity of the metropolitan area and maintains substantial white majorities in desegregated schools.

The basic forces generating both white and black suburbanization are multifaceted, and most are independent of school desegregation plans. There is no evidence that stopping school desegregation would stabilize central-city racial patterns. If the pattern of flight is to be significantly modified, however, positive, coordinated, and often metropolitan-wide, desegregation efforts dealing with both housing and schools will be required.

Notes

1. John Tepper Marlin, *City Housing*, Municipal Performance Report (New York: Council on Municipal Performance, 1973), 17. The data cited were developed by Karl Taeuber and associates at the Institute for Research on Poverty at the University of Wisconsin.

2. *Ibid.* The data are cited from Kurt Bayer, "A Social Indicator of the Cost of Being Black," unpublished dissertation, University of Maryland, 1971.

3. James S. Coleman, statement made at a symposium on "White Flight and Desegregation" held at the Brookings Institution, Washington, D.C., August 1975.

4. *New York Times*, October 17, 1973.

5. City of Detroit, Budget Department, *City of Detroit, Five Year Financial Forecast, 1975–1980* (Detroit: the Department, n.d.); Leonard Downie, Jr., *Mortgage on America* (New York: Praeger, 1974), 44.

6. *Catholic Schools in America*, ed. Chris Ganley (Denver, Colo.: Curriculum Information Center, 1975), iv.

7. MetroPoll data reported in *Integrated Education* 13 (January–February 1975): 9.

8. Data from the U.S. Census Bureau and the Washington Center for Metropolitan Studies, reported in the *Washington Post*, May 18, 1975, and the *Washington Star*, May 18, 1975.

9. U.S. Department of Health, Education, and Welfare, Data Management Center, "SMSAs Student/Teacher Data by Ethnicity," unpublished memo, October 1973, 39.

10. District of Columbia Public Schools, Division of Research and Evaluation, *Data Resource Book, 1975–76* (Washington, D.C.: the Public Schools, n.d.).

11. District of Columbia Public Schools, "Pupil Membership in Regular Day Schools on October 17, 1974, Compared with October 18, 1973," unpublished report dated November 1975, 1.

12. U.S. Department of Health, Education, and Welfare, Office for Civil Rights, *Directory of Public Elementary and Secondary Schools in Selected Districts. Enrollment and Staff by Racial/Ethnic Group, Fall 1972* (Washington, D.C.: U.S. Government Printing Office, 1972), 115. Current district statistics are from files of the Office for Civil Rights, and earlier statistics are from the Los Angeles Board of Education, "Appeal Brief," in *Crawford* v. *Board of Education of the City of Los Angeles*, 21.

13. HEW, Office for Civil Rights, *Directory of Public Elementary and Secondary Schools*, 154. See also statistics for 1974 from school district reports.

14. *San Francisco Chronicle*, June 13, 1974, reported that the Korean population grew more than 100 percent and Filipino residents more than 50 percent during 1970–1973.

15. James S. Coleman, Sara D. Kelly, and John Moore, "Trends in School Segregation 1968–73," unpublished working paper for the Urban Institute, Washington, D.C., 1975, 53. Coleman suggests that extrapolation from his data shows a far more dramatic initial loss in desegregation of a system like Detroit, with nearly three-fourths black enrollment. Since no such city-wide plans have been implemented, this conclusion is untested.

16. *Ibid.*, 59.

17. Leroy F. Aarons, "Compton, California, Looks Uneasily over Its Shoulder at Watts," *Washington Post*, August 8, 1975.

18. Edna Bonacich and Robert F. Goodman, *Deadlock in School Desegregation* (New York: Praeger, 1972), 3-4, 26, 95-97.

19. *Ibid.*, 86.

20. HEW, Office for Civil Rights, *Directory of Public Elementary and Secondary Schools*, 783.

21. "The State of the Region: A Digest of Selected Trends through 1974," *Regional Plan News*, No. 97 (March 1975): 26-27.

22. The impact of these expectations on housing prices is discussed in Charles T. Clotfelter, "The Effect of School Desegregation on Housing Prices," unpublished paper, 1974.

23. Conrad Weiler, *Philadelphia: Neighborhood, Authority, and the Urban Crisis* (New York: Praeger, 1974).

24. Gary Orfield, "Federal Policy, Local Power, and Metropolitan Segregation," *Political Science Quarterly* 99 (Winter 1974-75): 784-790.

25. U.S. Commission on Civil Rights, *Home Ownership for Lower Income Families: A Report on the Racial and Ethnic Impact of the Section 235 Program, 1971* (Washington, D.C.: U.S. Government Printing Office, n.d.).

26. Brian D. Boyer, *Cities Destroyed for Cash: The FHA Scandal at HUD* (Chicago: Follett Publishing Co., 1973), 171-172.

PART TWO
Magnet and Alternative Schools in Cincinnati, Houston, and Chicago

   This part begins with information on one of the largest and most vigorous alternative or magnet school programs in any big-city school district in the country. ("Alternative school" in this book generally follows the Cincinnati usage, where it is defined in terms of the "magnet" type of school, which offers attractive special programs. It is not used in the more limited sense of "free" or "open" schools that was common several years ago.) Cincinnati is attempting to implement an extensive alternative school program in order to provide attractive, integrated educational opportunities intended to help stabilize the city's schools and neighborhoods.

   Virginia K. Griffin provides background material on the desegregation controversy in Cincinnati and shows how developments in the court case there helped stimulate development of the alternative school program. The following chapter, by Donald R. Waldrip, includes a description and analysis of the components of the program, and then Joseph L. Felix and James N. Jacobs raise issues regarding problems of implementation. Experience in Cincinnati suggests that there are three important problems to consider in developing alternative or magnet school programs in big-city school districts. In Chapter 7, Duane Holm describes the metropolitan setting in which the Cincinnati alternative program is being carried out. He concludes that regional approaches (inclusion of suburban school districts) are required to achieve the desegregation goal of the alternative program and other desegregation efforts.

Next to Cincinnati and, possibly, Minneapolis, Houston probably has initiated a larger and more comprehensive magnet school program relative to its size than any other big-city school district in the United States. Chapter 8, by Connie Campbell and John Brandstetter, provides background material about this program and also describes the manner in which it was developed and implemented. The final chapter, by Campbell and Levine, is the only chapter in this book devoted to a single school — the Whitney Young Magnet High School — in Chicago, a city that does not have an extensive magnet school program. Like many other big cities, however, Chicago could benefit greatly from long-range plans tying urban renewal to the development of magnet schools. Chapter 9 attempts to pinpoint and illustrate some possibilities that could be explored by educators and planners in other big cities.

4. Desegregation in Cincinnati: The Legal Background

Virginia K. Griffin

The Cincinnati Board of Education first became defendant in a desegregation suit filed in 1963 by the National Association for the Advancement of Colored People on behalf of Tina Deal, a pupil in the city schools.[1] That suit resulted in a judgment in favor of the board. The U.S. Court of Appeals, Sixth Circuit, affirmed that judgment, but remanded the case "for further findings on the issues of claimed discrimination in specific schools and programs and claimed harm to Negro students, allegedly caused by racially imbalanced schools, and for the taking of such additional relevant evidence as either party may offer."[2]

On remand in 1969, the U.S. District Court found "that neither gerrymandering nor any other alleged discriminatory practice on the part of the board brought about such racial imbalance as existed." That general finding was supported by eighteen detailed findings in favor of the board on specific issues of claimed constitutional violations. All of the findings on remand were affirmed by the court of appeals.

During these years the board and the administration of the Cincinnati schools were acutely aware of the issues of the lawsuit and of the force of the civil rights movement itself. By 1971 none of the board members who had been party to the suit of 1963 remained on the board, and the office of the superintendent was also filled by a different person. New ideas and enthusiasms abounded.

There were a number of significant initiatives concerning desegregation policy. For example, the Cincinnati Board of Education strenuously resisted routine transfers of territory from the Cincinnati district to suburban districts made by the State Board of Education. These transfers involved small white areas that were seeking separation from the city schools. The U.S. District Court upheld the resistance of the Cincinnati board in one case and denied it in another. The latter involved two or three students whose homes had been cut off from the district by the construction of an expressway.

A report published in March 1969 by a community task force on education and race contained the recommendation that the board declare it to be "the policy of the Cincinnati Board of Education that quality integrated education is the highest goal of the Cincinnati Public Schools. While this purpose shall remain clear, devices used to achieve this goal may vary with time and circumstances. Whenever a relevant decision is made, the potential for achieving integration shall be assigned a higher priority than any other single factor."[3] Four years later, on March 26, 1973, the board adopted this policy statement.[4]

Meanwhile, the Planning, Program, and Organization Committee of the Cincinnati Board of Education had reported on June 8, 1970, that it believed the board should include among its stated goals that of fostering "better intercultural understanding." On June 29, 1970, the board adopted the following statement as part of its "Program Goals for 1971":

Intercultural Understanding.
. . . it will be one of the goals of the Cincinnati Board of Education to provide interracial and intersocioeconomic educational understanding for both the students and the teachers of the Cincinnati Public School system thereby giving the students and the teachers a more realistic knowledge of the multicultural nature of our society.

Recognizing that provincialism contributes to misunderstanding among groups separated by geography as well as other factors, the schools must devise methods for regular dialogue among representatives of different areas, bringing differences and even conflicting views into open discussion and examination.

Ohio law requires the equal opportunity for every child to attend the most convenient school regardless of race, creed or national origin. With this in mind, the Board of Education supports the neighborhood school concept. Nothing in the goal set forth in this Section F shall conflict with the legal requirements of convenience nor require the voluntary or involuntary transportation of students.[5]

On July 9, 1973, the superintendent reported to the board as a matter of record on steps toward implementation of the policies described above:

The incidence of racially identifiable staff will be reduced through attrition and transfer. New teachers will be assigned to schools on the bases of: 1) their area of training and certification, and 2) their race. The intent will be to have the racial balance of each school staff approach the racial compositon of the staff of the entire school system with ten percent leeway in either direction. A number of years will be required to reach this goal through attrition; therefore, we will work with teachers and the recognized teacher organization to encourage volunteer transfers so that the goal will be reached as rapidly as possible.

An open enrollment plan for students will be implemented in September, 1973, under the following conditions: 1) that the receiving schools have available space, and 2) that the transfers will improve racial balance.[6]

An application for funds under the Emergency School Assistance Act (ESAA) was drawn up during the summer of 1973. The requested funds were to be used to assist the board with a massive integration effort in one high school district. The regional office of the U.S. Department of Health, Education, and Welfare and the Office of Civil Rights verbally assured the superintendent that, with regard to eligibility based on staff assignment, student transfer, alternative schools, and school building construction, the Board of Education was making sufficient efforts to warrant the application.

On December 10, 1973, a lame duck Board of Education passed a resolution to abolish school district lines and to assign pupils to school buildings so that each school would have approximately the same racial balance as the district as a whole—approximately 50 percent black and 50 percent white.[7] Although the new board did not rescind the resolution, the new president detailed extensive plans for affirmative programs to provide students with quality integrated education consistent with its statutorily mandated and judicially approved neighborhood school policy and the evolving policies of the board prior to the action of the lame duck board. Responding quickly, HEW officials reduced the allowable amounts in the ESAA application.

After several months of written and verbal contact with HEW officials, the Board of Education determined to challenge "the right of the U.S. Department of Health, Education, and Welfare to withhold emergency school aid for the purpose of coercing the Cincinnati Board of Education to abandon its policy of providing a quality integrated education to the children of Cincinnati through the maintenance of neighborhood schools, and for the purpose of coercing the Board to overturn and restructure the system of public education now in operation in Cincinnati."

The U.S. District Court denied the board's motion for summary judgment and granted instead summary judgment in favor of HEW. Pending the outcome of an appeal, however, HEW was ordered by the court to set aside and hold available $1.2 million for the ESAA grant to Cincinnati. On March 31, 1976, the U.S. Court of Appeals, Sixth Circuit, reversed the judgment of the district court.[8] It sent the case back to that court to determine the issue of discrimination on the basis of evidence to be considered by that court in the *Bronson* case. Racial and economic integration of the public schools in Cincinnati and Hamilton County was the issue in this suit, which was filed in the U.S. District Court on May 29, 1974, by attorneys of the National Association for the Advancement of Colored People on behalf of Mona Bronson and all persons similarly situated. The attorneys requested that the court order the Cincinnati Board of Education to implement the integration plan passed by the preceding board on December 10, 1973, and to desist from implementing its own plan adopted January 14, 1974.[9] The attorneys further requested that the court order the Cincinnati Board of Education and the State Board of Education to consider the development of a county-wide integration plan.

The integration plan of the outgoing board was loaded with legal consequences for an incoming majority elected on a neighborhood school platform. In the preamble to its resolution, the lame duck board confessed to a long list of segregative acts, charged its predecessors with similar illegalities, and assumed a responsibility to desegregate the system completely. To right these wrongs, the board prescribed a racial and income balance for each school substantially proportionate to the district as a whole. School attendance districts were to be abolished, but not the pupil assignment to each school, and a redistricting was to be instituted by September 1974. The board sketched the administrative and financial machinery to accomplish the redistricting and noted that transportation could be one of the tools.

This desegregation drama was based on the scenario played out in Dayton. There, the outgoing Board of Education, anticipating the stance of the incoming majority, passed on December 8, 1971, a plan that became the pattern for what occurred in Cincinnati. The same

NAACP attorney who charted the course in Dayton served as the consultant in preparing the outgoing board's resolution in Cincinnati. In Dayton the incoming board rescinded the three resolutions embodying the plan of the outgoing board on January 3, 1972. The NAACP filed a suit in the U.S. District Court on April 17, 1972.[10] The trial was conducted from November 13 through December 1, 1972. On February 7, 1973, the district court found three sets of facts that were cumulatively in violation of the Equal Protection Clause. It is significant that one was the rescission of the resolutions of December 8.

In Cincinnati the incoming board projected its course on January 14, 1974, by adopting a resolution consisting of two major parts: "Findings," and a "Plan for Quality Integrated Education." Among the "Findings," the most important reiterated the *Deal* decision of 1969 holding that racial imbalance had not been caused by action of the Board of Education. The remaining "Findings" refuted the items in the resolution of December 10. The "Plan for Quality Integrated Education" set forth these major goals: racial balance of the staff; open enrollment to improve racial balance; alternative schools; and program improvements such as enrichment of the reading program, restoration of secondary school hours from 120 to 160, and other related proposals. In the preamble to this plan, the board set forth its position concerning the resolution of December 10: ". . . [it] is not being rescinded but rather it will stand as the action of the outgoing 1973 Board to be judged in the light of all the circumstances and of the foregoing findings."[11]

At this point two momentous decisions supervened to change the course of events. The first decision, handed down August 20, 1974, by the U.S. Court of Appeals, Sixth Circuit, in the Dayton case, greatly diminished the force of the alleged act of rescinding the December 10 resolution on integration passed by the Cincinnati Board of Education. The court ruled that the rescission by the board in Dayton was not in itself an unconstitutional act.[12] This prompted the district judge to advise the NAACP attorneys (on the *Bronson* case) that they could not rely on the rescission charge and would have to prove other alleged acts of segregation. The judge announced that he would hear at the same time evidence on both the original request for a preliminary injunction—the one that would require the board to implement the resolution of December 10—and on the merits of the entire complaint. He asked the attorneys to complete their gathering of evidence by November 1, 1974, and he indicated that he anticipated a lengthy and complex trial.

In the second momentous decision the U.S. Court of Appeals, Sixth Circuit, decided in favor of the Board of Education of the City of Grand Rapids on December 6, 1974.[13] The court upheld the neighborhood school concept and cleared the board in Grand Rapids of any responsibility for the displacement of whites by blacks in the established neighborhood attendance grid. The court would not require the board to take affirmative action to improve racial balance because there was no evidence of complicity by school officials in the allegedly segregative acts. Further, the board could not be held in violation of civil rights laws for its failure to foresee the possibility of racial imbalance.

Following these two decisions, arguments in the *Bronson* case have centered on how far back in time NAACP attorneys could go in attempting to show that segregation that may exist in the Cincinnati public schools is due to intentional action (or inaction) on the part of the Board of Education, rather than to neighborhood school patterns. On September 24, 1975, the U.S. Court of Appeals, Sixth Circuit, ruled that plaintiffs could not go beyond July 26, 1965 (the date that Judge John Weld Peck gave his findings of fact and conclusions of law in the first *Deal* decision [14]) in attempting to prove violation of constitutional rights. The court of appeals affirmed Judge David Porter, who presided in the *Bronson* case, but with modifications. One of the three appellate judges said that under no circumstances could the plaintiffs go beyond July 26, 1976; another said that it could be done for background purposes; and a third indicated that it could be done for newly discovered evidence, but observed that it was highly unlikely that such evidence would materialize. In the summer of 1976 Judge Porter asked the opposing attorneys to prepare their own interpretations of the confusing decision by the court of appeals.

The accumulation of laws, litigation, and practices throughout the United States provided the background for the actions of the Cincinnati Board of Education over a protracted period of time. The early date of the *Deal* case encouraged concern and care in many policy decisions involving desegregation. Such routine actions as the acceptance of periodic transfers of territory from the city district to suburban districts for the alleged convenience and safety of the pupils residing in the territory transferred began to be scrutinized.

In the late 1960s the board made some decisions that were based, at least in part, on a fear of promoting unfavorable court reaction. For example, an interracial camping program was held intact through several extensive budget-cutting sessions in which athletic programs were eliminated, high school hours were cut 20 percent, and foreign language was dropped at the junior high school level. The interracial camping program was retained simply because it was interracial.

Also, decisions concerning construction of every school building have required great attention to the assignment of pupils so that the most favorable conditions might exist for racial balance. Vocational annexes in five high schools have been planned in such a way as to offer programs that would promote cross movement of races in the school district. Transportation has been provided so that free and convenient service is available for open enrollment and for attendance in the unique programs. Staff balance is mandated by the board to ensure broader interracial contacts.

What is most important, magnet and alternative schools have been established in significant numbers so as to provide "quality integrated education." Acceptance in these programs is based on racial quotas, and much care has gone into planning the schools so as to promote stable, meaningful integration.

Notes

1. I appreciate the considerable assistance of Frederick E. Ewing, director, Department of Governmental Research, Greater Cincinnati Chamber of Commerce, in the preparation of this chapter.

2. *Deal* v. *Cincinnati Board of Education*, 244 F. Supp. 572 (S.D. Ohio 1965), aff'd 369 F. 2d 55 (6th Cir. 1966), cert. den. 389 U.S. 847 (1967), aff'd on other issues, 419 F. 2d 1387 (6th Cir. 1969), cert. den. 402 U.S. 962 (1971).

3. Cincinnati Board of Education, "Minutes of the June 29, 1970 Board Meeting."

4. Cincinnati Board of Education, "Minutes of the March 26, 1973 Board Meeting."

5. Cincinnati Board of Education, "Minutes of the June 29, 1970 Board Meeting."

6. Cincinnati Board of Education, "Minutes of the July 9, 1973 Board Meeting."

7. Cincinnati Board of Education, "Minutes of the December 10, 1973 Board Meeting."

8. *Cincinnati Board of Education* v. *HEW*, U.S. Court of Appeals No. 75-1918, (6th Cir., 1976).

9. *Mona Bronson et al.* v. *Board of Education of the City School District of Cincinnati et al.* (S. D. Ohio, Civil No. C1 74-205, 1974).

10. *Brinkman* v. *John J. Gilligan et al.* (S. D. Ohio, Civil No. 72-137, 1973).

11. Cincinnati Board of Education, "Minutes of the January 14, 1974 Board Meeting."

12. The ruling on Dayton makes clear that the rescinding of an integration plan is illegal only if the board that enacted it was under a constitutional duty to enact it. This was the situation in Dayton. The district court there had found violations in the form of racially imbalanced schools and in the use of optional attendance zones. Because of this, the resolution of December 8, 1971, by the outgoing board in Dayton was obligatory, and its rescission was an element in the cumulative violation of constitutional rights. This kind of illegality has not been found to be the case in Cincinnati; it has not been proven that the outgoing board was obliged to enact the resolution of December 10. Rescission is not illegal in itself.

13. *Higgins* v. *Board of Education of the City of Grand Rapids,* 508 F. 2d 799 (6th Cir., 1974).

14. *Bronson* v. *Board of Education of the City School District of Cincinnati,* 525 F. 2d 344 (6th Cir. 1975). Certiorari denied by the U.S. Supreme Court, April 19, 1976; case remanded to the district court for trial.

5. Alternative Programs in Cincinnati

or,

"What Did You Learn on the River Today?"

Donald R. Waldrip

In the last quarter of the twentieth century, Cincinnati parents might well ask the same question that Aunt Polly might have asked Tom Sawyer and Huck Finn. It seems that there is a new program in Inland Waterways Occupations, complete with operating craft, that is part of Cincinnati's expanding effort to provide educational options for elementary and secondary students.

Alternatives to traditional public schools have always existed. They have ranged from schools with a religious or some other private orientation to the extreme alternative of no school at all. The 1960s saw a proliferation of parent-controlled "free" schools, and, for some middle-class dropouts, free schools provided a hopeful alternative. For youth in the inner city, storefront schools and street academies also emerged. usually supported by businesses or philanthropic organizations. For the·most part, however, the alternative school movement had low priority and experienced limited growth until the 1970s, when the movement gained momentum and the range of alternatives widened, especially in large urban school districts.

The alternative school differs from more traditional approaches primarily in that the school system is seen as being responsible for fitting the program to the student, rather than the student to the program. No single curriculum can possibly capitalize on the talents and abilities or satisfy the needs of all students. Many educators believe that alternative schools offer new hope that urban school systems can meet their obligation to serve every student well. In Cincinnati and throughout the country the touchstone of plans for alternative schools is a flexibility that enables schools to adapt both to the diverse needs of students and to the ever-changing requirements of society. Alternative schools generally attract teachers with similar instructional styles who are willing to work together to create a given kind of learning environment. And students tend to choose a school where the learning environment is most suitable for them.

The Cincinnati Public School District has been among the leaders in offering alternatives that provide a wide range of options to all students. Both optional courses of study and alternative programs are available at no cost to all students in the district, and transportation is provided. More than eleven thousand students in Cincinnati were enrolled in full-time, optional courses of study during the 1975–76 school year, and approximately half of this number were enrolled in programs in alternative schools. It is estimated that by 1980 alternative programs will include over twenty thousand students, or 40 percent of the projected enrollment. Preliminary estimates indicate that, on the average, alternative schools cost only about 10 percent more than regular programs, exclusive of transportation.

One of the primary reasons for the adoption of alternative programs in Cincinnati has been to allow students and parents to choose what best suits them from among a range of options. The schools' administrators are convinced that alternative schools offer a means of improving racial balance in schools that is more acceptable to the public and more cost-effective than any other approach. Strong alternatives attract students to integrated school settings and can draw suburban youngsters to urban public schools. In contrast, mandatory desegregation plans in large cities frequently promote segregation rather than integration, as those who resist integration flee to the suburbs.

ALTERNATIVE PROGRAMS FOR HIGH SCHOOL STUDENTS

Students attending high school in Cincinnati can choose a college preparatory program. For many years the Walnut Hills High School, founded in 1918, offered a special program intended for college-bound students from the entire school district. That six-year program is still offered at Walnut Hills, but there are also comparable programs in neighborhood schools for qualified students who prefer to attend school near their homes. Admission to this special program is, however, highly selective. It is based on the results of a test taken by all sixth-grade students in the district.

There is a Junior High College Readiness Program that offers a related option. It was designed for students who desire extra encouragement and help that will eventually enable them to enter a college preparatory program with confidence. This program provides strong academic training for qualified students in grades seven, eight, and nine, as well as an alternative program intended to improve students' basic skills.

At the same time vocational options have expanded dramatically. As the birthplace of cooperative education, Cincinnati has traditionally been considered a front-runner in offering programs that stress career preparation, and the recent addition of modern vocational wings to district high schools has made it possible to increase the number of programs. In addition to the Inland Waterways Program mentioned at the beginning of this chapter, there are programs that concentrate on the care and housing of animals (offered at the zoo) and on horticulture, electronic communication, millwork, cabinetry, and other specialized areas.

High school students can also choose to attend a Citywide Learning Community Program where the curriculum combines learning with practical experience in urban life. The metropolitan area and its resources help students see practical applications for the subjects they are studying, and course requirements are met in various ways. The student, who works as part of a team consisting of ten to fifteen students and a staff member, reaches an agreement with the teacher regarding what is to be studied and how the work will be evaluated. Students may work with businessmen, artists, farmers. They can learn to build stage sets at Playhouse in the Park, help get out a newspaper, work alongside a member of the city council. One student spent a year as "assistant" to the superintendent of schools.

The Cincinnati Academy of Mathematics and Science, in turn, provides an opportunity for students to concentrate on science and mathematics. Scientists and mathematicians in the community provide lectures and demonstrations to supplement the wealth of field and laboratory experience. Most of the activities in this program are individualized. In addition to in-depth studies in mathematics and science, the program emphasizes the interdependence of all subjects studied in the school. Mathematics and science courses may, for example, present social implications of applied principles, while an English course might deal with the nature of writings in mathematics and science. As the student continues in the program, there is specific career emphasis.

The School for Creative and Performing Arts Program has gained national recognition in only three years. Presently available in grades four to nine, it will ultimately extend to grade twelve. The program combines a strong emphasis on basic skills with courses in the humanities, the sciences, foreign languages, visual arts, instrumental and vocal music, dramatics, dance, and creative writing. In 1975-76 the program had 556 students, with 362 others on the waiting list. This school, which operated in temporary quarters for its first years, is scheduled to move into Cincinnati's historic Union Terminal Building.

ALTERNATIVE PROGRAMS FOR ELEMENTARY SCHOOL STUDENTS

Cincinnati has introduced bilingual programs at the elementary level in French, German, and Spanish. Each of these alternatives is offered in two schools, but presently includes only the primary grades. The plan is to extend the alternatives upward by one grade each year so that they will ultimately continue through grade twelve. The objective is to develop skills in a second language that will enable students to speak two languages fluently by the time they are in the sixth grade. In bilingual classes students spend more than one hour of each school day with a specially trained language teacher participating in activities designed to develop listening, speaking, reading, and writing skills in the language and to foster an appreciation of the culture and history of the people who speak the language.

Three schools have special programs at the elementary level for students in grades four through six who require the special challenge of an accelerated and enriched curriculum, along with the basic skills required to enter a college preparatory program at the secondary level.

The Montessori method of instruction, which emphasizes motor coordination, cognitive learning, perceptual skills, and social interaction, has been offered to young children for decades. In Cincinnati, however, this kind of instruction was available only in private schools until 1975. Then the Cincinnati public schools established Children's House, where children from five to eight years of age participate in an all-day program of Montessori instruction. A second Montessori school opened in 1976, and three other schools have selected Montessori equipment combined with other materials and use manipulative learning aids in an interracial primary program.

Two elementary schools have Reading Intervention Centers where students with reading difficulties receive special diagnosis and instruction. The staff at these centers seeks to determine why some children with normal intellectual ability do not read well. The children are thoroughly examined by trained psychologists and reading specialists. After diagnosis, reading specialists work with each child to build vocabulary, phonic skills, and comprehension. A specific instructional program is prescribed for each child. Language arts, social studies, mathematics, and science are integrated into the child's reading program.

Another type of schooling available in Cincinnati responds to the needs of those who believe that learning occurs more readily in a tightly controlled, traditional environment. The Fundamental Academy stresses reading, language, mathematics, and science, along with good manners, personal grooming, proper behavior, and patriotism. The program emphasizes structure, self-control, and discipline in learning. Instruction is given in age-graded, teacher-centered, and self-contained classrooms, and homework is required. Student progress is reported in letter grades, and a student must meet established standards in order to be promoted to the next grade. These schools expect parents to cooperate with the work of the school through reinforcement of school requirements, attendance at parent-teacher conferences, and involvement in a parent-teacher organization.

Three alternative elementary schools offer the Individually Guided Education Program (IGE) developed by the Wisconsin Research and Development Center for Cognitive Learning. Students attending an IGE magnet school learn in a program designed for their individual capabilities. They study in nongraded "family" units taught by teachers and aides. A fourth alternative elementary school has a strong multi-age, nongraded program of team teaching and individualized instruction. These magnet schools are neighborhood schools that are open to students outside the neighborhood.

In the Individual Progress and Social Impact Program, a special program for children in kindergarten through grade four, children learn by working and playing with children of different races and cultures. Selected Montessori equipment, formal reading readiness materials, and manipulative learning aids are used for instruction. The interracial and intercultural experiences begun in kindergarten are continued through grade four under the direction of teachers specially qualified to work with young children.

INFORMING PARENTS ABOUT AVAILABLE ALTERNATIVES

If alternative school programs are to succeed in attracting applicants from differing racial groups and in providing options for students with various interests and abilities, there must be a large-scale, well-organized campaign to inform parents of available alternatives and to persuade them to enroll their children in appropriate programs. Massive efforts to provide such information in Cincinnati have been seemingly successful. Special sections have been prepared and distributed in the Cincinnati *Post*. There is a pocket-sized packet containing descriptions of all alternative programs. Announcements have appeared on television, have been broadcast on the radio, and have appeared in newspapers. Many community meetings have been held. Descriptive materials have been provided for students to take home.

The following excerpt from an item that appeared in the Cincinnati *Post* provides answers to questions most frequently asked by parents and others about alternative programs.

Questions and Answers Concerning the Cincinnati
Public Schools Alternative School Programs

Choosing a school program for your child is one of the most important decisions you will make. The following questions and answers may assist you in making this decision.

1. *Will my child learn the basics in an alternative school?*
   Whatever the philosophy, methods, or subjects, all Cincinnati Public Schools are committed to excellence in the teaching of basic skills. Results to date show that children in alternative schools do as well or better than they did in regular schools.

2. *Who can help me decide which option is best for my child?*
   Your child's teacher and principal will be able to help. Specific questions and additional information should be directed to the staff of the alternative school. If you do not know how to get in touch with these people, call the Hotline, 369-4037, for help in arranging contacts. Many of these people will be available at the scheduled meetings.

3. *Who can apply?*

Any child may apply for enrollment in any alternative program or magnet school. Each program has its own eligibility requirements. These requirements are described in this report.

4. *How are students selected for an alternative school?*

All applicants must meet the eligibility requirements set for that program or school. These requirements are applied equally to all children. Every attempt is made to ensure that the population in each program is racially balanced.

5. *If my child or I become dissatisfied with an alternative program, can we return to our neighborhood school?*

If you accept enrollment in an alternate program or magnet school, your child will be expected to complete the school year in that program. In exceptional circumstances, the parents of the child and the principals of the alternative and neighborhood school may agree to a transfer during the school year.

6. *Is it more expensive to attend an alternative program?*

There are no tuition charges for any alternative or magnet school for residents of the Cincinnati Public School District. These are public schools.

7. *Can children who do not live in the Cincinnati Public School District apply?*

Yes. If they are accepted, they will pay a tuition fee of approximately $800 per year.

8. *How is staff selected for alternative programs and magnet schools?*

Staff requirements are determined by the area directors and the personnel department. Staff is then selected from both inside and outside the system to provide the best teachers and administrators available.

9. *Can parents become involved in alternative schools the way they do in neighborhood schools?*

Each alternative program and magnet school values parent support. An outstanding feature of all the new programs is commitment to parent participation.

10. *Will transportation be provided?*

Transportation for alternatives is the same as that for the neighborhood school. Elementary school children are generally provided yellow school bus transportation to the public school nearest their home. Reimbursement may be provided to parents who drive their children. This is in accordance with state and local formulas. Junior and senior high school children use the Queen City Metro routes and are provided reduced fare tokens in accordance with state and local formulas.

11. *How do I apply?*

Application forms are available from any neighborhood school office or by calling the Hotline (369-4037). The earlier the application is received the better will be your chances of acceptance.

Meetings have been scheduled to provide interested parents and students an opportunity to get additional information regarding alternative programs. The meetings are scheduled at the school location of the alternative programs to offer parents and students an orientation to the specific program. All meetings will begin at 7:30 except those noted.

Table 5-1

Enrollment in selected alternative school programs, by race, for 1975-76, as well as the number of applications and anticipated maximum enrollment for 1976-77

| Program | Enrollment | | | | Number of applications 1976-77 | Anticipated maximum enrollments Sept. 1976a |
| | By race | | | | | |
	Black	White	Other	Total		
Montessori	84	106	1	191	411	465
Fundamental Academy	87	156	0	243	172	737
Elementary college preparatory	131	89	0	220	683	423
French bilingual	78	64	0	142	343	529
Spanish bilingual	136	133	0	269	405	386
German bilingual	136	137	0	273	209	715
Multi-age	308	270	22	600	119	453
Individual Progress and Social Impact	108	110	1	219	265	1,897
Individually Guided Education (IGE)	1,403	265	2	1,670	271	170
Reading Intervention Centers	52	280	0	332	375	As many as apply
Cincinnati Academy of Mathematics and Science	61	24	4	89	101	200
City-wide	31	103	0	134	82	360
Junior High College Readiness	246	187	2	435	458	780
Creative and Performing Arts	(Racial breakdown unavailable)			523	546	Capacity not determined)
Totals	2,861	1,924	32	5,340	4,440	Not calculable

aMany of the enrollment assignments for 1976-77 will be made as a matter of course as students currently enrolled continue in a program, particularly in the case of larger programs like IGE. Applications for 1976-77 are running ahead of the number received for 1975-76.

Source: Enrollment Memoranda, Cincinnati Public Schools, April, June 1976.

A PRELIMINARY APPRAISAL

How well are Cincinnati's alternatives accomplishing their purposes? During the 1975-76 school year, 1,076 white students returned to Cincinnati public schools from private and parochial schools. Coupled with the open enrollment policy, the alternative programs have done much to further integration in the schools. Open enrollment allows students to select any school in the district where their membership will improve racial balance. By definition, alternatives (other than vocational or magnet programs) are racially balanced. Table 5-1 shows that enrollment by race in various alternative programs (excluding IGE) was well balanced in 1975–76, with approximately 47 percent of the enrollment consisting of black students and approximately 53 percent of white students.

The other major purpose of alternative schools is to make choices available to students and parents. Participation in Cincinnati's diversified programs is high. During the 1975–76 school year about 1,000 students applied for open enrollment, 1,500 for full-time vocational programs, and 4,210 applied for other alternatives. The Walnut Hills enrollment was 2,800, and 450 elected the special college preparatory program at neighborhood junior high schools. Of those who enrolled in alternatives, 90 percent remained in their selected programs.

Although data are not yet available that show the achievement of students attending programs that were new in 1975–76, measures of achievement in previously established programs have shown noticeable gains averaging at least one month per month of instruction. In programs that tend to attract the more capable students, the gains in achievement are considerably larger.

Alternative schools can provide opportunities for success in attaining goals and gaining recognition in areas that correspond to the student's strongest interests and talents. In the School for Creative and Performing Arts, for example, students have gained national recognition of their talents. They have appeared in national and local television productions, have toured with dramatic companies, and have participated in every facet of the arts.

As with all programs involving change, the alternative school plan poses new problems and gives rise to new challenges. Declining enrollments, attributable to declining birth rates as well as to transfers to alternative schools, have made it difficult to maintain a full range of programs in several neighborhood schools. Often the soundest educational decision is to close the neighborhood buildings and absorb the students in surrounding schools, but such a decision sometimes disturbs the community.

Also, many of the district's most knowledgeable and strongly motivated parents are choosing to send their children to schools with alternative programs. Some families have as many as five children attending five different programs. Often the brightest and most talented students elect to leave their neighborhood schools, thus dispersing school leaders throughout the district. It would appear, however, that a spirit of wholesome competition is developing in neighborhood schools. In an effort to increase their appeal for students and parents, they are trying to improve their programs.

6. Issues in Implementing and Evaluating Alternative Programs in Cincinnati

Joseph L. Felix and *James N. Jacobs*

Donald Waldrip argues in the previous chapter that alternative education can be a powerful means of improving educational opportunity in a big-city school district such as Cincinnati. He presents evidence suggesting that the availability of alternative schools is helping to improve instruction and attain racial balance goals in the Cincinnati public schools.

Three major problems, however, still require constant attention in working to expand and solidify alternative programs in the Cincinnati public schools. First, not all parents and children value the alternatives now available, at least not to the extent that the children leave their neighborhood school for an alternative program. This might prove that an ever-expanding array of alternatives is needed to capture the special interests of more and more children, but this takes time and resources.

The second problem arises if parents perceive conventional school programs to be poor. They might feel it necessary to leave the school district and enroll their children elsewhere. Since the option to leave is often limited to the more affluent, the enrollment in the school reflects the lower socioeconomic status of the families, many of which are black. When this happens, racial balance becomes an academic issue.

It would appear that conventional programs in existing neighborhood schools must be viewed as having a quality educational program in order to maintain the racial balance that already exists in many schools and avoid the exodus of the more affluent families.

The third problem involves monitoring and evaluating the development and effects of alternative programs. The goals of the programs may be assessed in a number of ways, and decisions must be made concerning the indexes to be used in trying to measure their effects. In particular, racial balance data may appear much more favorable if one examines enrollment within the alternative programs or the number of students in schools affected by the programs than if district-wide figures on the percentage of racially balanced schools are used. Data collected should make it possible to determine whether the programs are developing as planned, or whether steps need to be taken to reorganize or expand them. The three problems outlined above are now considered in turn, together with illustrative information on how they are being handled in the Cincinnati public schools.

EXPANDING ALTERNATIVES

The ideal situation for achieving voluntary racial balance would be to have such a wide array of attractive alternatives that all students would be motivated to attend one rather than to stay in their neighborhood schools. Also, equal proportions of each race should ideally opt for each alternative, which is not likely to occur. When parents in Cincinnati, for example, were asked, "Would you send your child to another Cincinnati school for an alternative program?" about 40 percent of the parents of students in the elementary schools and about 50 percent of the parents of students in the secondary schools answered affirmatively. Black parents, however, answered affirmatively about twice as frequently as white parents.

In addition, many parents and students who indicate initial interest in alternative programs ultimately do not elect to enroll in them for various reasons ranging from inertia to uncertainty concerning the racial composition of the alternative schools. These responses indicate that the potential market for alternative school enrollment is between 20 and 40 percent of the total enrollment, depending upon resources and promotion. If one counts the students in magnet-type schools such as vocational high schools, which existed before the advent of the alternative program, approximately 11,000 of 68,000 Cincinnati students (16 percent) attended alternative schools during the 1975–76 school year. It is expected that alternative programs will be expanded in the future, and recruitment will be vigorous in an effort to attain racial balance. It is not expected, however, that enrollment in the alternative programs will exceed 40 percent of the district's school population in the foreseeable future. This leaves a lot of children in neighborhood schools.

SUPPORT FOR NEIGHBORHOOD SCHOOLS

Neighborhood schools must be strong to contend with alternatives for student enrollment. When they are not, the alternatives also will fail for lack of public support. In Cincinnati there is a group of citizens who fear that alternatives will draw off district resources at the expense of neighborhood schools. This fear is largely without foundation and grossly magnified, but it persists nonetheless. It is fed by an egalitarian concern that neighborhood schools will be neglected or treated unfairly. To avoid losing support and, more important, to render these fears groundless, steps must be taken to strengthen neighborhood schools at the same time that the alternative program is being initiated and expanded.

Strong neighborhood schools also have the advantage of attracting students under an open enrollment plan designed to improve racial balance. Most conventional schools have distinctive features of one kind or another than would attract some students. A school staff may be known for its strong science department, its athletic teams, its good discipline, or the high academic achievement of its students—attractions for students in the same way that alternative schools are. Attractions of this sort should also be expanded and promoted in working to achieve the goals of effective integrated education.

What steps are being taken to safeguard the quality of education of neighborhood schools in Cincinnati? There is, in one instance, a large-scale effort aimed at improving reading skills in all schools of the city. Over $2.5 million were invested in this program in the 1975–76 school year. A listing of expenditures by category is shown in Table 6-1. A mathematics improvement program that it is hoped will be funded under the Emergency School Aid Act will be similarly administered in qualified schools.

Table 6-1

Expenditures for Cincinnati's city-wide reading program, 1975-76

Item	Cost
Program coordinator	$ 21,750
Coordinating teacher	14,500
Reading resource teachers (74)	1,050,800
Instructor assistants (187)[a]	673,200
Secretary (1)	7,500
Fringe benefits	291,680
Basic textbooks	446,000
Instructional supplies	18,500
In-service	74,100
Total	$2,598,030

[a] Ninety-six aides were paid in full from the General Fund. The remaining ninety-one were aides paid through the Comprehensive Employment and Training Act Program, at a cost to the General Fund of $103,465.

Teacher-pupil ratios in alternative schools are kept at about the same level as in conventional programs. There are, however, some unavoidable exceptions to this rule. Individually Guided Education (IGE) schools, for instance, require additional staff to qualify for the program.

Conventional schools should not be deprived of leadership personnel by permitting too many teachers from one school to be assigned to alternative programs. Although there are no definitive procedures for selecting alternative teachers, the open availability of these positions to teachers throughout the system decreases the likelihood that too many will be drawn from a single area. There is, in addition, a conscious effort to avoid transferring more than 20 percent of a school's staff in any one year. Transferring too many teachers of recognized excellence would have an immediate and negative effect on parent perceptions of the quality of local neighborhood schools.

There is a related concern when selecting students to attend alternatives. If the selection process favors academically talented and motivated students, neighborhood schools suffer in terms of student leadership and achievement. It is the achievements of the student body, after all, that largely determine community perceptions of the quality of the school program.

RACIAL BALANCE

Measurement

The student population of the Cincinnati public schools is about 51 percent black and 49 percent white. The few students belonging to other minority races comprise less than 1 percent of the student population. The major concern, it would seem, is how well distributed the two major races are, and any consideration of the distribution seems to rely on enrollment percentages, racial balance indexes, and the number of students affected at the school, program, or classroom level.

Enrollment Percentages

Racial enrollment percentages are most often done on a city-wide basis, so that it is possible to talk about the number of schools falling at various points in the distribution according to percentage of black or white students. Such data for Cincinnati schools in the academic years 1974–75 and 1975–76 are shown in Table 6-2. The data indicate

Table 6-2

Number of schools showing changes in percentage of racial balance
from 1974–75 to 1975–76

Black enrollment 1974–75 (percent)	Less balanced	No change	More balanced, grouped according to percent change		
			1–4.9	5–14.9	Over 15
90 or more	5	5	13	1	0
71–89	12	0	6	2	0
50–70	8	0	0	0	0
30–49	4	0	2	0	0
11–29	1	0	8	1	1
10 or less	7	3	13	3	4
Total	37	8	42	7	5

a Change in racial balance is defined as percent change in movement toward a fifty-fifty ratio of black to nonblack students.

that 63 percent of the schools that were 90 percent or more black or nonblack in 1975 moved at least slightly closer to a racially balanced enrollment in 1976, as measured in terms of movement toward an equal (50-50) ratio of black to nonblack students. The big changes—15, 20, and 30 percent or more—have occurred in schools where the alternatives are housed (not shown in the table). Other schools show smaller differences, but many of these are also in the direction of improved balance. Even with this improvement, in 1976 more than 20 percent of the schools in the system still had student enrollments 90 percent or more black or nonblack. There is still some distance to go, then, in improving the balance in some of the schools.

There is a second way to consider enrollment percentages by race—that of instructional programs. A racially balanced population is a prerequisite for each of the alternative programs in Cincinnati. Students were admitted to these programs on a one-to-one basis (one white for one black) as far as possible, thus ensuring that the programs started the year with a racially balanced population. Fortunately, withdrawals from the program have also been relatively balanced, so that a desirable ratio has been preserved.

A third means of considering enrollment percentages by race is in terms of individual classrooms. Racial balance at the classroom level has not been a specific criterion for evaluation in Cincinnati, but it does have importance in relation to Office of Civil Rights guidelines.

Racial Balance Indexes

The second major criterion a school system can use in measuring racial balance is the index that relates percentages at one level to those at a higher level. The first example of such an index is one that compares each school's racial balance to that of the total school system. For example, a school in which 20 percent of the population is black might be considered well balanced in a school system having a similar percentage of black population. In a district like Cincinnati, though, where the distribution of students by race approximates fifty-fifty, the same school would be seen as considerably less balanced. Such a relationship can, of course, be mathematically represented.

The most useful example of such a representation is the Index of Segregation, originally set forth by Karl and Alma Taeuber in their book entitled *Negroes in Cities: Residential Segregation and Neighborhood Change* (New York: Atheneum, 1969). This index reflects how well pupils of different races are distributed throughout the schools in the system. It is simply a composite representation of the degree to which black and white pupils are disproportionately distributed among the schools. From the Index of Segregation one can easily compute an indicator of the percentage of black and white students who would have to transfer to schools that are predominantly of the opposite race in order to desegregate the system completely.

This index was computed for the Cincinnati public schools by representatives of the Metropolitan Area Religious Coalition of Cincinnati. This study showed declining segregation indexes for the school system at all levels. The elementary index for 1975–76 is lower than at any time during the thirteen years covered by the study. Even so, the total school system index of 67 means that two-thirds of the black students in the district would have to transfer to white schools (or vice versa) to achieve perfect racial balance.

It is also possible to compute indexes that relate to the racial balance of programs to that of the school in which they are located, or to that of the system as a whole. In Cincinnati this would set the ideal goal for any alternative program approximately at a fifty-fifty ratio. On the other hand, one might use an index that compares the racial balance of an alternative program to that of the school in which it is located.

Finally, the balance within a classroom can be related to that of a program, a school, or the school system. This is one of the basic interests of the Office of Civil Rights in assessing the school district's qualifications for funding under the Emergency School Aid Act. With only those exceptions that are justified by instructional considerations, the racial balance of each classroom must approximate that of the school.

Number of Students Affected

A third major kind of criterion for measuring racial balance is student count. If one counts the number of students in schools with improved balance, impressive figures can be obtained on the effects of integration. In Cincinnati, the total number of students affected by integration efforts is a little over twenty thousand. That is, more than twenty thousand students, or approximately 30 percent of the population, attend schools that were better balanced racially in 1975–76 than they were in the preceding year. This same concept can be applied to counting students by program or classroom.

Effect on Participants

Beyond the question of racially balancing schools lies one that ultimately has even greater importance: How does balancing schools affect students and others whom the schools serve? There are many ways of approaching this question. Attention here is focused on approaches to measuring five categories of effects: social integration, attitudes, achievement, holding power, and school board-defined objectives.

Social Integration

Most educators and sociologists feel that the goal of helping students of different ethnic backgrounds get along with one another is an important reason to strive for racial balance. In this perspective, the measurement of social integration becomes at least as important as simple racial balance criteria. In several Cincinnati alternative programs, sociograms are being used to measure changing patterns of interracial relationships. These sociograms are usually built on students' identification of their best friends. Several years ago this technique was used with students of preschool and kindergarten age in an early childhood education project in Cincinnati, and some evidence was found that interracial educational experiences were helping to promote integration in friendship patterns. This same sociometric approach is being used in evaluating several of the existing alternatives. Measures taken early in the 1975–76 school year tend to confirm the notion that segregation in friendship increases as students advance in age, but it is too early to be able to report the extent to which the experience of an integrated alternative has had a beneficial effect for the year as a whole.

Attitudes

Closely related to the social integration goal is the question of attitudes. In any program aimed at racial balance, a goal worth measuring is the improvement of attitudes toward people of other races. Other kinds of attitudes can also be affected in the integration process. Both racial and nonracial attitudes are measured by Cincinnati's surveys.

The Cincinnati public schools annually administer surveys to students, parents, teachers, and administrators throughout the district. Some of the items on these instruments are of special interest with respect to integration. On the student survey, which offers response choices of "yes," "no," and "undecided," students reacted to the statement, "It is important to go to school with students of other races." Responses to this item have been rather consistent for the past two years. At the sixth- and twelfth-grade levels, about 65 percent of the responses are affirmative; at the ninth-grade level, 50 to 55 percent are affirmative. Responses of students in schools with alternatives tend to be more affirmative on this item, with some of the elementary alternatives showing 90 to 97 percent "yes" responses.

Parents are also asked questions with "yes," "no," and "undecided" response choices. For the sake of economy, parents of elementary students are surveyed one year; those of secondary students are surveyed the next. In 1974–75, 65 percent of the parents of elementary children who responded answered "yes" to the question, "Would you keep your child in the Cincinnati Public Schools if all schools were racially balanced?" In 1975–76, the affirmative response among parents of secondary students was 67 percent. When asked, "Do you believe children should have interracial experiences in their school program?" a "yes" response was given by 64 percent of the parents of elementary students, whereas only 57 percent of the parents of secondary students responded affirmatively.

Teacher administrator surveys call for items to be rated on a 7-point scale, from 1 (poor) to 7 (excellent). Teacher judgments about the effectiveness of alternatives seem sharply divided. Those working in alternative programs rate them very high; others, for the most part, rate them low. Consider, for instance, the item dealing with "Effectiveness of alternative programs in improving interracial understanding." Teachers in elementary alternatives gave this item a mean rating of about 6.0 on the 7-point scale. Those in schools without alternatives rated it 3.6.

Other measures of relevant attitudes, used mostly in connection with Title I evaluation, have given additional helpful baseline data for assessing the effects of racial balance in the alternative programs. A primary-grade instrument, *Attitude toward Self and School*, was developed in the Cincinnati public schools ten years ago and has been adapted by many school systems and several commercial publishers. This instrument consists of eighteen questions dealing with students' feelings toward various aspects of their personal and academic life. The child responds by marking the nose of either a smiling or a frowning face. Several other kinds of student questionnaires and teacher-rating instruments have been used to get at very elusive attitudinal dimensions. Evaluators in Cincinnati, like researchers elsewhere, have found it difficult to develop valid, reliable instruments for measuring attitudes.

Achievement

Eventually all eyes seem to focus on the matter of achievement. In assessing the impact of integration efforts on student achievement, it would be wise to include both norm-referenced and criterion-referenced measurment. The norm emphasis of standardized tests is important to ensure that student learning is keeping pace with expectations that emerge from broadly based comparisons. In other words, standardized tests answer the question, "Are students in our integrated settings keeping pace with other students nation-wide?" Criterion-referenced measurement is also important in establishing how well students are achieving the specific learning objectives included in the curricula of their specific program.

In looking at standardized achievement data, Cincinnati is concentrating on individual student gains. The process of comparing a student's results from one year with those from another has been extremely difficult because of limited computer capability. At this time, therefore, no data are available to indicate the achievement impact of current integration efforts.

Holding Power

In evaluating the alternatives, an additional question involves the holding power of the programs. The question to be answered is "Once enrolled in an optional, integrated program, to what extent do students tend to stay?" Preliminary indications are that, once beginning-of-year problems of transportation and adjustment have taken their toll, most students seem to stay. About 85 percent of the students initially enrolled in the alternatives finished the 1975–76 school year in the same programs. The percentage of students remaining in the programs is running slightly higher for blacks than for whites.

Board Objectives

Evaluators will be looking at other data that are related to the specified goals of the Cincinnati Board of Education. These involve student and staff safety, discipline, and attendance. The effort to achieve racial balance, itself a board goal, may also be looked at as a means of attaining these and other related goals. It will be important to determine the impact of the alternative programs on the total spectrum of goals related to integration.

CHOICE AS A GOAL

Increasing the range of choices available to students and their parents must be a goal for the entire school district, whether in regular neighborhood schools or in officially designated alternative schools. To be more responsive to a wider range of clientele needs and expectations, all schools must assume a more flexible posture. Mass production through standardization built our industrial society, but this idea is no longer appropriate in educating large numbers of people. The challenge of serving every student well demands a strong effort to provide creative and effective programs in all schools.

In light of this, the best alternatives may be those that are least correlated with academic achievement and ability. The best examples of these types of alternatives in Cincinnati are the German, French, and Spanish bilingual programs, the Montessori alternative, and the School for the Creative and Performing Arts. In each of these, it is reasonable to assume that both more and less able children will benefit from their respective programs. We are working to ensure that the range of academic talent among students at these schools will be similar to that in the district as a whole.

In working to achieve racial balance through voluntary enrollment in alternative programs appropriate for individual students, the Cincinnati schools are attempting to develop and use a variety of measures that apply not just to desegregation patterns, but also to student attitudes, achievement, and other aspects of program implementation and performance. Most of these measures will require years of data collection before any conclusions can be reached about the success of the programs, but preliminary results provide encouraging indications that some of the goals are being advanced during the first full year of operation in many of the schools.

7. The Metropolitan Context for Reducing Racial Isolation

Duane Holm

Strategies for reducing racial isolation in schools are used in metropolitan areas and have an impact on those areas. This chapter is concerned with efforts of the Cincinnati public schools to reduce racial isolation, the impact of their strategies (quality education in neighborhood schools, new alternative schools, and board of education policy changes) on other school districts in the metropolitan area, and solutions being developed in other metropolitan areas and their potential for Cincinnati.

REDUCING RACIAL ISOLATION IN CINCINNATI

The Cincinnati school district is one of twenty-three separate school districts (four different kinds) in Hamilton County.[1] The districts vary widely in area (see Figure 7-1), and few conform to city, village, or county boundaries. Some even cross county lines. The Cincinnati public schools constitute an arrested metropolitan school district that failed to keep up with urban growth as the city stopped annexing new communities. Most of the school districts in Hamilton County were formed through successive consolidations arranged over the years in response to court orders, state standards, and local wishes. Twenty

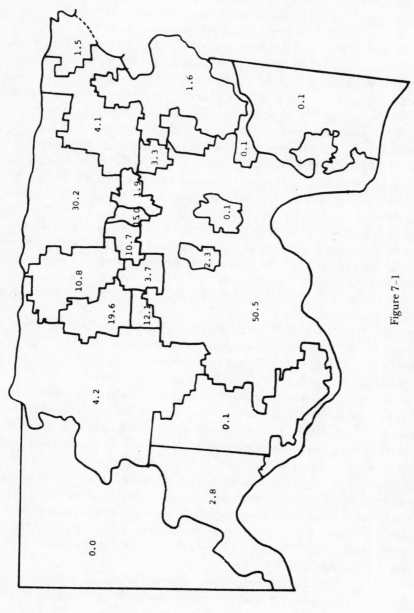

Figure 7-1

Black pupils as percentage of total pupil membership in 1974–75, Hamilton County School Districts

(*Source:* Ohio Department of Education)

years ago there were twice as many school districts in Hamilton County. Awkward, arbitrary boundaries have required continued readjustment, and there have been many petitions for transfer.

Enrollments in school districts in Hamilton County vary from over seventy thousand to less than one thousand pupils,[2] and they have been decreasing. The shift to the suburbs has not, however, been as pronounced as it has been in some cities since much of Cincinnati is suburban in nature. (Characteristically, Cincinnatians use the term "suburb" to refer to a residential community either inside or outside the city limits.) Enrollment declined in most districts in Hamilton County in 1975. In a number of districts enrollment is decreasing in older, more established neighborhoods, and increasing in newer areas that house young families. As a result, some districts are being forced to close schools and transport pupils.

Cincinnati is a hilly, southern community with a black population scattered through a number of city neighborhoods and some older suburban communities. The enrollment of black pupils among the school districts in Hamilton County varies from zero to 50.5 percent (again see Figure 7-1), and the county pattern is essentially an expanded version of the city pattern.

The percentage of black teachers among Hamilton County school districts, all of which draw from the same metropolitan labor pool, ranges from zero to 30.2. Of the administrators in Hamilton County, 15 percent are black, but they are all in two school districts.

Indexes of segregation measure how evenly black pupils are distributed throughout the schools of a district. These indexes allow one to compare a district over time, or one district with another. Indexes of segregation have been calculated for Cincinnati, but calculating the index of segregation for smaller suburban districts with very small percentages of black pupils is not helpful. Reynolds Farley infers that, where city schools are segregated and where city schools and suburban schools differ substantially in racial composition, the index of segregation for the metropolitan area would be as large as that for the city.[3] Our calculations give Hamilton County schools a 1974-75 index score of 75 as compared with 69 for Cincinnati.[4]

Most school districts in Hamilton County have had difficulty in passing tax levies. There is wide variation among the school districts of Hamilton County in assessed valuation per pupil (from $95,532 to $10,963), expenditure per pupil (from $1,704 to $799), and school tax rates (from 56.32 mills to 23.62 mills).[5] There is also wide variation among the school districts of Hamilton County in median family income (from $19,630 to $7,015). There is a close positive relationship between the median family income and the tax rate for school districts in Hamilton County, which would tend to indicate that voters respond to tax levies in terms of their ability to pay, rather than in accord with the size of the tax base (in terms of valuation per pupil) in their school districts.[6] Because Cincinnati is a fairly "rich" district in terms of valuation per pupil but "poor" in terms of median income, the new Ohio Equal Yield Financing Formula, which has no income factor, will result in decreased state aid for Cincinnati and increased state aid for many of the other districts in Hamilton County. This situation compounds the problems associated with providing superior instructional programs as integration proceeds in Cincinnati schools and with paying costs involved in desegregating the schools.

THE EFFECT ON THE METROPOLITAN AREA

Cincinnati's strategies for reducing racial isolation, although they are specifically designed to deal with the situation in Cincinnati proper, affect the entire metropolitan area.

Maintaining Integrated Education in Improved Neighborhood Schools

The improvement of neighborhood schools should have some success in Cincinnati, which is a rather lovely city with cultural advantages, a viable downtown, and a number of residential neighborhoods. Dramatic improvement would, however, take a lot of money, and many of the families that could afford to make the improvements decide to move on the basis of the reputation of the school district (percentage of black pupils is frequently a consideration). The reputation of a school, which often lags behind particular improvements being made, often becomes a self-fulfilling prophecy since it affects where families buy houses and in so doing helps to concentrate the more affluent, educationally concerned families into the same school districts. The effect of this strategy on the metropolitan area will, however, be limited because the concentration of black pupils in some suburban neighborhood schools and suburban school districts will increase racial isolation in the metropolitan area.

Creating Alternative Schools to Achieve Racial Balance

Alternative schools may succeed in holding some students and rearranging others in Cincinnati's public schools; they may also draw some pupils from private schools. The creation of alternative schools, by improving the reputation of Cincinnati schools, besides helping to hold some families, might attract others that would help to achieve that reputation. And, if participation in alternative school programs is not limited to city residents and can draw pupils from suburban school districts, such an approach could help reduce racial isolation in the metropolitan area as a whole. Alternative schools do, however, tend to take money, interest, the most talented teachers, and the most concerned parents away from the neighborhood schools.

Board Policy Changes

The actions of the Cincinnati Board of Education, although they are meant primarily to deal with the problems of the city, may well be the strategy that has the greatest impact on the entire metropolitan area. In their efforts to prevent white pupils from being transferred to other districts, the Cincinnati Board made other boards in the metropolitan area wary of any actions that might affect racial isolation in Cincinnati, and a recent county-wide meeting of interested citizens on city-suburban cooperation has increased awareness of the metropolitan dimensions of the problem of reducing isolation. Many suburban districts have been cautioned by counsel not to have dealings with Cincinnati; some have examined the Metropolitan Educational Collaborative Program (METCO) and the Metropolitan Planning Project in Boston, both of which are designed to bring about voluntary integration in schools in the metropolitan area. The action of the Cincinnati Board that may have the greatest ultimate impact on the entire metropolitan area will be the decision to file suit against the state over the Equal Yield Formula. More equal and more adequate funding is essential to any strategy to reduce racial isolation.

OTHER SOLUTIONS

Although there have been only tentative gropings in Cincinnati, excellent examples of metropolitan solutions have been developing elsewhere. For example, Kettering, a suburban district outside Dayton, has worked to increase black faculty and to arrange limited faculty and classroom exchanges. In the Boston area, the METCO program transports some 2,400 black Boston pupils who volunteer to some thirty-seven suburban school districts that agree to receive them, and also to integrate and train their faculty. The state pays transportation costs. There are similar programs in Rochester, New York, and in Hartford and New Haven, Connecticut. The Metropolitan Planning Project has developed shared, integrated programs involving Boston and some seventy-seven suburban districts. Wisconsin has provided financial incentives for pupil transfers that improve the racial balance between city and suburban school districts.

The metropolitan-level efforts mentioned above have been voluntary, but the main source of metropolitan desegregation efforts has been the courts, particularly in the South where there has been a scattered black population and a tradition of large county school districts covering much of the metropolitan area. For this reason, desegregation orders in the South frequently have resulted in metropolitan, or at least regional-level, integration plans. In the North, the U.S. Department of Health, Education, and Welfare and state agencies like the Ohio Civil Rights Commission have been slow to look at the problem of desegregation on a metropolitan basis.

Contrary to some early opinion, however, the Detroit case did not rule out metropolitan remedies in the North. The Supreme Court said that if there is to be a metropolitan remedy, the suburban districts involved must have their day in court, and it must be proved that actions in the districts increased segregation in the city district. Following proof of such action, Louisville and Jefferson County, Kentucky, were desegregated in September 1975. Wilmington and Newcastle County, Delaware, have been ordered to desegregate by September 1977. Indianapolis and Marion County, Indiana, are waiting for an appeals court ruling on a metropolitan solution.[7]

In Atlanta, the American Civil Liberties Union is preparing a clustering plan for a metropolitan case involving seven counties. The Kansas City School District is considering bringing a desegregation suit against the surrounding suburban districts and the state of Missouri. In Cleveland, the NAACP has called for a metropolitan remedy, citing state involvement in separate vocational schools and school district boundary changes. The apparent strategy of the NAACP is to show a pattern of state involvement in causing school segregation in city school districts in Ohio, and then to call for the state to develop metropolitan remedies. If this happens, a metropolitan solution could be ordered in Cincinnati.

If metropolitan desegregation were ordered in Cincinnati, it would be for the purpose of reducing racial isolation. But it could have other side effects. Racial isolation in schools has often been viewed as a result of housing patterns. Efforts like those in Louisville, Kentucky, where the city and Jefferson County have joined in action to encourage low-income suburban housing, partly in order to reduce busing in the future,[8] indicate that desegregated schools in a metropolitan area can be used to encourage integrated housing. Such a development would fit in with Robert Manley's analysis of historical stages of metropolitan housing patterns, in which American cities, like the older European cities, will, as they mature, open up economically desirable city housing that middle-class families will reclaim—if those neighborhoods are not tied to neighborhood schools.[9] Since outstanding magnet schools drawing on a metropolitan population base could help attract middle-class families back to the central city, Manley believes that metropolitan desegregation plans providing magnet alternative schools would allow the economic system to develop more desegregated housing in the metropolitan area.

Desegregation of metropolitan area schools could free educators and legislators to design a more rational system for delivering educational services in the metropolitan area as a whole, an effort that has been postponed partly because of the fear of becoming involved in school desegregation. By eliminating school districts that are too small or too large and by drawing on the tax base of the entire area, better curricula for regular, alternative, and specialized education could be provided; overlapping of special programs by district could be reduced; and existing personnel, buildings, and transportation could be more effectively utilized at a time when the educational system is shrinking.

Notes

1. Metropolitan Area Religious Coalition of Cincinnati, "A Proposal to Study the Financial and Administrative Organization of School Districts in Hamilton County" (Cincinnati: Metropolitan Area Religious Coalition of Cincinnati, 1975, mimeo).

2. Ohio State Department of Education, *Fall Pupil Membership and Ethnic Composition in Public Schools, 1974–1975* (Columbus: Ohio State Department of Education, 1974).

3. Reynolds Farley, "Racial Integration in the Public Schools, 1967 to 1972: Assessing the Effect of Governmental Policies," *Sociological Focus* 8 (January 1975): 11-12.

4. Metropolitan Area Religious Coalition of Cincinnati, "Racial Isolation in the Schools of Hamilton County" (Cincinnati: Metropolitan Area Religious Coalition of Cincinnati, 1976, mimeo).

5. Ohio Education Association, *Basic Financial Data on School Districts* (Columbus: Ohio Education Association, 1975).

6. Median income figures calculated from 1970 census data are from an April 1975 presentation by the Metropolitan Area Religious Coalition of Cincinnati to the Ohio Senate Education Committee.

7. More information about these three cases can be found in Daniel U. Levine, "Recent Court Cases Bearing on Regional School Integration," in *Citizen Guide to Desegregation* (Cleveland: Citizens' Council for Ohio Schools, 1976), 10-12.

8. "Sec. 8 to Aid Busing Plan," *Trends in Housing* 19 (Winter 1975-1976): 4.

9. Robert E. Manley, *Metropolitan Interaction between Housing Markets and School Integration Policies* (Evanston, Ill.: National School Boards Association Council of School Attorneys, 1975).

8. The Magnet School Plan in Houston

Connie Campbell and *John Brandstetter*

The origins of the magnet school program in Houston can be traced to a 1970 court order mandating major actions to promote integration. This court order included a majority-to-minority transfer policy with free transportation and the imposition of equidistant zoning. When applied, however, the equidistant zoning formula left twenty-seven schools in the northeastern section of the city essentially all black, and so the Fifth Circuit Court of Appeals modified the zoning policy and paired schools to increase integration.

Eleven pairs of schools were established, but the level of integration within those schools deteriorated rapidly between 1970 and 1974, largely because a loss of white students paralleled and partly accounted for the decline in white enrollment in the district as a whole. Table 8-1 shows the change in racial composition of paired schools between 1970 and 1974. It is evident that equidistant zoning produced some integrated schools, but they soon became one-race schools.

Texas law also required the identification of Mexican-American students, and in 1972 the Houston Board of Education responded to community appeals and recognized these students as a minority group, whereas they had previously been considered "white." This change in definition further reduced "integration" in the schools

Table 8-1

Enrollment by ethnic group in schools paired in the Houston
integration plan, 1970 and 1974

	Enrollment	
Racial group	August 1970	November 1974
Black	12,958	9,957
Brown	5,947	4,923
White	1,763	539
Total	20,678	15,419

paired by court order. By 1974 the school district was essentially mix-ing black students with Mexican-American students, and white stu-dents were withdrawing from the attendance areas served by the paired schools.

In November 1974 General Superintendent Billy Reagan recom-mended that the board appoint a triethnic task force of community and school representatives to consider alternatives for integrated edu-cation beyond the court-ordered pairing. The board-appointed task force was to make recommendations intended to halt the flight of resi-dents from Houston schools, to promote integration and provide al-ternatives to involuntary busing, and to improve educational oppor-tunities for students.

After consulting with numerous individuals, organizations, and representatives of the U.S. Department of Justice, holding public meetings at strategically located places, visiting programs in other cities similar to Houston, and examining the results of a comprehen-sive needs survey recently undertaken by the district, the task force re-commended that a magnet school concept replace the paired school program. Seventeen members of the task force (six black, five brown, and six white) supported the recommendation; three Mexican-Ameri-can members refused to sign the final report and issued a minority statement.

TASK FORCE RECOMMENDATIONS

The report of the task force outlined twenty-six proposals for pro-grams. The proposals ranged from expanding existing programs, such as the High School for Visual and Performing Arts and other "Vanguard" schools providing a specialized curriculum for gifted children to the establishment of fundamental schools emphasizing basic educational and social skills and the development of year-round programs. Other recommendations were concerned with a strong basic education foundation, early bilingual education, and a long-range goal to reduce the pupil-teacher ratio in the primary grades to fifteen to one. The task force also recommended that bilingual and bicultural programs be extended to all Houston schools, and that human relations and cultural interaction should be emphasized in the curriculum.

The task force also tried to identify factors that might affect the success of a magnet school plan. The plan was to include (a) a strong component for staff development, including an incentive plan to promote creativity; (b) policies for student transfers designed to ensure that both magnet schools and traditional schools would benefit; (c) free transportation for students enrolled in magnet school programs; (d) maintenance and promotion of triethnic student distribution within the magnet schools and 108 other schools already integrated by legal definition; and (e) the encouragement of majority-to-minority transfers through incentives.

In February 1975 the report of the task force was accepted by the Houston Board of Education and by the Biracial Committee, a monitoring body acting on behalf of the federal district court. The final magnet plan received judicial approval in July, six weeks before the opening of school. Despite this tight schedule, school officials were able to implement the program in September, partly because the situation in Houston was somewhat unusual.

First, the original court order of 1970 called for limited rather than massive integration. The school district was in compliance with this order and was not involved in litigation regarding integration. Any proposal intended to increase integration without coercion could, therefore, be viewed as voluntary affirmative action. The court's approval of a rather conservative magnet plan may have been influenced by the fact that the initiative was taken by the school district. In other urban situations, where districts have been deemed not in compliance with court orders or where the original decrees for integration are more demanding, approval of magnet programs may require that integration be much more extensive than was envisioned under the Houston plan.

Second, the Houston plan had wider support among community groups, including ethnic minorities, than any legitimate alternatives to the paired school plan for integration.

Third, the task force already had an up-to-date and comprehensive needs assessment that was taken into account in developing its recommendations. Furthermore, some successful pilot programs were already operating in Houston.

Despite these advantages, it probably would not have been possible to implement the magnet program at the beginning of the 1975-76 school year without the efforts of a newly appointed administrative team. This sixteen-member team, comprised of central office staff, assistant area superintendents, and building administrators, represented the major ethnic groups and geographical areas of the city. The objective of the team was to design the magnet plan so that it could ultimately be carried out through normal administrative channels. The members of the team were retained in their regular positions, thus enabling them to preserve their contacts in the community and in the schools. The team was organized into four committees: budget and funding; facilities, location, and transportation; program development and staff in-service training; and dissemination and evaluation. The committee responsible for dissemination and evaluation had a systematic plan for releasing progress reports on a scheduled basis. It planned media programs, advertising, and expositions and used nontraditional methods of dissemination designed to reach all parents. All members of the team were given high priority in the allotment of materials, the use of facilities, and the availability of secretarial assistance, and the team worked long hours in rented office space that was isolated from routine distractions. Some of the responsibilities assigned to the various members of the team, taken from the *Report to the General Superintendent and the Board of Education of the Houston Independent School District* (Houston: Independent School District, 1975) are listed below:

General coordinator
1. Overall project coordination under the Superintendent of Instruction.
2. Public relations and information.
3. Management of planning, budgeting, organizing, staffing, and operations, and evaluation of the Task Force Project.

Assistant general coordinator
1. Program development.

2. Coordination of funding and program development.
3. Supervision of project staff.
4. Other assigned tasks from the General Coordinator.

Funding consultant
1. Locate funding sources.
2. Prepare proposals for funding.
3. Advise Budget Officer.

Budget officer
1. Prepare budgets.
2. Coordinate funding with Funding Consultant.
3. Manage budgets.

Facilities and location officer
1. Identify sites.
2. Plan selection and modification of facilities.
3. Assist in program design and implementation.

Transportation officer
1. Plan transportation to accommodate programs.
2. Locate transportation sources.
3. Negotiate contracts, manage services.

Program officer
1. Plan program of studies suitable to area needs.
2. Select models for implementation.
3. Design strategies for program installation.

Staffing and in-service officer
1. Design criteria for in-service training and staff selection.
2. Coordinate with other component officers.
3. Plan and conduct in-service training.

Information or dissemination officer
1. Development of a public relations program.
2. Disseminate information to community and to staff not directly involved in the project.
3. Develop programs for feedback from community and educators.

Evaluating and assessment officer
1. Plan and conduct program monitoring.
2. Conduct process evaluation.
3. Plan and implement a comprehensive evaluation.

DEVELOPMENT OF THE MAGNET SCHOOLS

To begin implementing the magnet school concept the administrative team first gave every building principal a list of programs proposed by the task force. Requests for magnet programs were made by the principals after they had discussed the list with staff, parents, and community organizations. In preparing their requests, principals were asked to consider the needs assessment survey submitted earlier from their school. All magnet programs that actually developed were located in schools with grass-roots support and with the ability to implement the program physically. Proposals for magnet programs were submitted by 116 schools, nearly half of Houston's 247 public schools.

When reviewing initial requests, the administrative team gave particular attention to whether each proposed magnet program would: increase the number of children attending integrated schools, decrease the number of schools with more than 90 percent of their enrollment members of one race, and improve the quality of education. Other considerations were: accessibility, physical space, potential utilization of programs already established, and stabilization of enrollments already integrated. Thirty-four magnet programs on thirty-one campuses were implemented in Phase One, which began in September 1975. Eleven additional programs were to be implemented in Phase Two, which was to begin with the 1976–77 school year.

Enrollments were projected by estimating the number of children each school would have had without magnet programs and then determining the probable increase in student population due to magnetization. The physical accommodations available in each school and a designated ethnic ratio for the student population in magnet schools were other considerations. The regular and magnet enrollments were combined to estimate the total projected enrollment of each school. Examples of the four types of programs are described below.

Add-on Programs

In some instances specialized classes and staff have been added to the existing curriculum. All students transferring to attend the "add-on" magnet program are totally integrated within the regular school enrollment, and the total school population generally participates to some degree in the specialized classes. Enrollment in these programs is limited by the classroom space available in each school and the lower teacher-student ratios mandated for magnet sites. A percentage of students in these programs also tends to be absorbed into the existing school population.

Foreign Language Academy

Most of the add-on programs are in elementary schools, the one exception being the Foreign Language Academy at the Bellaire Senior High School. There were 150 add-on positions open at the academy the first year for students wishing to enroll in Hebrew, Chinese, Italian, or Latin. Other languages were taught upon request if a teacher was available. Bellaire's add-on program does not affect foreign language instruction offered in other Houston high schools; it affords the opportunity for individual students to go beyond traditional instruction. The academy study units focus on jobs, professions, or careers in which foreign language skills would be advantageous. Academy students who enroll in a foreign language class for at least two quarters a year can follow either a vocational or a college preparatory program in the school.

Ecology and Outdoor Education Academy

The James A. Berry Elementary School combines nature study and a regular curriculum in basic skills in what is called the Ecology and Outdoor Education Academy. Because it has a nature area behind the campus and a city park adjacent, Berry has excellent facilities for outdoor ecological studies. Specialists provide at least one instructional session per week in an outdoor setting for all interested students and teachers, and the science, music, and art classes incorporate nature themes. Students have developed a campus nature trail by planting and labelling hundreds of trees and shrubs. A garden area is available for growing plants.

Music Academies

Bruce, Garden Villas, and MacGregor Elementary Schools are sites for add-on programs in music. The Bruce and Garden Villas programs provide thirty minutes of string instruction a day for interested and capable students in the primary grades. Minicourses on instruments like the ukulele, autoharp, and resonator bells are offered to intermediate students in general music classes. Students in grades four through six can also take individual and group instruction for beginning band and orchestra. Approximately one and one-half hours of the school day are spent in some kind of music instruction.

Science Academies

In addition to a music program similar to that of Bruce and Garden Villas, the MacGregor Elementary School includes a science curriculum emphasizing laboratory instruction in biology, earth science, and physical science. MacGregor facilities include well-equipped laboratories and closed-circuit television.

Wainwright Elementary School emphasizes science through its Science Careers Academy. Approximately 100 academy students attend special mathematics and science classes during a school day that is extended to 4:00 p.m. for additional laboratory work in science and mathematics. Students are selected on the basis of interest, teacher recommendation, and aptitude in science and mathematics. A major emphasis is on the participation of resource people from the community.

School within a School (SWS)

Students who transfer into a School within a School participate in programs quite different from the regular curriculum in the schools in which the programs are located. The degree of specialization within the programs means that SWS students are integrated with the regular students in just a few classes, such as physical education. This arrangement is based on the rationale that SWS programs, such as the School for the Engineering Professions, Vanguard Schools (for the gifted), or the Petrochemical Careers Institute, require specified standards in order to be effective.

Contemporary Learning Center

All SWS magnet programs do not necessarily compete for successful students already highly motivated and goal oriented. The Contemporary Learning Center at the Miller Junior High School campus has positions for as many as five hundred high school students who may have a history of absenteeism or a record of conflict with classmates, who may read at least two years below grade level, or who are failing two or more academic subjects in their regular schools. The Contemporary Learning Center emphasizes academic individualization, continuous progress, and various options in learning activities.

Milby Petrochemical Career Institute

The Petrochemical Career Institute at Milby Senior High School was established in response to a shortage of skilled technicians in Houston's petrochemical industry. Its vocationally oriented physical science program stresses career information and interaction with community members active in various petrochemical fields. A main thrust of the program is to provide on-the-job training for each student. The institute may be viewed either as a job-training program ending with a high school graduation or as technical preparation for further study. The institute, which began with an enrollment of thirty sophomores in 1975, now includes grades ten through twelve.

Sterling Aerodynamics Program

Another magnet SWS program based on a large Houston industry is the Aerodynamics Program at Sterling Senior High School. Interest in aerospace careers and background in mathematics and science are the basic prerequisites for students applying for approximately one hundred openings in the program. Some of the specialized studies include basic aviation, history of aviation, flight rules and regulations, meteorology, navigation, aerodynamics, and flight systems. The instructional program emphasizes field trips to airports and to aerospace industries. Female as well as male students are recruited.

Booker T. Washington School for Engineering Professions

Offering a rigorous college preparatory program centering on mathematics and science, the High School for Engineering Professions admits students with superior school achievement and recommendations. Beginning with about two hundred freshmen and sophomores in 1975, the program was to be expanded to include grades seven through twelve by 1977, and the scientific curricula are being balanced with more work in language arts and humanities in order to attract students interested in law, medicine, business, and other fields. A continuous progress plan in mathematics and English and a schedule with five instead of four periods per day allow students to complete regular high school requirements a year early. Senior courses can be taken for college credit. Each student meets with a faculty adviser once a week for discussion and assessment of progress.

Scroggins Literature and Art Program

The SWS magnet program students at Mary Scroggins Elementary School spend two and one-half hours of the school day in literature and art classes. Included are art history, art as it relates to literature, creative writing, and crafts such as pottery, stitchery, puppet making, and puppetry. The remainder of the school day is spent in regular classes. Participating grade levels have been expanded from the original grades three through six to include kindergarten and primary students. There are no student admission requirements beyond parental approval, but a racial-ethnic quota is required, as it is in all magnet programs in Houston.

River Oaks Vanguard Program

River Oaks is one of several SWS programs for the gifted at the elementary level. It is open to 230 students in grades four, five, and six who have standardized achievement scores at least one and one-half years beyond grade level and a grade average of at least B in language, reading, and mathematics. The Vanguard Program centers on special interest activities. A specialized team of fine arts, science, and foreign language teachers helps develop and supervises a variety of electives such as dramatics, debate, chorus, painting, newspaper production, and ecology. Vanguard elementary schools recruit students with acceptable ratings in school and social behavior and with a regular attendance record.

Cluster Center Programs

In Cluster Centers students from schools where one race heavily predominates are integrated in special programs ranging in duration from one day to a week. In addition, the schools that send students to attend the program receive orientation materials and carry on follow-up activities so that the experience can be incorporated into the regular curriculum when the children return to their home school. Clearly, the goal of cluster centers involves not total integration but enriched education on a part-time integrated basis for racially isolated students.

People Place Center

The People Place Center at Anson Jones Elementary School is organized around the study of diverse cultures. Intermediate students participate in simulation activities designed to give them the feeling of being in the country they are studying. Most instructors have strong ties to or extensive experience in the culture they teach.

Children's Literature Center

Located in Briargrove Elementary School, the Literature Center provides a four-day learning experience for first-, second-, and third-grade students. Instructors incorporate as much verbal stimulation as possible in presenting award-winning children's classics. Auditory and visual presentations range from simple puppet dramatizations to closed-circuit telecasts and videotaped interviews with the children. Group discussion centers on the ethnic traditions of the children coming to the center, and group activities extend literature themes through drama, art, song, dance, and stories.

Career Orientation Center

Fourth-, fifth-, and sixth-grade students come to Sinclair Elementary School to learn about careers in food, communication, business and industry, science, foreign language, travel, and transportation.

Complementary careers are clustered together, and student exercises involve planning, problem solving, and decision making. The Career Center emphasizes production, application, and operational aspects of the work and careers being explored.

Separate and Unique Schools (SUS)

New programs have been organized around specialized curricula such as health, fine arts, or business in the Separate and Unique Schools. The total school population participates in these programs. Several Separate and Unique Schools, such as the High School for Health Professions organized jointly with the Baylor College of Medicine, were already established in Houston with outside support prior to the magnet plan. Others were regular or traditional schools with reduced teacher-student ratios and an explicit added emphasis on discipline and basic skills.

The high degree of specialization that exists in some SUS programs may make the conversion of an existing school almost impossible. The High School for Visual and Performing Arts, for example, specializes in training artistically or musically gifted students. The curriculum of such a school demands a new or converted physical plant, a large staff, and student recruitment from a very special population, none of which may be available in small cities. On the other hand, fundamental schools may need few building changes and minimal staff adjustments and most of the students are drawn from the surrounding neighborhood.

Fundamental Schools

Looscan School is an example of a Fundamental School. Discipline, grooming (including dress codes), good manners, and grade promotion based on mastery of skills are the goals stressed at Looscan and the other elementary and secondary fundamental schools. The faculty and administration stress traditional values in education, patriotism, brotherhood, pride, and respect for others and oneself. Looscan's primary and bilingual classes are self-contained, but intermediate students exchange teachers for some subjects. A traditional grading system is used. Since the whole school population participates in the fundamental program, applications are limited only by considerations of classroom space and teacher-student ratio.

High School for Visual and Performing Arts

With an enrollment of 550 students, the High School for Visual and Performing Arts provides specialized and concentrated work for students talented in art, dance, drama, media, and music. Opportunities are also available to learn behind-the-scenes skills such as lighting and stage management, camera and media technology, costume and scenery design, and set construction. Admission standards are rigorous and are based on an interview and an audition (dance, music, drama) or on the presentation of a portfolio (art, photography). A board of consultants selects students for a final interview and matriculation. Artistic talent and academic success are the main criteria for continuing at this school. Traditional district secondary courses are offered, but staff members also help establish a curriculum in which the arts and academic areas are closely associated.

High School for Health Professions

Because of present and future demands for health personnel on a local and national scale, Houston and the Baylor College of Medicine have developed a high school curriculum for students interested in medical professions. In addition to traditional courses that meet high school requirements, the High School for Health Professions aims to provide entry-level skills to health professions or specialized academic background for continued career or professional training. Because the campus site is at the Texas Medical Center, students have unique access to health care and medical facilities. Established in 1972, the High School for Health Professions was the first of its kind in the country and has grown from an initial enrollment of 45 sophomores to approximately 350 students.

FUNDING THE MAGNET PROGRAMS

Houston officials projected the actual costs of Phase One (1975–76) and Phase Two (1976–77) for the magnet programs as $7,557,514, of which the total additional local cost was estimated at $5,243,664. Table 8-2 provides a summary of the project budget. Actual additional costs for implementing the first thirty-two programs during Phase One (1975–76) amounted to $4,200,000, according to estimates made in January 1976. A significant part of this money was spent for planning and coordination of the new programs. For example, one or two curriculum planners were assigned to many of the schools, and an instructional coordinator was selected to help assistant principals in each participating school.

Table 8-2

Projected budget summary for magnet programs in Houston, 1975–76 and 1976–77

Expenditures	
Program budgets	$ 8,112,464
Transportation	625,246
Staff development	298,560
Portable buildings	70,000
Total	$ 9,106,270
Total, less program implementation factor [a]	$ 7,557,514
Revenue from external and existing sources	
Estimated external funding	$ 2,200,000
Existing proposed budget	113,850
Total	$ 2,313,850
Total additional cost to Houston Independent school District	$ 5,243,664
Total	$ 7,557,514

[a] The program implementation factor of approximately one-sixth represents the fact that part of the budget for a new program is not spent in the first year because enrollment does not immediately reach 100 percent.

Source: Detailed Program and Budget Information for Quality Integrated Education Report: Magnet Schools (Houston: Independent School District, June 1, 1975).

Staff development expenditures include the cost of over sixty-eight in-service training hours in connection with individual programs. These workshops focused on group process skills, human relationships, curriculum writing, research using problem-solving skills, and specializations pertinent to the needs of individual skills. Administrators of the programs attended training sessions dealing with the use of management models. The total budget for staff development in magnet schools, including funds from the district budgets for 1974–75 and 1975–76, amounted to $298,560.

Individual program budgets incorporate most minor building costs, as well as the staffing expenditures based on lowered student-teacher ratios. Transportation costs are difficult to estimate accurately since the school district attempts to coordinate transportation of magnet school students within an already complex busing system intended to fill the need for special education services, majority-to-minority transfers, and regular transportation. Transfers in and out of the magnet schools occur almost daily, causing numerous route changes and scheduling problems that affect expenditures for transportation.

PRESENT STATUS OF THE MAGNET PROGRAM

Despite the short time available to inaugurate the magnet school program in September 1975, the school district was able to coordinate all staff assignments, complete curriculum guides, and handle requests for transfer of students through normal administrative channels. There was some pandemonium when school opened because supplies were not always available, some assignments of students to magnet schools were still uncertain, and there was the complex problem of coordinating fluctuating bus routes. Houston had shifted from traditional school buses to smaller passenger vans to make the voluntary busing more manageable in a vast city.

It is believed that the magnet programs, involving 25,204 students and 3,167 approved transfers in Phase One, helped to retain some students who might otherwise have left the district. Houston also may be achieving some stable integration in the magnet schools. During the 1975–76 school year, for example, 587 minority students (black and brown) and 670 white students had transferred (as of December 12, 1975) into magnet schools with enrollments that had been between 25 and 75 percent minority during the previous year. The student population in one school increased from 1.5 percent white to 9.5 percent; in another, from 12 percent white to 28 percent, partly as a result of the magnet programs in those schools.

It should be noted, however, that many of the magnet school programs in Houston provide for very limited contact between pupils of differing social and ethnic backgrounds. At the elementary level, for example, a large proportion of the students in the cluster program join students of differing background for only one week or less in a school year. This limited contact may well be useful in acquainting students with others from different groups, particularly if there is opportunity for additional contact outside the school in neighborhood activities, at athletic events, in summer recreation programs, and so forth. It should be clear, however, that such an approach cannot be considered a promising remedy for solving the learning problems of masses of students of low socioeconomic backgrounds in inner-city schools.

Furthermore, as Houston school officials are the first to point out, the magnet school program there is not a plan for racial integration for the district as a whole but rather an attempt to move toward integration to an extent commensurate with what was envisioned in the court-mandated pairing arrangements, which had not succeeded in achieving meaningful integration. This goal seemed particularly important because Houston, like other big-city school districts, was declining in overall enrollment (from 236,220 in 1970 to 211,780 in 1975) and in white enrollment in particular (from 125,432 in 1970 to 82,805 in 1975). Much of this loss represented withdrawal to other districts in the county. Given this pattern, it seemed more important to expand integration where possible, rather than to devise a very large integration plan that might hasten resegregation.

Several features that characterize Houston's magnet program deserve emphasis. There was cooperation between the courts and the school district in establishing the program. The development of the programs and the administration of them was accomplished internally on a district-wide basis. There was free transportation for all students transferring to magnet schools. Most programs were limited in size. Diminishing enrollment left empty classrooms scattered around the district, providing available space for small magnet programs side by side with regular school schedules and populations. By using such space, students in magnet programs can take part in an integrated school program, and regular school programs can benefit from the additional funding, the specialized staffing, the in-service training opportunities, and the lower student-teacher ratios provided in the magnet program.

9. Whitney Young Magnet High School of Chicago and Urban Renewal

Connie Campbell and *Daniel U. Levine*

The public school system in Chicago has operated selective magnet-type vocational and technical schools for decades. During the past ten years it has established some highly innovative magnet schools, including the Disney Elementary School, the Metro High School, the Hyde Park Career Academy, and, in the fall of 1975, the Whitney Young Magnet High School. The opening of Whitney Young marked the beginning of an important experiment in urban education. An estimated $31 million was spent for this new school facility. Its enthusiastic staff and student body and its attractive new building and equipment win the admiration of visitors who are pleased to see a big-city high school offering superior educational opportunities. Yet below the surface are some important fundamental issues worth the serious attention of those concerned about education in other large cities. Much of the information about Whitney Young included in this chapter came from interviews with members of the teaching and administrative staff of the school during its first year of operation.

A SELECTIVE HIGH SCHOOL

Some would refer to Whitney Young as an elitist school, but to do so would prejudice the issue of whether considerable sums of money should be spent for a big-city high school serving only a relatively small number of students who must meet the high standards of admission. There are many types of magnet or alternative schools. Some serve local neighborhoods, while others serve an entire metropolitan area. Some provide programs that are new and different, while others merely dress up old programs in new terminology. Some cost little more than conventional schools, while others consume large amounts of resources that are thus unavailable for other purposes. What is the justification for a school that provides a new and expensive program for a highly selected group of students drawn from all parts of a big city?

One must understand the functions that such a school is (or might be) designed to serve and the contributions it could make in the renewal of deteriorating big cities. We shall consider Whitney Young in the context of urban renewal in Chicago, and we shall also examine several problems faced in the establishment of the new magnet programs in that school.

URBAN RENEWAL

In many large cities, much of the middle class has moved to the suburbs. Large segments of the city have become difficult, unhealthy, or even dangerous places in which to live. Public services have declined in quality. Blight has spread from one neighborhood to the next. Renewal has occurred rather spottily, which has resulted in a few enclaves of middle- or mixed-status areas in the inner core of the city. As a whole, however, the city barely holds its own or continues to decline.

Many public schools in big cities, like other social institutions, serve a population consisting largely of lower socioeconomic groups. The schools do not function very effectively and have lost much of their capacity to retain or attract middle-class residents. Some of the residents who do remain in the city wall themselves off from the larger community. They educate their children in private schools, and they withdraw from leadership roles in public schools and other institutions. Public schools may be a major factor in determining whether these trends can be arrested and reversed. Without good public schools, middle-class residents will continue to leave the city, and too few such families with school-age children will return to allow for systematic renewal of large sections of the city.

With attractive public schools, however, the future of the city could be different. Chicago already has several racially integrated middle-class housing developments close to its downtown section. These areas have become stable because residents are able to enjoy the benefits of living near the downtown in communities large enough to provide a sufficient number of school-age children for an elementary school — a school that parents can be assured will not become an inner-city school with a majority of students of low socioeconomic status.

The situation is different, however, with respect to secondary education. The absence of good secondary schools in which middle-class parents, both black and white, can have confidence places definite limitations on Chicago's chances for rebuilding and renewing its burgeoning inner city. Long-range plans call for the systematic renewal of much of the city as a racially and economically mixed community, particularly in some of the oldest neighborhoods. But all such plans may be doomed to failure unless they include the establishment of both elementary and secondary schools sufficiently outstanding to attract middle-class residents and upwardly mobile residents of lower socioeconomic status.

Whitney Young is designed to be such a school. The original stimulus for the school came from a proposal to establish several cultural and educational clusters (that is, magnet-type school complexes) that would reverse the trend toward racial and social isolation in the Chicago schools. For various reasons, including lack of funds, the other clusters did not materialize. Whitney Young, however, was built in a neighborhood just west of the downtown area and is easily accessible by public transportation from all over the city. Much light industry and many warehouses are located in this neighborhood, and the area already experienced the demolition of buildings. Not far away are several major urban renewal projects. In this setting, Whitney Young could become an important nucleus for further residential redevelopment. Unless other improved public school programs and facilities are established later, however, the potential for systematic renewal of a large section of Chicago will be severely limited. Whitney Young at least provides a start.

PROGRAMS AND STUDENTS AT WHITNEY YOUNG

Three main magnet programs are offered at Whitney Young: medi-

cal arts, science, and the performing arts. The courses needed to meet
requirements for high school graduation are, of course, also available.
In addition, Whitney Young houses a "school within a school" for students with hearing impairments.

The medical arts program provides opportunities for students to
train for work in medical fields related to business, to work in health
service jobs for which they can be certified upon graduation, and to
study basic premedical subjects. The science program, which emphasizes varied subject matter, minicourses, and independent projects, is
designed to complement the medical arts program. The performing
arts program stresses behind-the-scenes skills in television and stage
production, ranging from lighting technology to makeup and costume
design. Each of these programs is developed sequentially in the ninth
through the twelfth grade, with increasing specialization in the later
grades. All three programs will draw heavily on the resources of major
institutions in science, medicine, and the performing arts that are located in or around downtown Chicago.

Students with hearing impairments from throughout the city are accepted with no further admission requirements beyond a need for the
school's special facilities. These students participate with other students in the magnet programs in nonacademic activities and in regular classes whenever it is possible to do so.

Standards for admission into the science, medical arts, and performing arts programs are such that 80 percent of the students have
scored at the fiftieth percentile or above (based on city-wide norms) on
achievement tests. Students are chosen to represent a geographical
cross section of the city. They provide their own transportation to and
from school. Enrollment is closed by September, and there is a general
policy against accepting students after the beginning of the school
year. In its first year the school enrolled 950 ninth- and tenth-grade
students and 225 hearing-impaired students. The enrollment for
1976–77 was 1,784, including 274 students with impaired hearing.
Future enrollment is planned to be 2,650, including 650 with hearing
impairments.

The Chicago Board of Education originally established a quota system for Whitney Young under which 40 percent of the students would
be black, 40 percent white, and 10 percent of Spanish background. Of
the remaining 10 percent, 5 percent were to be from other minority
groups, and 5 percent could be admitted by the principal at his discre-

tion. The actual enrollment in 1975-76 was 43 percent black, 34 percent white, 16 percent Spanish, and 7 percent "other"—a higher percent of minority students than was anticipated. Bernarr Dawson, the school principal, expects a closer approximation to the original quotas in the future as the school establishes its reputation for excellence and as recruitment of students is more vigorously undertaken.

PLANNING THE INSTRUCTIONAL PROGRAM

Whitney Young is a newly built school, with specialized facilities for carrying out its magnet programs. The principal began work there in January 1974, more than eighteen months prior to the scheduled opening of the school. He feels, however, that it would have been desirable for him, as well as for other administrative and supervisory staff, to have begun earlier, since the architects and designers of facilities needed recommendations at an early stage from those who would be working in the building daily.

Experience at Whitney Young suggests that a new magnet school requires considerable lead time and coordination to develop courses and assignments for students in the new programs. Whitney Young administrators found it difficult to attend to all the details of doing this when they had only three months before school opened in fall 1975. In addition, the program was designed to make extensive use of community resources such as universities and medical centers in the area. Some staff at Whitney Young think that this kind of coordination requires the services of a full-time staff member.

The administrators at Whitney Young agree that staff members must have considerable leeway in the development of innovative courses and programs of instruction. They also believe, however, that it has been desirable for the staff to work within the general requirements set by the Board of Education in order to minimize conflict within the faculty on such issues as courses to be offered and the delineation of subject matter for those courses.

Even with the limitations mentioned above, the faculty had considerable autonomy in the development of its programs. The administrators believe, however, that the intelligent use of this freedom requires time—as much as a full year prior to the opening of the school—for planning by the full staff of a new magnet school. In the case of Whitney Young the resources devoted to instructional planning were relatively bounteous. Twenty persons were employed for curriculum planning during the summer of 1974 and were given priority in consideration for appointment to the permanent faculty. They participated in daily workshops on individualization, learning theory, and other subjects taught by university consultants. Teachers employed during the academic year 1974–75, but who were to join the faculty on a full-time basis in September 1975, worked part-time as volunteers during that year, sharing much of the burden of instructional planning and meeting weekly in two-hour sessions with the original planning group and the outside consultants.

While these planning activities proved valuable, it was still felt that the part-time arrangement permitted too little time for meetings. Some of the participants tended to consider the theories underlying individualized approaches to learning as nebulous and impractical. More time was needed by the faculty itself to discuss and analyze these theories and to explore their implications for programs such as those to be developed at Whitney Young.

RECRUITMENT OF STAFF

The staffing of a magnet school frequently presents problems because of the highly specialized personnel needed to develop and implement the kinds of programs to be offered. Recruiting for Whitney Young, however, was not a major problem. In the first place, there was ample time to select persons who met the requirements for appointment: adaptability, previous teaching experience, and certification. Furthermore, the central office of the Chicago public schools, neighboring universities, and other institutions helped to identify persons suitable for the special magnet programs. It is likely that a smaller school district with fewer community resources upon which to draw could have more difficulty in staffing a magnet school.

A second problem encountered in selecting staff arises because a magnet school frequently drains off outstanding teachers from other schools in the district. Depriving these schools of their most creative and vigorous teachers can lead to friction between them and the magnet school. This friction could, in turn, reduce the cooperation upon which administrators of magnet schools depend in the recruitment of students. Because of the size of the Chicago school system there seems to have been no major problem of this sort in recruiting the staff for

Whitney Young. In smaller districts, or in larger districts with a greater number of magnet schools, administrators would need to exert care in recruiting staff in order to avoid the harmful side effects associated with the transfer of outstanding teachers to a new magnet school program.

SELECTION AND RECRUITMENT OF STUDENTS

Potential students must be informed of programs available and must be persuaded to apply for admission. Selection of students can be difficult and time consuming especially when, as at Whitney Young, there are many applications and there are constraints on admission because of established racial quotas and academic guidelines.

Because too few resources were available to provide adequate publicity about Whitney Young before the school opened, the targets for racial composition of the student body were not quite met in its first year. Administrators at the school believe that problems of selecting and recruiting students could be alleviated if there were a full-time director of publicity and community relations to work directly with elementary schools. At present students learn of the school's programs through guidance offices in public elementary school and through mailings to private and parochial schools. Lack of extensive publicity, coupled with a general reticence on the part of whites to transfer to an inner-city school, seems to explain the initial low enrollment of white students at Whitney Young. Principal Dawson reported that "there is a tremendous competition among blacks to get into Whitney Young, whereas white students generally have more acceptable options than black students." For the school year 1976–77 there were 5,400 applications for 500 openings at the ninth-grade level. Approximately four-fifths of these applications came from black students.

Competition from other schools can also complicate the problem of securing the kind of student body a magnet school seeks to attract. In Chicago, for example, competition for high-achieving students comes not just from private and parochial schools but also from fifteen other specialized public high schools (including vocational and technical schools), all of which require good academic performance.

HOW LARGE A MAGNET?

The question of how large a magnet school should be is related to issues involving recruitment of students and faculty, types of program offered, and the purposes for which the school is established. In Chicago, for example, the success of large-scale renewal activities will in part depend on the ability of schools like Whitney Young to attract middle-class residents to redeveloped neighborhoods near the downtown area. But the availability of space in magnet high schools may be of little value unless students are persuaded to apply for admission as a result of an effective recruitment program.

Perhaps Whitney Young should be larger. A magnet high school with its advantageous location might attract many more than the 2,000 (exclusive of the hearing-impaired students) now anticipated. To have built a larger school at this time would have been extremely expensive, and it would also have presented more difficult problems of instructional planning and recruitment of staff and students. Principal Dawson agrees with this assessment and notes, furthermore, that the school would not have been successful had it not received significant additional funding.

We believe that there is no ideal size for a magnet school. Rather, size should be determined by the availability of staff and funds, the nature of the problems anticipated in planning the instructional program, the role of the school in relation to the total school system, and the relation of the school to comprehensive plans for renewal of urban neighborhoods.

THE MAGNET SCHOOL IN RELATION TO THE LOCAL COMMUNITY

A critical issue in making a magnet school part of plans to renew urban neighborhoods involves its relationship with the community immediately surrounding it. One important question that must be answered is whether students from the surrounding community should be allowed to attend the school on an unrestricted basis or whether they should at least receive some type of preference in admission.

The main disadvantage of giving preference to such students is that the attractiveness of the school may be diluted so that potential students would view it as just another neighborhood school, and perhaps as an inner-city school as well. Thus, if these students were to be admitted along with those who meet the high admission standards of the magnet school, the school may lose much of its magnetic force. But there can also be disadvantages in closing the school to enrollment from the surrounding community, particularly in the eyes of those living there. Whitney Young was viewed by some residents of the area as a neighborhood school. They believed that their children should have the highest priority in admissions decisions. This view was reinforced by the overcrowded conditions of the nearest neighborhood high school, where large classes contrasted glaringly with the small ones at Whitney Young. A further complication arises when one considers the function of schools like Whitney Young in the process of urban renewal. If substantial neighborhood renewal takes place in nearby areas, should not local residents then be given preference in order to help attract a middle-class and a racially mixed population to the area?

Early in the planning for Whitney Young it was decided to give no preference to students from the local community. In order not to tip racial percentages irreversibly, the Board of Education chose to keep enrollment low rather than fill all vacant positions at the school in its first year. Even if more vigorous recruitment had been undertaken and the enrollment goals met for the first year, the dilemmas posed by restricted enrollment still would have been only partly resolved. Perhaps a reexamination of policies concerning admission will be called for as neighborhood renewal proceeds near the downtown area of Chicago. It is possible that a less selective companion magnet high school should be established to serve the community in which Whitney Young is located. Again, the underlying point is that planning and development of big city magnet schools should be part of a much larger and more comprehensive plan for school and community renewal.

WHO GOES TO WHICH SCHOOLS?

Implicit in the foregoing discussion is the basic problem of developing a comprehensive framework for improving the educational opportunities available to students from all social backgrounds. Rather than maximizing opportunity, the big-city educational system, together with other urban social systems, now operates to limit opportunity. For reasons beyond the control of the schools, social welfare agencies, private housing developers, or any other single component in the network of urban social systems, middle-class students in large cities frequently do not have attractive public schools available, and children of lower socioeconomic backgrounds are piled up in inner-city schools that do not function effectively.

Fragmentary efforts have been made to change this situation, particularly with the development of magnet schools for high-achieving students and compensatory education for low-achieving students. Overall results, however, have often been unproductive if not positively irrational. Millions of dollars have been poured into inner-city schools, but little has been accomplished, partly because such schools are not good places in which to teach or learn. Efforts to stabilize mixed-status schools have been made, but, without coordinated city-wide and metropolitan policies, such schools continue to become isolated racially and socioeconomically. Special opportunities have been provided for relatively high-achieving students from inner-city neighborhoods. An example of one such opportunity is new vocational high schools where the academic admissions requirements help to keep them from being regarded as inner-city high schools. As a result, some high-achieving students with aspirations to go to college attended these relatively attractive schools only to find themselves unprepared for college because the required vocational courses did not allow them to take a full college preparatory program. An excellent college preparatory magnet high school provides new alternatives for some whose only previous choices were between vocational programs and the arguably "high" track in neighborhood schools with abysmally low academic standards and expectations.

It is unrealistic, however, to expect that fundamental inadequacies in educational opportunities in big cities like Chicago can be alleviated merely by establishing a number of selective magnet schools. The roots of the problems in big-city school districts involve city-wide and metropolitan-wide forces that have produced concentrations of poor families in the city and in some suburbs, particularly in the first-ring suburbs in the path of the expanding inner city. Unless these forces are dealt with, the establishment of magnet or alternative schools may only exacerbate irrationalities in the provisions for educational opportunity in big-city school districts.

If selective magnet schools are established on a sufficiently large scale, for example, more "regular" city high schools, even those vocationally and technically oriented schools with high standards for admission, will become still more of a dumping ground for students whose academic performance is far below the level attained by students in a middle-class elementary school. As this happens, middle-class parents who are unable to place their children in the selective magnet schools will transfer them to nonpublic schools or move to the suburbs.

Conversely, if too few selective magnet schools are established, middle-class white and black families will be encouraged to withdraw from big-city schools and neighborhoods. The underlying problem, of course, is that the population of many big cities, including Chicago, is already largely composed of people of lower socioeconomic status. This prevents, of course, socioeconomic integration in the schools.

The perfect number — whatever that is — of selective magnet schools could aid in slowing the flight from the city and could even help to make large-scale renewal of the city feasible. Meanwhile, the existing inner-city schools continue to provide inadequate educational opportunities, and nonpublic and suburban schools function as magnets in their own right, drawing middle-class and upwardly mobile students from lower socioeconomic classes away from central-city schools and neighborhoods. Perhaps the establishment of a network of magnet schools could overcome these trends. It is more likely, however, that the pace of decline would simply be slowed down. Only when magnet schools are components of a comprehensive plan for improving existing inner-city schools and for reversing the trend toward deterioration of neighborhoods throughout the city is it likely that there will be any overall improvement in the educational opportunities for the next generation of youth in the big cities.

PART THREE
Desegregation Developments and Instructional Reform in Boston

The desegregation controversy in Boston has received more national attention than any other in the country, but there is no clear understanding about what actually happened there, why and how it happened, or the implications for big-city schools elsewhere.

Many people, for example, are not aware that most of the schools in Boston have already been desegregated with little or no strife or turmoil, or that, largely as a result of Federal Judge W. Arthur Garrity's desegregation order, Boston is now undertaking a wide-ranging and thorough attempt at instructional reform. The degree to which this effort will succeed is still highly speculative, and the lessons that may have been learned with regard to peaceful and constructive desegregation are even more uncertain, but sufficient time has elapsed since desegregation by court order began in 1974 to allow for examination of developments in Boston in terms of their meaning and implications for educators elsewhere.

Accordingly, Chapter 10 provides a detailed account, by Charles W. Case, of the events leading up to and following court-ordered desegregation, as well as a description of the major components of the desegregation plan. Robert A. Dentler then develops a broad view of the desegregation process and the lessons that have been learned in

Boston. It is based on the author's firsthand acquaintance with many of the developments that occurred there.

Finally, Marvin B. Scott provides a description of one of the main components: the most sizable effort that has been made anywhere to involve higher education institutions, in this instance through court initiative, in working to improve educational opportunities in big-city elementary and secondary schools.

10. History of the Desegregation Plan in Boston

Charles W. Case

Planning for desegregation in Boston was met by active resistance on the part of school authorities and some citizens' groups and by legal tenacity on the part of the plaintiffs and the state of Massachusetts. After years of struggle, however, Boston finally had a comprehensive plan by the fall of 1975, and many parts of the community were participating in its implementation. This chapter describes the circumstances under which the plan was developed.

Of Boston's approximately 85,000 public school students, 40 percent were black, and most of them attended schools that were at least 85 percent black. The Massachusetts Racial Imbalance Act of 1965 defined any school with a nonwhite enrollment of more than 50 percent as imbalanced and gave the state commissioner of education the right to refuse state aid to districts that failed to correct such imbalance. As a result, in the fall of 1971 the Massachusetts State Board of Education withheld $21 million in state aid from the Boston public schools and demanded that the Boston School Committee (the Boston school board) produce a desegregation plan for the school year 1973–74 that would comply with the Racial Imbalance Act. For six years the state board had, in fact, sought such compliance. The mayor of Boston intervened at this time and brought about a temporary compromise, which was soon ignored by the school committee. When the state board then decided to withhold $52 million in state aid, the school committee entered a suit against the board in Suffolk County Superior Court. A countersuit by the state followed. At the same time, the National Association for the Advancement of Colored People filed a federal suit against the Boston School Committee. In June 1972 the U.S. Department of Health, Education, and Welfare notified the Boston schools that formal proceedings were being instituted to examine Boston's school desegregation efforts; $10 million in federal aid was at stake. Hearings were held, and early in 1973 a federal administrative judge ruled that Boston was operating a dual school system. Thus, within a year's time state courts, a federal court, and HEW had become actively involved in the desegregation problem in Boston.

During 1972 the state commissioner of education was directed by the State Board of Education to draft a desegregation plan for Boston. This plan, which was adopted by the state board in the fall of 1972, was concerned primarily with the distribution of students on the basis of racial percentages and not with broader educational matters. In December 1972 the Suffolk County Superior Court ordered the state board to restore state aid to Boston and ordered Boston to comply with the Racial Imbalance Act by implementing the state plan for desegregation. The school committee immediately appealed the decision to the Massachusetts Supreme Judicial Court. In October 1973, after eighteen days of quasi-judicial hearings conducted by court-appointed experts on the question of whether the state plan should be altered, the Supreme Judicial Court upheld the state board.

Simultaneously, Judge Arthur Garrity was hearing the NAACP suit against the Boston School Committee in the U.S. District Court. In June 1974 he concluded that the school committee had deliberately promoted segregated conditions for nine years through decisions regarding school construction, assignment of pupils, policies concerning transfer of pupils, feeder patterns, and policies for selecting students for the largely black vocational schools and for the largely white and exclusive "examination schools." The judge stated that segregation "permeates schools in all areas of the city, all grade levels, and all types of schools." He noted that the Boston School Committee had consistently rejected proposals to redistrict for racial balance, but did redistrict at times when there were no racial implications. The defendants' position was that the present segregation was not a product of their intent. It was due, rather, to factors over which they had no control or to the policy of providing neighborhood schools, a constitutionally permissible policy that predated any present segregation. The court maintained that inaction in the face of racial segregation involved intent to segregate as much as actions actually designed to segregate the schools. Judge Garrity ordered the school committee to implement a partial desegregation plan prepared by the State Board of Education by the following September, which was only twelve weeks away. The partial plan focused only on the reassignment of students and teachers and was limited primarily to Irish South Boston and black Roxbury, both low-income communities.

PLANNING FOR PHASE ONE: SUMMER 1974

With twelve weeks left prior to the implementation of Phase One, the school committee immediately appealed Judge Garrity's decision in the U.S. Circuit Court of Appeals. In December 1974 that court affirmed the decision of the district court, holding that patterns of selective action and refusal to act in light of the foreseeable racial impact, when accompanied by statements of express intention not to counter antisegregation sentiment, constituted evidence of an intention to create or maintain a dual school system. The court concluded likewise with regard to feeder patterns, policies of open enrollment and controlled transfer, changing of attendance zones, and placement of provisional teachers in predominantly black schools. (The U.S. Supreme Court subsequently upheld Judge Garrity's decision in May 1975.)

In mid-July 1974 Judge Garrity gave the school committee two more weeks to submit an alternative to the state plan. In the meantime, the participants in the antibusing movement, led by ROAR (Restore Our Alienated Rights), were having protest demonstrations and were promoting a boycott of the schools in September. ROAR's position was adamant: "You are either with us or against us." After a two-week period, at the end of July, the school committee refused to submit an alternative plan. The judge then ordered that the state plan be implemented. Six weeks remained before school was to open.

The school committee decided early in August to appeal the court's orders denying a delay in implementation as well as the exemption of high school seniors. When attorneys for the school committee threatened to withdraw from the case if the appeal was filed, the school committee backed down. Also, early in August, Judge Garrity found it necessary to issue two court orders to release state and city funds to the schools for the implementation of Phase One. The school committee decided to delay the opening of school for one week, and the judge approved the decision.

In mid-August the school committee and the mayor's office began to arrange for extra buses, to plan bus routes, to anticipate traffic problems; to organize safety plans with the police and fire departments; to prepare training programs for teachers, principals, aides, and monitors; to organize school security plans as well as an information and rumor-control center; and to reassign students and teachers. Many transitional aides had to be hired and trained to ride the buses and to assist in the schools during the day. Traffic supervisors for street crossings also had to be hired and trained. In addition, the mayor continued his series of "Kaffeeklatsches" in neighborhoods throughout the city to discuss implementation plans and concerns. The mayor's office also established seventeen neighborhood desegregation task forces to coordinate the efforts of the police department, fire department, schools, clergy, home-school associations, community agencies, and the street workers in those areas.

A coalition of black groups organized safety plans, rumor control, and dialogues between black and white parents. Plans were also made for neighborhood parents to be available to bused children who became ill in school. The coalition was facilitated by Freedom House, a black community organization with a twenty-five-year history in Boston. Common questions and concerns of parents included: "Where does my child catch the bus?" "How do I get my child enrolled?" and "How will the buses be protected?"

ROAR continued to march and demonstrate. Some white antibusing parents changed the address of their children to that of a relative in an area that would not be affected by the plan. Some parochial schools obeyed Cardinal Medeiros's order that such schools were not to become havens for those seeking to avoid desegregation; others did not. The training programs in human relations for teachers, administrators, aides, and monitors were hurriedly prepared and, therefore, were poorly done and ineffective.

Late in August Judge Garrity requested assistance from the Community Relations Service of the U.S. Department of Justice to monitor the implementation of the plan. The Community Relations Service, which functions as conciliator and mediator, began working in communities attempting to desegregate in 1970. In Boston it had attempted to work quietly early in 1974 in order to help the schools prepare for implementation, but at that time the prevailing attitude there was "Why plan? There will be more appeals and delays." The Community Relations Service had had experiences in other communities where the school professionals had done contingency planning even though the appeals process was in motion. The Community Relations Service is free to work with any group in a community. Judge Garrity issued a court order for all parties to the suit to work with the service.

During this time there was a vacuum of leadership. Business, higher education, churches, and civic organizations showed little interest in becoming involved. There were notable exceptions, but they were few in number. The news media in Boston emphasized balanced coverage so as not to inflame emotions by focusing only on negative factors.

IMPLEMENTATION OF PHASE ONE: SCHOOL YEAR 1974–75

In this climate of defiance, fear, and unpreparedness, the schools opened. It is unnecessary to dwell on the violence and harassment that occurred. Demonstrations, damage to property, stoning of buses, and boycotts began immediately. Each day the acts were repeated as the buses carrying black children rolled into South Boston in the morning and departed in the afternoon. It is important to note, however, that serious disorders took place in only four out of the eighty schools included in Phase One.

The police immediately escalated the security force, quadrupling manpower in South Boston. Orders were given that groups of three or more were to be dispersed, and those resisting were to be arrested. The Community Relations Service had advocated that the police presence be obvious initially in order to establish a tolerant environment, but one that would not reinforce the antics of demonstrators. ROAR continued its marches and directed some of its emphasis toward the "liberal" media.

In late September Judge Garrity ordered that hearings on Phase Two begin. A coalition of black organizations — Freedom House, Lean Park Community Development Corporation, and Roxbury Multi-Service Center — increased its efforts. A Community Information Center was established for informational meetings, rumor control, protection, and emergency help such as transportation, child care, and legal services. A Coordinated Social Services Council was formed, involving over forty community agencies and organizations that met weekly to share information and to plan for social services related to desegregation. Other assisting organizations included the Boston University Consultation and Education Program, the YMCA, the Education Task Force, the Elma Lewis School of Fine Arts, the Massachusetts Council of Churches, the Boston Ministerial Alliance, the Archdiocese of Boston, the Family Service Association, the YWCA, and the City-Wide Education Coalition.

In October the violence escalated, spreading from the streets into the schools. Police were assigned duty in the schools, and the force on the streets was doubled. Incidents also occurred in other locations in the community. Many antibusers began to direct their epithets toward the police. Each day the battered buses continued to run the gauntlet.

At this point the mayor asked Judge Garrity to bring in federal marshals, whereupon the judge responded that this action would have to be a last resort after all local efforts had failed. He recommended that the mayor request the governor to send in state police. The Boston Teachers Union asked the superintendent to close the affected schools; the superintendent refused. President Ford stated at a news conference that he was not in favor of sending in marshals or troops, or of busing. Meanwhile, the governor was deciding whether or not to call out the National Guard. The U.S. Department of Justice sent in prosecutors, who one week later made two arrests related to earlier incidents of violence. When a stabbing occurred in a school, the governor ordered in the National Guard. In late October, as these events were taking place, Judge Garrity issued an order that Phase Two was to include the entire city and that a plan was to be submitted by the school committee by December 16, 1974.

By November the violence and harassment began to abate somewhat. The number of guardsmen was reduced by two-thirds. About 4,500 high school students continued to boycott four high schools, and white high school students still refused to elect representatives to the biracial councils as ordered by the judge. State police patrolling the school corridors were replaced by city police.

There was a distinct advantage in using the state police because they were not neighbors in the South Boston community. In December, a short school month owing to a number of holidays, the state police force was reduced by two-thirds. At this time, however, the enrollment of white students began to increase, especially among seniors thinking of graduation. Fighting began to escalate again, and another stabbing occurred. The superintendent closed the schools.

Judge Garrity ordered the exclusion of all persons from the schools except those assigned to be there. Also, he ordered that no groups were to be within fifty yards of the school or of the bus routes and that racial slurs were not to be made on school property. If these orders were disobeyed, he would close South Boston schools permanently; he further ordered that a contingency plan for such an eventuality be prepared immediately.

Also in December, the school committee voted three to two to defy the court order regarding Phase Two. The attorneys for the schools then requested to be removed from the case. The judge ordered the school committee to appear before him, and he accepted with regret and understanding the resignation of the attorneys. The three-person majority on the school committee was given a week to show cause why they should not be held in contempt of court. During this time much effort was expended in investigating an alleged plot to blow up the bridges around Boston; such a plot was never verified.

In January 1975 the police commissioner urged that the schools remain closed. The superintendent, under duress, complied temporarily. Also in January the U.S. Court of Appeals (First Circuit) ruled on an appeal that had been filed by the Boston Teachers Union challenging the part of the Phase One decision requiring that one black teacher be hired for every white teacher hired. Prior to Phase One only 7 percent of Boston's teachers were nonwhite, while the student enrollment was about 40 percent nonwhite. The court of appeals affirmed the district court's decision, holding that the district court had not exceeded the scope of its remedial powers. The union's earlier request to intervene as defendants in the original action in the district court was denied.

The majority of the school committee returned to court to respond to the contempt charges, indicating that they would obey the strict letter of the law, but would not approve a plan involving involuntary busing. Ruling that they were in contempt of court, the judge gave them the weekend to reconsider. When they returned, they offered to prepare a completely voluntary busing plan, but no more. The judge reluctantly agreed, but he proceeded to consider individuals who might be appointed as masters and experts to aid the court in preparing a plan for Phase Two for the fall of 1975. A plan had also been submitted by counsel for the plaintiff, and fragments of plans were submitted by other parties who were allowed to intervene.

During the first four months of the school year 1974–75 the average daily attendance in the Boston schools was 75 percent of the enrollment compared with 85 percent in the previous year. Attendance in the elementary grades was 82 percent. During the first term 185 new black teachers began working. Four out of the eighty schools included in Phase One where disorders occurred were in white neighborhoods. All desegregated schools in black communities were peaceful. Altogether, police were used in only three schools. Eighty percent of the court-ordered biracial councils were formed.

In February Judge Garrity appointed a panel of four masters and in addition two experts to assist the masters in preparing a plan for Phase Two. The panel completed its work in mid-March. Upon the release of the plan, the NAACP and the state board of education filed briefs stating that the plan would not sufficiently desegregate the schools. In April Judge Garrity told the court-appointed experts to redraw attendance district lines so that no more than 60 percent and no less than 40 percent of any race would be represented in any of the districts except in East Boston, which is separated from the rest of the city by a river, tunnels, bridges, and an airport. Meanwhile the opponents of busing were finally successful in securing the repeal of the Racial Imbalance Act. Because Boston had been found to be violating the U.S. Constitution, however, repeal could not affect the current effort at desegregation. In May Judge Garrity made his final ruling on Phase Two. The amended master's plan was approved and was ordered to be in effect in September 1975. In the final months of the school year tensions in the schools and the streets decreased significantly, but ROAR continued to oppose desegregation and told the community it would seek an antibusing amendment to the Constitution.

PLANNING FOR PHASE TWO

The panel of masters consisted of two attorneys and two educators, all of whom were experienced and distinguished. Judge Garrity's order to the panel included the charge that "the goal of the master's report shall be the recommendations of a plan meeting constitutional standards that includes system-wide desegregation of vocational and examination schools, athletic and other programs, and makes provision for bilingual education for special needs. . . . Magnet schools, metropolitanization, and other options may be recommended as part of a plan to the extent they are compatible with the essential objective of prompt system-wide desegregation." (Report of the Masters in *Morgan v. Kerrigan*, U.S.D.C., March 31, 1975, Civil Action No. 72-911-G, U.S.D.C., D, Mass Order of Appointment and Reference of Masters, Appendix A).

The role of the panel was to determine the facts and to make recommendations to the judge. Though a panel cannot collect information personally, it can direct experts to gather specific information. These experts are usually retained into the implementation period to provide continuity and to assist the judge who is provided with a very small staff.

The experts began their work by collecting all the information and data that had been made available to the courts over the previous ten years. For a number of reasons, the various data packages conflicted with one another. It is significant to remember that courts received their information from opposing attorneys who received many of their data from cross-examination. The Boston schools had withheld factual information for ten years. As specific allegations were made in court, the schools would release some data to counter the allegations. After two and a half years the court still did not have accurate information on the number of children, building capacities, and the like. Finally, at the request of the panel, Judge Garrity issued a court order demanding that the school district provide computer printouts indicating the name, address, sex, ethnicity, and school attendance of all 85,000 children in the district.

The panel of masters began its deliberations with eleven days of evidentiary hearings and one day of visits to school sites. The experts drafted a proposed plan that was distributed to all parties to the suit for their reaction; they also received all the memorandums given to the masters by the experts. The parties to the suit were given the opportunity to cross-examine the experts. An order was also issued permitting any organization that had filed desegregation proposals or comments before the hearings began to present documents in support of or in addition to its submission, including comments on the draft of the master's report. On February 26, 1975, the panel heard arguments of counsel for the parties.

The masters concluded that the various plans submitted by parties to the suit were inadequate and unacceptable. There were some specific objections to the various plans, among them:

— Plans advocating total freedom of choice were unacceptable.
— The pairing of schools or the creation of one-grade schools would cause an excessive number of changes in assignments of students.
— Magnet programs must be limited in number, of high quality, and carefully placed so as to promote desegregation.
— Part-time integrated schooling could not substitute for a desegregated education.
— A plan should assure not just the proper assignment of students, but also educational programs appropriate to the special needs of students victimized by segregation.

THE PHASE TWO PLAN

In the introduction to their report, the masters set the theme for the Phase Two plan by stressing the reestablishment of quality education, which, they noted, had been declining steadily in Boston for many years. They focused on the vast number (75 percent) of students who did not go on to postsecondary education. They noted that course offerings had remained unchanged for many years. They also stressed that black students generally attended schools that were the most crowded, the oldest, the least well maintained, and the most poorly staffed.

The masters acknowledged the elements they had accepted from proposals submitted by the school committee, the NAACP, the State Board of Education, the mayor, and the Public Facilities Commission. Some of the "borrowed" elements follow:

— Parents and students should be offered alternatives.
— Geographic assignments that provide sure and predictable desegregation should be used.
— The school system should be divided into smaller units, which would lend themselves to identification with the community, and emphasis should be placed on programmatic education.
— Some schools should be consolidated if it was determined that certain buildings were unfit for use.
— Compulsory busing should be kept at a minimum, yet managed so that it would achieve the desegregation required by law.

The major features of the Phase Two plan recommended by the masters were:

—Attendance options for students and parents that would include, first, being automatically assigned to the community school district wherein they resided, but with no guarantee as to which school in the district; second, remaining in the current school if it had been among the schools included in Phase One; third, attending a city-wide magnet school; fourth, attending a specific program available in another community school district if the ethnic composition was within the established limits; fifth, attending a school external to the school system such as one included in the city-suburban exchange program in the Boston area. It was noted that these options would give coequal importance to the preferences of the students and parents and the obligations of the school board.

—There would be nine community school districts (later changed to eight) and one city-wide school district.

—Programs would stress variety and innovation.

—Twelfth graders could remain in the school they attended the preceding year, if they so desired, and kindergartners would be exempted from busing wherever possible.

—Reorganization of the administration of the schools would be carried out to ensure accountability to the community and to the court.

—Schools would be paired with specific colleges, businesses, and labor organizations.

—Twenty-five buildings (this number was later reduced) would be closed to upgrade the quality of services and to consolidate students for the furtherance of desegregation.

The plan also emphasized that some mandatory busing was necessary to desegregate the schools effectively. Neighborhood assignments would not desegregate the schools because of the geography of the city and the racial and ethnic distribution of its population. The revision of attendance zones and grade structures, the construction of new schools and the closing of old ones, and majority-to-minority transfer were not seen as sufficient. An analysis of the projected busing costs indicated that they would be less for Phase Two than for Phase One.

Implementation of Major Features of Phase Two

In Phase Two students' and parents' options for school attendance are exercised through a three-step procedure: first, the family files its preference; second, the school administration analyzes all the applications under court review; and, third, the ethnic ratios having been determined, the student is notified of his assignment. With the application for filing, the family receives a multilingual booklet describing program options and how to apply for them. There is an information and guidance center in each community school district, and in some neighborhoods community organizations also provide assistance to parents. The application includes information on the student's age, ethnicity, residence, last school and grade, special learning or treatment needs, Title I eligibility, and home language. Families have ten days in which to file a preference, and the school district must notify the student of his assignment within twenty-one days of filing.

The eight newly established community school districts correspond rather well with the boundaries of the wards, the precincts, and the natural residential units or combinations of units of the residential communities of Boston. The school planners used geocoded information from the police department in drawing the boundaries of new school districts and in assigning children to schools. Assignment of students within community districts provides more community control and minimizes the amount of transportation. The average distance traveled by bus within a district is less than two and a half miles, and the longest trip is less than five miles.

Each community school district has a community superintendent and a community council, and each school facility has a principal or headmaster. Some principals were previously responsible for more than one school, which tended to force them to emphasize only managerial functions, rather than programmatic and community concerns. Under the new plan principals in each district form a council of principals, chaired by the community superintendent. Each district, within the constraints of state standards, policies of the school administration, and contractual obligations with a paired college, is to develop its curriculum, programs of instruction, and extracurricular activities in response to the needs and interests of parents and students.

The high school in each community district is to be a four-year, comprehensive institution that also is engaged in vocational and postsecondary education; it is also to serve as an adult or multipurpose community education facility. As occurs in many school districts, a rigid separation had previously existed among the students, staff, and curriculum for vocationally oriented programs and the regular high school curriculum. Such a separation tended to lock students into tracks that greatly influenced their options for postsecondary education. Such a system made it difficult for students to take advantage of opportunities in the "other" program.

There are to be variable styles of instruction in elementary and middle schools ranging from an emphasis on traditional education to open education. This is an attempt to encourage alternative teaching styles to fit the different learning needs of individual students. Much of the assistance from higher education and business is to be directed toward the development of these options.

The district office, located in a convenient school in each district, includes the community superintendent, community secretary, and professional staff charged with district-wide servicing of ancillary programs in special needs diagnosis and referral, counseling, social work, and adult or community education. The office serves as the meeting place for the community council and the council of principals.

There are now uniform grade structures: elementary schools comprise the first through the fifth grade, the middle schools comprise the sixth through the eighth grade, and high schools comprise the ninth through the twelfth grade. Most elementary schools have a kindergarten. Previously there were many different patterns of grade progression that had been gerrymandered, partly, perhaps, in an effort to keep the schools segregated over the years.

The plan designates ethnic ratios for each school in each district and allows for an 8 percent variance. The panel felt it was necessary to be specific to ensure equitable desegregation throughout the city and to recognize particular geographic constraints and ethnic concentrations. Thus the Phase Two plan sets somewhat flexible goals for desegregation and yet guarantees that there will be a significant number of minority students in each school.

The city-wide magnet school district is comprised of those schools offering unique programs for students residing anywhere within Boston. Twenty-five of the 162 schools in the city are designated as magnet schools. Applicants to magnet programs must meet established standards for admission. Each school was to have an enrollment that is

40 to 60 percent white, 30 to 50 percent black, and 5 to 25 percent other minorities. The magnet schools have made progress toward these goals. Enrollments in the twenty-five schools as of September 1976 are shown in Table 10-1.

Table 10-1

Percentage of racial distribution of students attending
twenty-five magnet schools in Boston,
September 20, 1976

School	Racial distribution (percent)		
	Black	White	Other
Elementary			
Curley	39	52	10
Guild	31	69	—
Haley	48	48	5
Hennigan	38	42	21
Hernandez	14	7	80
Jackson-Mann	38	40	22
McKay	34	63	3
Ohrenberger	47	51	3
Trotter	44	49	7
Middle			
Boston Latin	23	65	12
Latin Academy	27	66	7
Mackey	31	47	22
Mann	40	42	18
Mario Umana	32	61	7
Martin Luther King	48	45	7
High			
Boston	39	46	15
Boston Latin	6	86	8
Boston Technical	35	50	15
Boston Trade	57	40	3
Copley Square	34	50	16
English	43	45	12
English Language Center	23	46	31
Latin Academy	11	76	14
Madison Park	54	38	8
Mario Umana	54	38	8

Note: Some percentages do not add up to 100 because of rounding.

Source: Boston Public Schools, "Boston Public School, Monday, September 20, 1976-9th School Day," mimeographed report.

The magnet approach provides the opportunity to offer special programs that would be too costly to duplicate throughout the city but are feasible if located in one place and available to all students. The magnet schools have been placed in locations where many people would not normally go. While magnet schools are not used as the primary means of desegregation, they are part of the total plan, and they add an element of choice on the part of parents and students.

Monitoring the Plan

In each community district an advisory council has been established to advise and to plan with the community superintendents and the council of principals. Each council has thirteen members, including five parents, two high school students, one teacher, the superintendent, and one person from each of the following fields: business, higher education, labor, and the police. The powers of the council are limited to guiding the desegregation process and reporting to a city-wide coordinating council of forty-two members.

This coordinating council monitors the implementation of the desegregation plan and all related subsequent orders of the court, including policy making by the school committee, administration and staffing, planning, curriculum and instruction, discipline, transfer procedures, police-school relations, budgets, expenditures, and the training of students and teachers in human relations. The members of the council are appointed by the court. The council has a full-time paid executive director, seven additional professional staff members, and two clerks. Members of the council attend all meetings of the Boston School Committee, including executive sessions.

For the external monitoring of the plan, only this council may notify the court or request court action on issues of noncompliance or deviation from the objectives of the court's orders. The council receives information and inquiries from the community school district councils. The detailed items to be monitored have become part of current court-ordered desegregation plans elsewhere and reflect the interest of the courts in results.

Many consider the city-wide council unwieldy, and it has been criticized because half its members either have no children in the Boston schools or live in the suburbs. It has been divided into six committees: an education committee to monitor partnerships, special education, and bilingual education; a school liaison committee to coordinate and evaluate the voluntary monitors who work in biracial teams that serve as fact finders and interviewers for the other committees; a district liaison committee to work with the eight community councils and the biracial councils in the schools and to review educational policy; a public safety and transportation committee to check out bus routes and to review safety plans; a public information committee to monitor all city departments on their descriptions of daily events and to foster a better understanding of Phase Two within the community; and a community liaison committee to help with linkages among various community organizations. The council submits monthly reports directly to the judge. If he deems it necessary, he issues court orders to correct deviations from the court plan. It is intended that eventually the coordinating council will replace the court-appointed experts.

The monitoring information submitted by community superintendents to the councils and to the court includes data on race and ethnicity of students, faculty, administration, and aides; infractions of the discipline code; evaluations of the human relations training; requests for police assistance and the activities and control of police in school buildings; the length of experience of the staff, number of permanent faculty, and the use of substitutes; achievement of students; attendance rates; discipline rates; suspensions and expulsions; facilities and their adequacy for particular school programs; types of programs available to students; budgets and allocations for books, equipment, supplies, and field trips; plans for improvements in programs; communications among parents, students, and staff; and satisfaction with school programs and facilities. This monitoring approach is similar to that used in Denver, where there is a timetable for implementation that is monitored by the court-appointed experts.

Phase Two and Higher Education

The idea of involving higher education in Phase Two came from the educators on the panel of masters in response to the concerns about the declining quality of education in the Boston schools. The panel asked the court experts to prepare a list of hypothetical pairings of colleges and schools by which institutions of higher learning could be linked with particular schools to assist in improving the quality of education. Judge Garrity contended that transporting children to different schools may eliminate current segregation, but would not erase the effects of past discrimination. Learning opportunities must be developed that would remedy the losses students had already suffered and lay a basis for improving the quality of education for all of the city. The attorneys on the panel felt that the involvement of institutions of higher education should be part of the court order so as to strengthen the plan.

The panel met with sixteen college presidents to present the idea before it was put into the plan. Many of the presidents were resistant, especially those of the private universities. The panel strongly requested that the sixteen presidents give a pledge to participate within thirty-six hours that would be used as an appendix in the masters' report. All sixteen did so. The judge appointed an ad hoc committee of lawyers to devise a contract for such partnerships. As this became public information, seven more colleges asked to be included in the plan. Judge Garrity later told the State Board of Education to provide $1 million for planning to take place during the summer of 1975.

The institutions of higher learning worked with the schools during the summer of 1975 to plan their partnerships for implementation in the fall. Some of the colleges are thus paired with particular community school districts, and with specific magnet programs in the city-wide magnet district. Harvard's commitment is to one school (Roxbury High School), while Boston University is paired with all sixteen schools in Community School District Number One. The colleges have had some difficulties in working with the teachers and parents in the planning phase. Often the fundamental issue concerns a disagreement over what constitutes a "quality education" and what the priorities should be. The one thing upon which there is agreement is that the school programs need much improvement.

Business and Civic Involvement

From the beginning, business leaders were divided in regard to the role they should play in the process of school desegregation. Some feared physical damage to their businesses should they become involved. Others saw themselves as national and international corporations with little relationship to the local community. Still others accepted the responsibility to participate in the magnet school partnerships.

The Tri-lateral Task Force is a partnership of the Metropolitan Boston Office of the National Alliance of Businessmen, the Greater Boston Chamber of Commerce, and the Boston School Department. Its efforts to assist in attaining quality education are embodied in five programs.

First, there is the Human Relations Program, which is directed toward achieving a peaceful implementation of the desegregation plan. The mayor was given $50,000 for a public relations campaign. Some businesses have released employees to serve as monitors in the schools. Another emphasis in this program has been a link with the school committee, the mayor's office, the Task Force on Public Safety, the media, and others to assure the availability of accurate data and information for public dissemination.

Second, the Skills Assessment Program, directed by an economist from the First National Bank, attempts to identify those occupations that will exhibit growth over the next several years. The data will be used for updating curriculum and for off-campus learning experiences. The program also works with the Personnel Managers Club of the Chamber of Commerce to explore the skills needed in the private sector and to determine how business can contribute or assist the school committee in meeting these needs through training programs, in-house teaching, and career guidance institutes.

The third one is the Partnership Program, which establishes a partnership between a business firm and a specific high school. The businesses provide staff time, money, and equipment to be used directly for students. Each partnership has a coordinator from the firm and a coordinator from the school and together they define its specific relationship. Most of the planning for these partnerships occurred during the summer of 1974. Some of the organizations participating in this program are the Prudential Insurance Company, Boston Five Cents Savings Bank, the Federal Reserve Bank, Boston Edison, Kennecott Copper, Honeywell, the Liberty Mutual Insurance Company, the National Shawmut Bank, New England Telephone, Massport Authority, the John Hancock Mutual Life Insurance Company, IBM, the First National Bank of Boston, Boston Gas, Travelers Insurance Company, the State Street Bank, the New England Merchants National Bank, the New England Mutual Life Insurance Company, the Gillette Safety Razor Company, and Blue Cross/Blue Shield.

The fourth program, the Administrative and Support Services Program, intends to provide a resource pool of business executives that could be made available to the school committee to respond to management needs. The school committee appears to have moved very slowly on this project.

The fifth program is concerned with funding, and a committee develops and writes proposals for funding programs for submission to public agencies and private foundations. For example, a proposal to the United Way resulted in an allocation of $95,000 to some of its agencies for their participation in the desegregation plan.

One problem encountered by the charitable foundations in Boston has been that many small groups want money to do what is already being done by another group. The Associated Foundations of Greater Boston, representing most of the foundations, has appointed one of its staff members to coordinate all requests dealing with the desegregation effort. This staff member also strongly encourages groups to work with the Tri-lateral Task Force, the Higher Education Partners, and the city-wide Coordinating Council, which works with groups of parents. The task force meets once a month to share experiences and problems; the steering committee and the project director meet more frequently.

Developments during 1975–1976

As fall approached, many in Boston were greatly concerned with the potential for trouble in South Boston, East Boston, Charlestown, and Hyde Park. These communities have strong, traditional ethnic identities. The Community Relations Service recommended that the school year begin with a heavy show of police that could be decreased at any time.

School opened in September 1975 with mothers demonstrating in Charlestown, sporadic incidents in South Boston, and 1,600 policemen, 6 federal prosecutors, 200 Metro police, 100 federal marshals, 50 FBI agents, 550 state police, and 600 national guardsmen ready. The police commissioner requested and received a court order giving him the sole authority for assigning safety personnel. Many reporters, photographers, and television technicians also took to the streets.

Because of the minimum compliance of the school authorities it was necessary for Judge Garrity to monitor the schools on a daily basis and to issue supporting court orders on a weekly basis. The Office of Implementation of the Boston schools operated eighteen hours a day, six or seven days a week, to arrange for legitimate transfers, transportation, security, renovation of facilities, collection of daily attendance reports, training of seventy-five new administrators and retraining of one hundred other administrators, movement of teaching materials, answering of requests and complaints, training of 900 transitional aides, and so forth—all with twenty professionals and some clerical help, and little assistance from the regular school administration.

In December 1975, following a request from the NAACP, Judge Garrity stripped the Boston School Committee of much of its control over school integration and placed South Boston High School in receivership. He noted that integration was not working at South Boston High and accused the school committee of thwarting his court order. He agreed with the NAACP that black students and faculty had been subjected to discrimination and abuse, including assaults and racial epithets. He ordered that the entire administrative staff and the football coach of South Boston High be transferred to other schools and named one of the district superintendents to be the receiver in charge of the school. The judge further ordered a review and evaluation of the qualifications and performance of all faculty, guidance, and other educational personnel, to be followed by their transfer if that was deemed necessary. He also directed that a plan and schedule be prepared for substantial renovation of the physical premises and that an effort be made to enroll students assigned to the high school but not attending it. He declared that, if necessary, separate catch-up classes and summer school classes should be conducted for these students. He also broadened the power of the superintendent to oversee integration without interference from the school committee, and he barred the committee from making personnel appointments until newly elected members took office in January 1976. In February 1976 the court ordered that more black faculty and administrators be hired and that all contracts and work orders for repairs be monitored.

The business community moved ahead to implement programs within the partnerships agreed upon, including tutorial programs, guest lectures, curriculum review, work experiences, career exposure, and job projection. Twenty companies have paired with sixteen high schools. The State Street Bank, for example, is working with Harvard University in Roxbury High School to develop a career education program for seniors, and the John Hancock Insurance Company is developing a career education program in English High School and is also providing computer and printing services to the school. Some businesses, like the First National Bank, have made extensive commitments of staff, money, and moral leadership to their partner schools. As with the institutions of higher learning, there is a wide range of commitment in the business partnerships, extending from plant tours to complete programs. All participating companies have, however, made a five-year commitment to the partnerships.

Some of the problems being dealt with include teacher resistance to working with outside agencies, lack of attention to job placement opportunities, little dialogue with community groups, and an insufficient number of cooperating companies. The business community is also directing attention to the need for stronger political leadership at the local level. Some business leaders are continuing to use their influence to support the United Way, which has been under constant attack for supporting agencies that are active in the desegregation effort.

The partnerships with higher education, which are also of a five-year duration, began to implement the programs that were planned during the summer and coordinated by the Lincoln-Filene Center at Tufts University. Some of the initial activities included English workshops, remedial mathematics, a theater arts program, establishment of diagnostic centers for students with special learning needs, and staff development programs.

The many cultural institutions in Boston have formed the Metropolitan Cultural Alliance, which is directed toward involving its 110 members with the schools. In Phase Two twenty institutions are participating. The emphasis is on educational programs rather than just field trips. The Museum of Fine Arts, for instance, has established an American crafts program for sixth graders; it includes portrait painting, quilt making, silver making, and programs for seventh and eighth graders to create wall murals, rugs, and ceramic reliefs. The Pocket Mime Theatre is teaching ninth graders basic mime techniques, observation skills, and techniques for dealing with stereotypes. The Children's Museum is working with fifth graders; it is using museum resources to center on four themes—living things, Japanese children today, bookmaking, and "a hundred years or so ago." In addition, it has a program on tribal rhythm methods. The New England Aquarium is involving eighth graders in the study of chemical properties, animal life, and the ecology of three local bodies of water. The Museum of Transportation takes sixth graders to different parts of the city to teach them to use maps, charts, and time-space calculations.

The Freedom House Coalition has expanded its efforts to include protection of legal rights of students and parents; a crisis intervention center for mental health; Saturday morning conferences on issues relating to education and desegregation for all interested citizens; information workshops for parents on educational issues; an educational counseling service for middle school and high school students; a radio show; and additional informational publications.

The Rumor Control and Information Center has continued into Phase Two. Most of the questions addressed to it have dealt with a teachers' strike, parents' meetings, special education, school assignment, legal matters, transfers, transportation, and volunteer service.

During Phase Two many parents recognized the benefits provided them by the decentralization into community school districts and expressed their concerns and interests through their district councils. (School administrators not accustomed to decentralization continued to check, often unnecessarily, with the central administration on matters of policy.) The range of immediate concerns included such matters as size of classes, maintenance and reliability of buses, emergency buses for sick children, crossing guards, rain shelters at bus stops, bus drivers, difficulties experienced by parents attempting to attend meetings at distant schools, schools' discipline code, hot lunches, disruptive students, and the need for late buses for students involved in extracurricular activities. Many parents were equally concerned in matters relating to curriculum and instruction, such as remedial reading programs, bilingual education, music instruction for elementary school students, use of teachers' aides and substitute teachers, art instruction, library resources and services, physical education for elementary school students, procedures for hiring and assigning administrators, unwillingness of schools to provide data to district councils, and the need for written communications to parents in many languages.

Every afternoon the Office of Implementation reported the data and events of that day to the news media. Though the local media continued to stress balanced coverage of events, the national media focused on the occasional disorders that occurred.

The implementation of Phase Two during the school year 1975–76 constituted a mixture of both positive and negative factors. The involvement and commitment of higher education, business, and the community resulted in increased opportunity for participation by most parents and students—a distinctly positive factor. On the negative side, however, were assaults, violence, and periodic school boycotts. Many of those arrested for these acts were dismissed outright. Some community organizations charged that the mayor spent more time criticizing than implementing orders from the court.

According to the vice-mayor, school enrollment had declined at the rate of 3,000 students per year prior to busing and had declined by 17,000 students during the two years of desegregation. Others claim that 17,000 is a greatly exaggerated figure and does not take into account chronic absences and nonexisting students. In November 1975, for example, 3,500 truants did not return to school. No figures exist on the actual number of students who transferred to Catholic schools or to private academies or who dropped out.

Similar debates over financial expenditures were also prevalent. The mayor's office claimed that $28 million was used for police overtime, extra teachers, and buses. Others calculated the expenditures at $12 million, with 50 to 90 percent of this figure attributable to police overtime. Some assert that police overtime was the result of unlawful resistance to the court order, that the busing expense (7 percent of the operating budget) was constitutionally necessary, and that expenses for programs and facilities simply brought the schools up to the state's minimum standards for all schools. Still others noted that Boston has three to four times as many administrators as comparable school districts.

In April 1976 the city of Boston filed suit in the U.S. Supreme Court requesting an order to require lower courts to consider the costs of desegregation and to take community reaction into consideration before handing down busing orders. Judge Garrity ordered the mayor in May 1976 to raise $17 million to keep the schools from closing six weeks early. (The Boston schools are fiscally dependent upon the city.) An attorney for the Massachusetts Board of Education noted that the city had paid school districts regularly when the schools were segregated, but now refused to cover the deficit when the schools were desegregated.

During Phase Two 20,000 out of 76,000 students were bused, but one out of six schools was still racially identifiable. Minority members among the school staffs became more prevalent, increasing from 5 percent to 11 percent. Along with the appointment of a new superintendent, a substantial turnover in central office administrators has occurred. There are, however, very few black principals. Only four of the 162 desegregated schools experienced any violence.

The Phase Two plan is a comprehensive plan based on some of the best available knowledge on desegregated education and the organization of education. It stresses programmatic options for students and parents and affords greater opportunities for the community's participation in educational planning and governance. The plan is dedicated to fulfilling the spirit and intent of the law. It was restricted by limited time for planning and retraining, by continued resistance from some school officials, and, of course, by the diversity of attitudes and beliefs that are still present. The decision by the court of appeals in 1974 that reaffirmed Judge Garrity's district court decision described the situation accurately: "Deep emotions have been stirred. They will not be calmed by letting violence loose, . . . submitting to it under whatever guise employed. Only the constructive use of time will achieve what an advanced civilization demands and the Constitution confirms."

11. Educational Implications of Desegregation in Boston

Robert A. Dentler

Most of the writing on public school desegregation since *Brown* v. *Board of Education of Topeka* in 1954 has concentrated on two subissues.[1] One body of literature asks whether desegregation affects the academic achievement of students. A smaller but currently more fashionable literature asks whether court-ordered desegregation produces undesirable effects upon residential mobility — the white flight issue.

One answer to both questions is often overlooked by those who ask and answer educational policy questions through scholarly books and journals. The educational and demographic outcomes of court-ordered desegregation rely heavily upon the degree of planning evidenced in the remedial order and upon how well it is implemented. One reason why this answer is generally overlooked may be that those who study school desegregation are rarely those who plan or implement it. In other words, for more than two decades educational researchers and policy scientists alike have tended to remain aloof from the critical intervening variables of planning and implementation, concentrating, instead, upon pre- and postobservations that neglect the process itself.

School desegregation plans ordered by the courts often determine the character of the demographic mixture and the learning environment in desegregated settings. The plans have often been poor in quality for at least three reasons. The first is that many judges have relied upon reluctant and incompetent boards of education to develop the plan, in keeping with civil procedures that require local initiatives. This means that the same policy makers who have caused or maintained segregation and who have repeatedly asserted their opposition to affirmative action are called upon to plan solutions to the very problems their policies created, and to do so upon very short notice.

Even where judges have devised plans themselves or have sought to modify plans submitted by reluctant defendants, they have been handicapped by judicial ignorance of public school policies and practices and about urban demographic processes—a second reason why the plans have been poor. This ignorance has, in turn, been reinforced by the absence of expertise among participating attorneys who base their recommendations and arguments upon prior experience with other kinds of equity cases.

A third reason is that efforts of federal and state agencies to train the planners have been deflected by political opposition, especially since 1969. Where centers and institutes were formed, most were discontinued or starved into inaction soon thereafter. Because the few that have survived have had to proceed with extreme caution, their impact upon the training of planners has been negligible. Civil rights organizations such as the National Association for the Advancement of Colored People have generated a group of effective lawyers, but they have not invested in the preparation of more than a handful of educational planners.

NATURAL HISTORY OF COURT INTERVENTION

Federal case law on school desegregation has broken into three stages of development of quality with respect to planning and implementation since 1954. The premise of this chapter is that these stages have directly affected the conditions under which students learn and under which households move or stay in place.

In the first stage, between 1955 and 1965, court orders were relatively gradualistic and amateur in nature. Partial or incremental desegregation was allowed under the principle of "all deliberate speed," and courts modified their remedies on a trial-and-error basis over a period of several years. During this decade, moreover, efforts in educational research and development did little to prepare educators and social scientists for service in planning for desegregation. Rather, they were busy designing studies of the effects of desegregation upon learning. This period culminated in the production of the Coleman Report, commissioned by the U.S. Office of Education, and the Weinberg Report, commissioned by Phi Delta Kappa.[2] The Coleman study failed to distinguish schools naturally unsegregated from those desegregated by plan. All were simply lumped together as integrated. There was almost no attention to either planning or implementing desegregation. With few exceptions the studies summarized and appraised by Weinberg also neglected the likelihood that desegregation might profit from well-conceived plans and their effective implementation.

The second stage extends roughly from the years 1966 through 1972. It was powerfully affected by the increased precision of decisions by the U.S. Supreme Court.[3] During this period planning became more sophisticated; courts began to retain independent experts to review or to make planning proposals; and the quality, scope, and speed of remedial orders improved. This stage reflected a growing awareness that the act of mixing students and staffs in ways that eliminated or mitigated racial and ethnic isolation does little or nothing, in itself, to improve learning conditions.

This chapter concerns itself with a third stage, which was foreshadowed in federal court orders for Denver and Minneapolis and reached its fullest maturity in *Morgan* v. *Kerrigan*, the Boston school remedial order.[4] In the Boston order, the memorandum of decision and the plan itself signal an evolution of quality that will most likely characterize the offspring of *Brown* v. *Board of Education of Topeka* in a positive way in dozens of northern cities through the next decade.

DESEGREGATION IN BOSTON

Phase One

On June 21, 1974, U.S. District Court Judge W. Arthur Garrity, Jr., issued an opinion holding that Boston's public schools had been unconstitutionally segregated by the purposeful actions of the school committee and the superintendents.[5] The only remedial plan available to the court at that time was a temporary plan devised by the state Board of Education and designed to achieve compliance with state law. The Boston School Committee and superintendents had failed to develop a substitute for the state plan.

Judge Garrity ordered the state plan into effect, beginning in September 1974, for want of alternatives and under the obligation imposed by the second *Brown* decision [6] to achieve immediate relief for the plaintiffs. Aware of the fact that the state plan permitted the continuation of virtually all-black schools in some neighborhoods and all-white schools in many more, the judge also defined this remedy as Phase One, or temporary. He called for immediate planning toward Phase Two, to take effect in September 1975, as a permanent remedy that would prove wholly acceptable under the Constitution.

The Phase One plan affected educational practice in a few minor ways by, for example, closing some dilapidated facilities. Overall, however, it was a partial design for achieving racial balance and nothing more.[7] State law, incidentally, defined a racially imbalanced public school as one in which the student body was more than 50 percent nonwhite. Thus, an all-white student body could be considered racially balanced! The same law set severe limitations on the extent to which a remedy could affect boundaries and busing as well.

Planning for Phase Two

On October 31, 1974, the court entered an order establishing the filing date and general criteria for a student desegregation plan to be created by the defendants. Judge Garrity decided that the use of a panel was advisable because of the complexity and multiplicity of the plans that were subsequently filed. Two members of the panel, retired Supreme Judicial Court Justice Jacob J. Spiegal and former state Attorney General Edward J. McCormack, Jr., were seasoned attorneys. Two others, Francis Keppel, former U.S. Commissioner of Education, and Charles V. Willie, professor of education and sociology at Harvard University, were experienced urban educators. In addition, the court appointed two planning experts, Robert A. Dentler and Marvin B. Scott, dean and associate dean, respectively, of the School of Education at Boston University, to assist the other members of the panel and the court. The composition of the panel, in addition to the appointment of planning experts, manifests the shift from the second to the third historical stage of court orders on desegregation, for four of the six appointees were educators. Judge Garrity sought to ensure that his intent "to express a deep educational concern" would be embodied in the work of the panel in taking evidence and in reviewing or making new plans.

All members of the panel worked to achieve the court's expressed goal. They sought to develop detailed, carefully planned situations that would allow public instruction to benefit and benefit equally all students. No federal court order issued in the twenty years between *Brown* and *Morgan* have ever wittingly ignored these concerns, but few had ever been so explicitly aimed at effective improvements in public education.

Phase Two A

The most important of the instructional and organizational changes mandated in the plan for Phase Two are described in the paragraphs that follow.

Community School Districts

In his liability opinion Judge Garrity had found that:

> The city has a complex maze of single school and multischool districts which vary widely in size. The elementary schools generally cannot be fairly characterized as neighborhood schools. District lines require some students to travel many blocks to school when there is another school much closer but on the other side of that district line.[8]

In this respect and in others the school system operated from a patchwork of confused districts that benefited some students and baffled or hindered others. The remedial order began, therefore, by redistricting the entire system into eight clearly identifiable, durable, partially autonomous, and ethnically well-mixed community school districts. Within the boundaries of each district students are guaranteed a place within a nearby facility at the elementary- and middle-school levels. They can then apply for a place in the community high school or for a seat in a city-wide magnet school. Because of insufficient space, however, preferences for high schools could not be guaranteed until new facilities were added.

The City-wide School District

Of the 168 public school facilities functioning in 1976-77 under court order, 25 were to serve as magnet schools unified within a single city-wide subdistrict (Community District Nine). In addition to contributing to the purposes intended for community districts, the city-wide district was designed to "facilitate the establishment of a substantial sector of the school system within which complete desegregation with relatively slight deviations from systemwide racial ratios is accomplished on the basis of the magnetic attraction of the programs of instruction."[9]

In the city-wide magnet schools the ethnic composition was designed to fall within a plus or minus 5 percent of the ethnic composition of the student enrollment for the system as a whole. Students enroll in city-wide district schools because they volunteer to participate in ethnically desegregated programs of instruction. Every parent of every student eighteen years of age or older may ask that the student be admitted to a city-wide magnet school through an application procedure designed by the court to approximate a college admission procedure. In 1975 orientation and application booklets printed in seven languages were mailed to 74,000 households. The booklets described the community districts and the city-wide magnet schools, and they provided an opportunity to select three ranked preferences per student. No family had to apply. Within one week of mailing, however, about 62,000 completed applications were returned. Never before had the Boston public schools described their services as fully and universally. The public response was overwhelmingly positive.

In 1975 the Boston School Committee adopted a hands-off attitude toward the orientation and application booklet. The response was so positive, however, that in 1976 the committee made sure its members' names appeared on the title pages of every edition of the booklet, and they added photographs as a point of pride. In the second year more than 65,000 applications were returned within eight days of distribution.

In both years nearly all of the magnet schools were oversubscribed. Where an excess of students from one ethnic group predominated in application preferences for a few schools, a computer program randomized the preferences in lottery fashion and also set a ceiling on enrollments so that each schools' student population was in keeping with the city-wide ethnic ratio. Only four of the magnet schools have been underenrolled as a result of that rule.

Citizen Participation

During the second stage of court experience with school desegregation in the nation, the federal courts, together with the Community Relations Service of the U.S. Department of Justice, began to realize that citizen participation was an essential precondition for achieving equal education. As with desegregation planning and practice itself, this lesson did not come from the findings of educational researchers

and developers, few of whom gave serious attention to citizen participation during the years from 1955 to 1965. Rather, it emerged
through trial and error in the process of court intervention.

Because all parties in the Boston case agreed with the proposition
that citizen participation was essential, Judge Garrity established an
elective racial-ethnic parent council in each school in October 1974 as
part of Phase One desegregation. These councils were continued as
part of Phase Two, when the concept of citizen monitoring, advisement, and involvement in the remedial process was elaborated by the
court. The court plan included a district advisory council for each of
the nine community districts. In addition to continuing a city-wide
parents' advisory council to support the local councils, the court also
established a city-wide coordinating council of forty-two members appointed by the court to be the "primary body to monitor implementation on behalf of the court."[10]

These units are more than parent-teacher associations. They have
prescribed powers to require accountability, to review, and to advise,
in addition to aiding the court by monitoring adherence to the court's
many directives. For the Boston public schools, these councils have resulted in a drastic redistribution of influence, away from the powerfully centralized and overwhelmingly dominant school committee and its
headquarters staff and toward a partially decentralized, district-
based system of school operations.

By the close of the 1975–76 school year, the first year under Phase
Two, the parent councils in more than half of the facilities and most of
the district advisory councils had taken substantial root in the city and
were affecting programs, policies, practices, and the allocation of resources in significant ways. Initial resistance to the elections establishing them and to the holding of early meetings was intense in a few districts, but by March of 1976 there was little doubt that a durable
structure for decentralized citizen participation was coming into being. In the high schools, moreover, student councils, which also contributed in a similar fashion, began to interact meaningfully with both
faculty and parent councils.

The city-wide coordinating council did not fare as well. It proved to
be quarrelsome, factious, and cumbersome, in nearly all respects. Its
staff workers were stalemated by contradictory directives from council
members. Only two or three committees made noticeable progress in
either monitoring implementation or in recommending ways to im-

prove educational opportunities. Judge Garrity had hedged his bets in
forming the city-wide council, however, by fixing an end date of August 1, 1976. At that time he set about reorganizing the council, limiting its membership much more tightly for the 1976–77 school year.

The model of a large city-wide council composed of well-known and influential citizens seemed to be predicated upon a theory of political consensus. Where a city's voters, through their elected officials, seem bent upon protracted conflict over desegregation, the model falters, however, for such councils tend to do little more than crystallize and then reflect the conflict. Perhaps a small council comprised of citizens knowledgeable about public education and committed to making school desegregation work would prove to be a better model for implementing court policies.

Chain of Command

Before September 1975, about 40 percent of the elementary schools in Boston were without principals. The chain of command above the level of area superintendent, a position that was not introduced until 1973, was rusty, knotted, and broken in many ways. Three studies recommending basic reorganization of the leadership structure had been commissioned, but none of the recommendations had ever been adopted.

The court ordered the development of a rational chain of command from a fully authorized principal in every building, to nine district superintendents, to a deputy superintendent for operations at headquarters. It created an office of implementation managed by an associate superintendent to oversee fulfillment of the order, and it required the appointment of a school security director. In addition, the court specified how administrators at all levels would account to citizens' councils and to the court.

The court assigned experts to maintain liaison with the office of implementation and other local and state agencies during Phase Two. As flaws and gaps in the decrepit chain of command were revealed, the city-wide council and the experts recommended further court actions to improve administration. Early in 1976 the court issued an order governing the appointment of school administrators, again with a view toward desegregating the staff. In this instance, the court required that candidates for the ninety-two open positions of principal, headmaster, assistant principal, and assistant headmaster, be screened by the district advisory council.

Upgrading Facilities

In *Morgan* v. *Kerrigan*, the court found that many Boston public school facilities were severely overcrowded; others were underutilized; yet others were extremely dilapidated but still in use. In Phase One, about ten school buildings were closed, but, according to evidence provided by the city's public facilities commission to members of the panel selected by Judge Garrity, more than forty-five other schools had been designated by one agency or another (including the school committee itself) as being unfit for school use for as many as thirty-three years. Of the 197 buildings that comprised the public school system in 1970, 60 percent had been erected before 1900, and no real program of replacement had been attempted since the 1920s. As of 1973 there had been no new high schools erected since 1934.

The court ordered twenty-two unsafe and unfit facilities closed during Phase Two, bringing the total number of schools closed by court action to thirty-two. The list changed a bit as student assignments and parent applications were completed, but the court was the first agency since 1942 to intervene in terminating the use of unfit and unsound buildings. In addition, the court required the repair and renovation of existing facilities. When the upgrading process was found to be unacceptably slow, the court began to review requisitions for repairs and all contracts and work orders. Upon occasion the court set aside normal bidding procedures in order to have the system ready for school opening.

The court also established a capacity limit on the maximum number of students that could be enrolled in each facility. This limit was designed by experts. It was based on data provided by state, city, and school departments, and it was intended to prevent overcrowding, just as school closings helped to eliminate underutilization. The capacity limit fixes a ceiling but not a floor on enrollments, so that, over time, administrators and teachers may modify class sizes and program uses of buildings. Finally, the court conducted a comprehensive review of plans for major new construction and renovation projects. It intervened to modify the intended uses of some new facilities and ordered the renovation of others.

Curriculum and Grade Structure

Instead of being free, inclusive, and universal as Horace Mann had intended, the curriculum in the public schools of Boston had by 1965 become exclusive and set. Uniformity is not, however, to be confused with universality. In Phase Two, therefore, the court directed:

Within the limits established by state standards, the policies of the School Department, and contractual obligations entered into with a paired college or university, each community school district shall develop its curriculum and programs of instruction and extracurricular activities in response to the needs and interests of the parents and students resident within the District, so that programs are nondiscriminatory and inclusive of all ethnic groups.[11]

In addition to enabling curriculum variations, the court ordered the creation of a fairly uniform grade structure. These two actions appear to contradict each other, but there were at least ten types of grade structures to be found in Boston schools that persisted through Phase One. They included single-grade schools, two-grade schools, and other variations arranged so that a student might have to attend as many as five different schools in order to move from kindergarten through twelfth grade. With but five exceptions, the court required all elementary schools to include grades one through five, middle schools to include grades six through eight, and high schools to include grades nine through twelve. Rational coherence and equitable consistency upon which parents could depend were substituted for an incomprehensible maze of grade structures that helped some and hampered others.

Bilingual Education

Under state law, Boston schools began to offer bilingual instruction to students whose first language was Spanish, Haitian French, Italian, Portuguese, Greek, or Chinese. Convinced that this type of instruction was of special value in remedying inequities in services to nearly 10,000 students, the court identified the schools throughout the districts where bilingual classes would be held, and it expanded the availability of such programs. The court also authorized the hiring of more bilingual teachers, and it allowed bilingual students to cross district boundaries for programmatic purposes.

The implementation of this improvement has been far from successful. Schools designated to offer bilingual instruction had to be changed as student assignment problems emerged. Fewer students entered bilingual classes than had been expected. Early in 1976 the city-wide coordinating council held hearings and aired the many grievances associated with this program, and by the summer of 1976 some of the problems were being resolved.

Some bilingual programs have stimulated the development of multicultural studies among both white and black students, and, as a result of parent interest, the bilingual program expanded further during the 1976–77 school year. It is possible that Boston could eventually have the most diversified bilingual educational programs in northeastern United States.

Students with Special Needs

The court also reinforced the school department's unfulfilled obligation to comply with state law requiring special educational services on an integrated and mainstreaming basis for all students with special needs who are not severely handicapped and disabled. More than 10,000 public school children had been classified as needing special services by March 1975 in a system that was providing for less than half that number. The court plan requires that:

Every school facility shall receive and educate mild and moderate special needs students. . . . No less than one resource room and one special needs services space shall be set aside in each school. Each school shall have special educators and materials. . . . At least three . . . special schools in each community district shall be identified (for severely handicapped students).[12]

Again, facilities were upgraded through repairs, and the court authorized the hiring of additional special educators. The reform in special education is, however, far from complete. As with bilingual education, the system was lagging in fulfillment as late as April 1976. Yet, in six months, the court accomplished more than the system had done of its own volition at any time.

Occupational Education

The courts also required that existing occupational and vocational training programs had to be properly, as well as equally, equipped and staffed. Boston Trade High School, at court insistence, was not only repaired from basement to roof and upgraded significantly, but it was also paired with a major university. By court order it was converted into a comprehensive school with an academic as well as a trade faculty.

What is even more important, the court directed the city, the state, and the school committee to coplan a modern, long-term occupational education program to be instituted between 1976 and 1980. The plan was submitted to the court and approved in August 1975. The plan will bring career exploration courses into all middle schools and will make job skill training available to all high school students, replacing and updating a gravely outmoded network of old programs. (Under court order, every high school now provides a comprehensive education.)

As with reforms in bilingual and special education, those in occupational education lagged sadly behind the court-approved schedule throughout the first year of Phase Two. The politics of funding and staffing, at both state and local levels, plagued program developers throughout the year. While some progress was made, it is not yet clear whether improvements will take effect in the decade ahead.

Phase Two B

Judge Garrity kept his experts and other planners in the city and state occupied throughout the first school year with the planning of modifications and additions to the Phase Two remedy in the light of experience gained in the course of 1975-76. On May 3, 1976, he issued a memorandum of decisions and modifications of the remedial orders, summarizing the recommendations of experts and planners and synthesizing his own appraisal of the tasks ahead.

Phase Two B, as this order came to be called, initiated no new features of educational policy. Its importance with respect to improving public education came instead from its deliberately explicit effort to ensure stability and continuity for the massively reorganized system. Magnet programs were kept in place, for example, and provision was made for continuing students in the schools to which they had been assigned the previous year, if their parents so desired, and for offering new opportunities to express preferences. The remainder of the order was given over to modifying facilities in order to close a few more ancient or dilapidated buildings, to upgrading other facilities, and to requiring the construction of new plants, including a large Occupational Resource Center.

Under the Phase Two order, there was much student movement as a result of liberal features in the policy that aided student transfers. The transfer policy was tightened considerably under Phase Two B. Ironically, however, the procedures that the school department developed and applied in implementing Phase Two B relocated one in every seven students in the system, many of them in ways that violated the intent of the court's Phase Two B order. Thus, careful planning for stabilized conditions was undone in the course of implementation, whereas poor initial planning undermined prospects for successful implementation. Both planning and implementation need constant attention if desegregation is to be successful.

What can be said in summary about educational improvement in Boston in the period following Judge Garrity's opinion of June 21, 1974? What should be extrapolated from that summary and applied for the remainder of the decade?

Only a few things can be stated with reasonable conviction. Educationally essential connections between professional staff, parents, and students have been created anew by the advent of the court-ordered desegregation plan and its implementation. These connections, while they are incomplete in the extreme, will expand and improve steadily over the next three years. The degree of parent participation and advisement has increased tremendously. The paths taken are authentically multiethnic for the first time in the history of Boston.

The court plan has both structured and decentralized the educational system. Community school district offices with district superintendents, councils of principals, and community advisory bodies have relocated the power structure in many respects away from headquarters and have returned control to the points of contact with clients. There is reason to believe that this shift in power will be countered desperately by the central school committee for another year or two as its historic mechanisms of control through job and program placement and through patronage wither away. But the shift probably will prove permanent. Already some school committee members are choosing to run for election to different city and county offices. Structural coherence and decentralization combined will not automatically provide improved educational results, but they establish a part of the necessary conditions for doing so.

Special programs for bilingual students, for students with special needs, and for instruction in occupational skills have been powerfully reinforced by the court plan. New teachers, greatly improved facilities, and some new materials and equipment have moved these programs toward equalization and upgrading of opportunities. The distance yet to go, however, remains great.

There is reason to expect that, by the end of the present decade, the Boston public schools will begin to become magnetic as they have not been since at least 1920. The ingredients required for a massive transformation in the provision of diversified, high-quality educational services have been carefully and thoughtfully introduced, and they are being adjusted constantly to fit changing needs. If the transformation continues, it will lay a basis for two events of great moment.

First, physical, commercial, and related urban reconstruction efforts that have been taking place in Boston since 1960 will be strongly reinforced, and the city will stand a chance, for the first time in sixty years, of reattracting households, businesses, industries, and service institutions. The city may go into fiscal default before that moment arrives, but that is true of at least half of the nation's cities with more than a half-million residents in their metropolitan areas. If Boston should go into default, it will certainly not be the result of the court-ordered desegregation plan. The city will, however, have been helped toward that precipice by the doubling of administrative and teacher salaries and benefits that were required during the last decade.

Second, the foundations for a metropolitan educational system, including many suburban districts, will have been established. This will be an evolutionary development, coming out of METCO, the voluntary busing program financed by the state, and the Metropolitan Planning Project financed for three years by the federal government. But the evolution will be speeded up tremendously by the impact of the court plan, which does not order but which enables interdistrict collaboration.

Careful planning can foster improvements in urban public education. We should look forward to the years ahead during which federal courts could provide the authority and the means to develop plans, after decades during which we have discovered that carefully planned change does not spring from boards of education and city halls. Future students of school desegregation should concentrate on the of planning and implementation as critical determinants of educational outcomes in the process of desegregating schools.

Notes

1. *Brown* v. *Board of Education of Topeka*, 347 U.S. 483 (1954).

2. James S. Coleman *et al.*, *Equality of Educational Opportunity* (Washington, D.C.: U.S. Government Printing Office, 1966); Meyer Weinberg, *Desegregation Research: An Appraisal* (Bloomington, Ind.: Phi Delta Kappa, 1970).

3. *Davis* v. *Board of School Commissioners of Mobile County*, 402 U.S. 33 (1971); *Swann* v. *Charlotte-Mecklenburg Board of Education*, 402 U.S. 1 (1971).

4. *Morgan* v. *Kerrigan*, Civil Action No. 72-911-G, Dist. of Mass., Memorandum of Decision and Remedial Orders, June 5, 1975. This chapter is a revised and updated version of "Improving Public Education: The Boston School Desegregation Case," *The Advocate* 7 (Fall 1975): 3–8.

5. *Morgan* v. *Kerrigan*, Civil Action No. 72-911-G, U.S. D.C., Dist. of Mass., June 21, 1974.

6. *Brown* v. *Board of Education of Topeka*, 349 U.S. 294 (1955).

7. Commonwealth of Massachusetts, Board of Education, "Short-Term Plan to Reduce Racial Imbalance in the Boston Public Schools," February 1, 1974.

8. *Morgan* v. *Kerrigan*.

9. *Morgan* v. *Kerrigan*, Part II, 43.

10. *Ibid.*, Part III, 87.

11. *Ibid.*, Part II, 3.

12. *Ibid.*, 5.

12. Pairings in Boston: Boston University and the District One Program

Marvin B. Scott

In 1849, the black community of Boston petitioned the Boston School Committee, stating that:

A number among us have more than once made application to members of your honorable board for the admission of our children to the district schools but are refused on the ground that there is an "exclusive school" for colored children. . . . This holds up a barrier against a portion of the people "solely on account of color," and encourages the worst of influences in the community. In no other place in the Commonwealth do we find "exclusive schools" in existence.[1]

More than 125 years later, many black residents were still objecting because their children were forced to attend segregated schools. They gained support for their views in 1965 when the Kiernan Committee, appointed by the Massachusetts State Board of Education to study the Boston public schools, reported that some Boston schools were predominantly black, that imbalance is harmful to black children educationally and serves to perpetuate low self-esteem and white racial bias, and that this imbalance harms white children as well by isolating them from healthy interracial contact.[2] The Boston School Committee voted, 3 to 2, to reject the report, primarily because there was a proposal in the report that 5,000 students, black and white, be transported to reduce racial imbalance.

In March 1972 attorneys for Mrs. Tallulah Morgan, her children, and a number of other black parents and children, filed a complaint with the U.S. District Court in Massachusetts. It was alleged that the Morgan children, as well as all black children enrolled in the Boston public schools, had been denied equal protection of the laws by the Boston School Committee. The committee, according to the complaint, had intentionally brought about and maintained racial segregation in the public schools of Boston.

The reply, filed by the committee, denied many of the statements contained in Mrs. Morgan's complaint. The case went to trial before Judge W. Arthur Garrity, Jr., who was randomly chosen to preside. During the trial the law imposed on the plaintiff the burden of proving the allegation against the committee. The hearing lasted fifteen days. Many witnesses testified, and several hundred exhibits were presented. On June 21, 1974, the judge filed a lengthy opinion containing his findings of fact and conclusions of law based on the testimony he had heard and the exhibits he had reviewed.[3] Simply stated, the judge said one thing: Mrs. Morgan and the other plaintiffs were right. The Boston School Committee had intentionally brought about and maintained racial segregation in Boston's public schools.

Chapters 10 and 11 have described the events that followed June 21, 1974, and the authors have summarized the major features of the court-ordered plan for desegregation of the Boston schools and for improving the quality of education in those schools. One of the distinguishing features of the plan called for colleges, universities, businesses, and other agencies to assist the schools. Under Judge Garrity's order there was to be pairing of elementary and secondary schools, on the one hand, and colleges and universities, on the other hand, and this was to be a particularly important part of the desegregation process in Boston. Colleges and universities were to help the Boston schools equalize educational opportunities and improve the learning of students. The concerns shared by the partners included staff development and training, the design of instruction, materials and methods, planning or other organizational processes important in the school or the district, and community relations.

An article in the *Boston Globe* summarized much of what happened during the 1975–76 school year when the collaborative efforts were being established:

For decades reformers had been saying that Boston's unequalled concentration of higher education and cultural resources and business talent should be used to improve the schools. Some joint ventures were underway. Colleges had been sending student teachers into Boston achools, and business firms, organized under the Tri-lateral Task Force, had been working in some schools for several years.

But it took the judge's order to organize, expand, and put the prestige of the court behind the unprecedented network of partnerships. . . . The judge named twenty-one colleges and universities in the order (two others were added later) and urged that the business partnerships (there are now nineteen) and the links between cultural organizations (there are now twelve) and the schools be continued and broadened.

[In the summer of 1975,] using $900,000 in funds allocated by the Massachusetts Board of Education, hundreds of college faculty members, cultural representatives, and Boston teachers spent weeks in meetings, workshops, and discussions. . . . [Only a few programs] were ready to go when school opened in September. . . . More were added over the fall and still others began early [in 1976]. The programs range from the simple and direct (college students tutoring, colleges lending film projectors or sending over a mathematics specialist to help with a new course) to the most elaborate (planning a new magnet technical school in East Boston).

So far, almost $2.8 million in state money has been allocated to finance the pairings — $1,047,480 to colleges, $130,000 to the cultural institutions, and $1,605,906 to the Boston schools. The business firms are providing their own financing.[4]

BOSTON UNIVERSITY PAIRINGS WITH THE PUBLIC SCHOOLS

One major goal underlying the pairing of an institution of higher education with a Boston public school is to formulate and implement innovative magnet-type educational programs. Boston University is working with the Brighton-Mission Hill Community School District (District One) and is also helping with bilingual Hispanic programs located throughout the city. The remainder of this chapter is devoted to a description of the range of activities undertaken under this pairing arrangement in order to illustrate how one institution of higher education can begin working very closely with local public schools. The purpose of these cooperative efforts is to develop educational programs that increase the quality of public education for all children, regardless of their race, ethnicity, or religious creed, residing in the boundaries of District One. In a sense District One has been ordered by the court to act like a community of schools. The task of the district and the university is to facilitate the development of cooperative community relations that will assist with the broad goal of improving the schools.

While many needs have been identified in District One, Table 12-1 shows the specific objectives that were selected at the outset as most

Table 12-1

Initial funding for projects undertaken in the Boston schools-Boston University pairing

	Source of funds	
Purpose	District One	Boston University
To improve reading and related communication skills	$ 29,471	$ 7,613
To upgrade services for children and youth with special needs	10,575	8,418
To improve mathematic and scientific literacy	4,900	8,757
To improve motor skills, physical development, and promote pleasure in movement	27,400	11,850
To strengthen guidance and counseling services for high school and middle schools; to expand awareness of alternative careers among high school students	34,485	10,733
To improve health care services	unfunded	unfunded
To improve the quality of bilingual teaching in Spanish and Chinese	—	3,200
To improve counseling and instructional support close to home and out of school (in the Mission Hill Housing Project)	(included in guidance)	
To provide workshops for strengthening skills in community participation	—	12,140
Administration and evaluation	13,500	30,064
Totals	$120,331	$ 92,765
Total District One and Boston University funds	$213,096	

Source: Boston University Pairing Program Office, *Pairing: An Information Booklet* (Boston: Boston University, 1976), 11.

pressing and most treatable. Initial funding was provided to pursue the goals shown in the table. The district contains fifteen public schools: Brighton High School, two middle schools, and thirteen elementary schools, with a capacity for a total enrollment of 6,890 students. The Boston School Department projected the ethnic composition of enrollment for 1975-76 in the district as follows: 44 percent white, 33 percent black, and 23 percent other minorities, including 640 Hispanic and 220 Chinese and other Oriental bilingual students.

A planning group decided to concentrate efforts during 1975–76 in five schools (Brighton High School, the Edison and Taft middle schools, and the Tobin and Garfield elementary schools), which together enroll about 3,680 students, more than half of the student population of District One. Plans called for adding other schools during 1977 as program components evolve to allow their extension. Several other schools are already involved through utilization of student teachers and unpaid student aides.

The administration of the program for Boston University is lodged in the office of the dean of the School of Education, while the administration of the program for District One is lodged in the office of the district superintendent. Cooperative programs are developed jointly by the office of the dean and an advisory council in District One. Communication with the five target schools is maintained by faculty members from the university who work directly with building administrators and their designated staff. Each component, developed around one of the objectives shown in Table 12-1, is being implemented by a university team led by a member of the faculty.

PROGRAM COMPONENTS IN THE
BOSTON UNIVERSITY-DISTRICT ONE PAIRING

The specific components of the collaborative program between Boston University and District One are briefly described below.

Reading and Communications

In order to develop a sound program of instruction in reading and related communication skills, accurate information must be obtained about each learner. A sound school reading program is one that coordinates teaching with knowledge about the abilities, ways of thinking, and needs of each student. The reading and communication component begins with an in-depth needs assessment of all children in the target schools in District One for which standardized and informal teacher tests are given. Test information is further developed into individualized reading profiles. Classroom teachers develop individualized reading programs, using technical assistance provided by the university: manpower to assist in the school reading laboratories, courses and special workshops for improving classroom reading instruction, in-service work for the development of experimental curricula, assistance in the evaluation of instructional materials and procedures. Activities in this component utilize the services of the Reading Clinic at Boston University. The clinic offers diagnostic and remedial services to all children in District One and specializes in the referral of special problems from the reading laboratories of the target schools. Diagnostic tests are administered by classroom teachers, with the assistance of graduate students and faculty from Boston University. Test scoring is handled by a computer under the supervision of the personnel from the Reading Clinic. Regular classroom teachers, reading laboratory staff, and Boston University faculty then coordinate the referral system.

The development of reading programs in the district varies considerably from school to school. Basic programs include diagnostic and prescriptive reading instruction in the classrooms, specialized instruction and services in the reading laboratories, and the use of clinical resources at the university for difficult cases. Student teachers and junior interns from the School of Education provide assistance to regular classroom teachers. The university also assists teachers in the middle and secondary school in developing reading programs appropriate for particular situations with the general intention of improving reading in content areas.

While learning to read well and to enjoy reading constitutes the prime objective of this component, there are also activities aimed at developing the related skills of speaking, listening, and writing, beginning with students at Brighton High School. Some of the resources and talent available at Boston University in theater arts, public communications through radio and television, creative writing, and other areas of visual and expressive communications are recruited in an attempt to share them with high school teachers and students. There are plans, for example, to collaborate in developing a student-operated radio broadcasting unit at Brighton High School.

Special Education

All parties agree that the services for children and youth in District One who have special needs require prompt and effective improvement. This challenge has been met in three ways. First, there is an attempt to provide short-term treatment for approximately thirty third-, fourth-, and fifth-grade children. Then the university sends people to assist the staffs of the Taft Middle School and the Garfield Elementary School in the diagnostic identification of children who may need special assistance. The third effort resulted in the setting up of workshops and credit courses at Boston University for the in-service training of teachers in the theories and methods of special education.

The students selected are those with serious learning deficits. They attend daily four-hour sessions, divided into shorter segments, in which specific learning problems are identified and then remedial treatment is given. Four Boston University graduate students, all experienced special educators, advise the school's faculty. In addition, four undergraduate special education majors assist. The main approach consists of the use of positive reinforcement schedules for rewarding effective mastery of instructional tasks and materials.

Specialists in diagnosis at Boston University again join with District One faculty to provide methods and a battery of tests for use in screening students currently not evaluated as needing special services. And the university's Department of Special Education offers workshops, in-service consultation, and credit courses for teachers, coplanned on a semester-by-semester basis.

Mathematics and Science

The objective of the mathematics and science component is to improve the mathematical and scientific literacy of students in the target schools of District One. Equipped with such literacy, the youth of Brighton, Allston, and Mission Hill are better able to take advantage of educational opportunities available to them at Brighton High School and, thereafter, to participate fully in the life of a region outstanding for its scientific knowledge and institutions.

The work of this component should range much more widely in future years, but, during 1976, university faculty and school staff collaborated in performing four activities that have been identified as needing further work. First, students in the four target elementary and middle schools were tested and evaluated to determine their individual skills and deficiencies in the area of mathematics. The testing was completed during November 1976.

Second, mathematics instruction laboratories are being designed and installed in the four target schools. University faculty and students are participating in the design and operation of these laboratories, where the results of diagnostic testing will be used in workshops where teachers demonstrate techniques for improving the skills of children in the elementary and middle schools. A third activity involves the conduct of workshops and the design of a curriculum for use in teaching mathematics and science to bilingual students at both the elementary and secondary target schools, including Brighton High School. The fourth activity is intended to develop a program of science education for use in an upper-level elementary classroom. When that program is in operation, it is to serve as a demonstration center for elementary teachers throughout District One.

Leadership for these activities is coming from the Department of Science and Mathematics Education of Boston University, with assistance from faculty members in the College of Liberal Arts, the College of Basic Studies, and the Bilingual Project of the Department of Reading and Language Education.

Motor Skills

Nearly all the elementary children in District One, like their counterparts throughout the rest of Boston, have no school-based experience with a program of physical education. There are no physical education teachers in elementary schools, and few schools have a gymnasium or playground. Middle and high school facilities are better, but programs are sparse at those levels.

For this reason, Boston University's Department of Movement, Health, and Leisure has conducted motor skill development programs since 1973 for Brighton, Allston, and Mission Hill children and youth at the Case Center for Physical Education. These programs have become widely accepted as good opportunities to learn everything from jumping and running to swimming and skating.

Under the pairing arrangement, this three-year-old component is being expanded and improved. Students and teachers from the Garfield, Hamilton, Taft, and Edison schools engage in motor skill activities under the direction of faculty and graduate students of the university two days out of every week. While at the Case Center, children are tested for fitness, perceptual motor coordination, and related development potential. The nine hundred participating students are helped to strengthen their skills in individualized ways on the basis of the test results.

There is a movement and motor skill program at Tobin Elementary School, where there are a good gymnasium and a playground. Teachers there are trained to guide students through track and field experiences, dancing, gymnastics, and outward-bound adventures that lead to cooperation and self-testing.

The Human Environment Institute joins with the Department of Movement, Health, and Leisure in a third activity. The entire faculty of Brighton High School participates in a program of planning and training at Camp Sargent in New Hampshire. The major purpose is to help high school teachers apply new techniques in integrating movement activities with environmental studies and other curricula. There is also a field program at the same camp for two hundred students from District One.

The long-range intention of this component is to provide outstanding programs of movement and motor skill development that are carried on by regular, well-trained teachers within the schools of District One. Such programs should go far beyond the conventions of traditional physical education to integrate concepts from the arts of dance, music, and theater and from a multicultural understanding of the sports and arts of the peoples of the world.

Guidance

The guidance departments at Brighton High School and the middle schools in District One are understaffed and poorly equipped to meet the new challenges created by desegregation. The aim of the guidance component is simply to augment the services of departments that already exist.

Initially, two doctoral candidates and one master's candidate have been selected and scheduled so as to provide services daily throughout the school year to Brighton High School. The team includes a bilingual member and a former Boston schoolteacher who previously had been working as a group facilitator for multicultural workshops. A teaching assistant from the Department of Counselor Education works two days a week with the faculty of Edison Middle School on a model for career education. Another teaching assistant is available one day a week to coordinate the career resource center.

Boston University's Department of Counselor Education has a role in augmenting the present guidance facilities in District One. Doctoral and master's candidates serve yearlong internships assisting and guiding the staff of the target schools. Teams of advanced graduate students are to be placed at Brighton High School, Taft Middle School, and Edison Middle School, and the feasibility of an analogous team in the elementary schools of District One is being explored.

The Department of Counselor Education provides additional individual and group counseling services to the schools. Further, the faculty and students of the department offer services in curriculum development and teacher training to further careers in education. Bilingual counseling for Spanish-speaking students is also available, and workshops dealing with cultural heritage and diversity are offered to students since it is felt that crucial issues involved in desegregation can be explored productively in this manner.

Child Health

The objective of the child health component is to improve the quality of health care services for children and youth in District One. This is to be accomplished through collaboration between the medical personnel of the Boston School Department and faculty and students from the Boston University School of Nursing, School of Medicine, the Sargent College of Allied Health Professions, the School of Social Work, the School of Graduate Dentistry, and related departments of the Medical Center.

The first activity related to this component involved the establishment of a Health Coordinating and Planning Group with representation from the above schools and departments. During 1976 this group prepared a proposal for a direct health care program involving community clinical facilities and started an evaluation research program to monitor the delivery of health care services to children.

There is a second activity that involves a collaborative program of student testing and parent health education at the Tobin Elementary School, which has requested help in establishing a comprehensive health services program. This program gives the planning unit a basis for direct action and experience in the community. The School of Nursing provides initial leadership for this program.

Bilingual

Boston University is already fulfilling its pledge to assist Hispanic bilingual education throughout Boston under a contract between the university, the Boston School Committee, and the U.S. Office of Education. The program funds the preparation of a cadre of undergraduate students whose first language is Spanish and a smaller cadre of graduate students in various specialties. The Bilingual Project within the university's Department of Reading and Language Education works closely with the Bilingual Department of the Boston Public Schools. University students do their practice teaching in schools throughout the city. The project is the largest of its kind in New England under the Federal Bilingual Education Act. It is therefore relatively easy to provide additional support and assistance in bilingual instruction as part of the pairing with District One, where large programs in Hispanic and Oriental bilingual instruction are currently underway.

The objective of this component is to make immediate improvements in the quality of bilingual teaching and learning in Spanish and Chinese and related Oriental languages. The first activity in this component involves the selection and development of appropriate tests and materials for use in assessing the reading skills of District One elementary and secondary bilingual students. District teachers are to be trained in the use of these tests and materials and helped in their efforts to individualize materials of instruction by university specialists. In addition, the university conducts workshops to teach basic Spanish to interested teachers and parents who are not bilingual.

As part of this unit, there is special emphasis on preparing a reliable profile of the unique problems of Chinese students who are bilingual. Existing tests and materials for instruction, for example, fail to take into account the tonal aspect of Chinese and Chinese ideographic writing, much less differences in pronunciation and grammar between English and the various Chinese dialects.

A second activity in this component concentrates on identification of the needs of Vietnamese and Burmese students enrolled in Brighton High School. While federal funds are available to assist in the education of Vietnamese refugee students, their academic needs must be assessed systematically and intensively so that these funds are channeled most effectively for the benefit of the students.

Mission Hill Public Housing Project

The Mission Hill Public Housing Project is a large and densely populated neighborhood within District One that is remote from the public school facilities of the district, except for the Tobin and Farragut Elementary Schools. All of the residents of the project are members of low-income minority families whose needs cannot be met by public school services and programs alone.

During the summer of 1975 the Department of Counselor Education of Boston University established a collaborative association with the Roxbury Children's Service. The service, which operates as a social service facility in the housing project, is now aided by experienced graduate students doing fieldwork there as a result of that collaboration.

As part of the first activity in this component, the facilities of Roxbury Children's Service provide a base for the development of a "drop-in center" for teenagers in Mission Hill. The drop-in center contributes direct counseling services for individuals and families as well as a training program for adults and youths seeking skills in professional and peer counseling. The main purpose of the center, however, is to help resolve the problems presented by school conflicts that often result in withdrawal from school. The proportion of Hispanic youths who withdraw from middle school and high school in the district has been estimated to exceed 80 percent. Close attention, including tutorial help, is to be given to potential dropouts and their parents.

The second activity in this component is designed to help Mission Hill adults and youths who take training in counseling to apply their new skills to families and youths within the housing project. The development team is planning to generate volunteer services from within Boston University as part of a collaborative effort to improve opportunities for residents of the project.

Community Participation

The desegregation order of the federal court obligates the parents of Boston public school children to participate directly in the conduct of school affairs. The order establishes electoral and operating procedures for parent councils at each school and for district-wide advisory councils. Parent leaders and representatives are charged with monitoring fulfillment of the order and with guiding school administrators and teachers toward the achievement of equal education and the development of a curriculum that varies to meet the needs and interests of children from different parts of the city. At the suggestion of parent leaders in a summer planning workshop, this component has been designed to help strengthen the ability of adults in District One to carry out the court order.

One activity in this component has included the organization of workshops that were conducted during 1976. Each workshop was co-planned by an advisory group composed of parents, teachers, and university faculty and graduate students. University leadership has come from the Metropolitan College Program in Urban Affairs and from the Department of System Development and Adaptation and the Institute of Responsive Education.

The second activity includes workshops on such topics as:

1. Parent-School Relations: How can parents be involved most effectively in school affairs? What do they need to know about school programs, budgets, and staffing? What makes for good communication between public schools and parents?

2. Special Needs Programs: What does Chapter 766 of the state law dealing with special education mean for parents and children? How do core evaluation teams work? How can parents help at home to meet the special needs of children?

3. Helping Children Learn: How do children learn at school and at home, and how can parents help most? How can parents help children learn to read and to enjoy reading? How can parents help children develop good health habits and motor skills?

4. School and Community Relations: How can a community contribute to the learning of its children and youth? What are the community resources of District One? How can these resources be put to work effectively?

A LOOK AHEAD

Colleges and universities have assisted public schools in many parts of the United States over many decades. Few collaborative projects, however, have been undertaken on the scale of the Boston University-District One pairing. Few, if any, projects of this kind outside Boston have been initiated and carried out under a federal court order. It is the deliberate intent of this pairing to remain flexible and open to change in emphasis. New units within District One and within the university will doubtless seek inclusion in the project as it moves ahead.

Many difficulties surround and limit the prospects for effective support and assistance from higher education to public elementary and secondary education in the Boston desegregation plan. The federal court insisted, for one thing, that the Boston School Committee *contract* with each college and university, but the contract that has resulted is extremely tenuous and falls far short of providing a firm relationship in which Boston University might function with assurance. The Community District Advisory Councils that were formed in each district by court order and charged with monitoring and guiding fulfillment of the order are currently weak and in conflict—including the council in District One, where members have resisted university involvement. It will take time, moreover, to evoke and involve university talents in an effective and inclusive manner, for this work does not fit into university reward structures easily. There are also funding problems to resolve, although the State Board of Education has helped substantially.

The same article in the *Boston Globe* that was referred to earlier concluded with the following comments about pairing in the Boston schools:

The partnerships have had their problems. The combination of university, city, and state bureaucracy has meant months of delays and mounting frustration in getting programs approved and funded. . . . Most involved with the pairings regard them as at least three- to five-year commitments.

Many on both sides approached the pairings with misgivings. Universities have not had an impressive record in working with city schools in Boston or anywhere else. Boston school personnel were skeptical about "experts" who had never been inside a big city school. Colleges and cultural institutions worried about where they would find the money to finance the ventures and whether they would be expected to work miracles. Businesses worried about getting involved in the controversial school desegregation process.

But, on balance, the relationships between the schools and their new partners have gone well enough to surprise the early critics. One university coordinator says that he and his staff are not making any real impact on the basics of what goes on inside the school — who teaches what and how. But, he adds, "It is not a totally closed school any more. The administrators and teachers have to deal with outsiders." . . .

If the schools are more open now to new people and new ideas, college professors and artists and businessmen who thought they knew just how to "fix" the schools are more humble. They have seen first-hand the enormous problems of urban education and they realize now that there are no simple answers or magic cures . . . .

But Boston students, many for the first time, are meeting and talking and studying with college students, are going to downtown firms and seeing that individuals like themselves can have rewarding jobs and careers, are visiting zoos and museums, watching and experimenting with theater and mime. And, in the midst of racial tensions, they are seeing that persons of different backgrounds can study and work together. . . .

The partnerships will not transform the Boston schools. But they are a new and imaginative and hopeful aspect of the painful process of desegregation. And they might help to widen the horizons of Boston children.[5]

Notes

1. *School Reform: Past and Present*, ed. Michael B. Katz (Boston: Little, Brown & Co., 1971), 178.

2. *Boston Desegregation* (Boston: Massachusetts Research Center, 1974), 3.

3. John F. Adkins, James R. McHugh, and Katherine Seay, *The Boston Orders and Their Origin* (Boston: Committee on Desegregation, Boston Bar Association, 1975), 16-18.

4. Nina McCain and Susan Trausch,"Who's Paired with Whom in Boston's Phase 2," *Boston Globe*, February 29, 1976.

5. *Ibid*.

PART FOUR
Desegregation Policy, Urban Education Reform, and the Future of Big Cities

The chapters in this final section attempt to reach conclusions about the status of education in big-city schools and to identify policies that offer special promise for improving instruction and promoting stable, desegregated education in big cities. The first of the chapters, by John A. Finger, Jr., discusses desegregation plans in several cities and delineates policies that he believes differentiate potentially successful from unsuccessful desegregation plans in the various cities. The second chapter, by Eugene E. Eubanks and Daniel U. Levine, analyzes a significant effort now being initiated by the Reverend Jesse L. Jackson and his PUSH organization to improve teaching and learning conditions in big-city schools. In the third chapter, Robert J. Havighurst and Levine attempt to assess the status of instructional improvement efforts in big-city schools in general and in inner-city schools in particular. The authors conclude that encouraging gains are being made in at least some locations, but such gains should not be viewed as substitutes for racial and economic desegregation or for community development efforts aimed at making the inner city a better environment in which to live and learn.

The final two chapters draw on material from earlier parts of the book in deriving specific conclusions about policies and approaches for attaining desegregation and otherwise working to improve schools in big cities. The chapter by Levine and Connie Campbell on magnet schools concludes that such schools may be helpful in improving or maintaining racial and economic balance in city schools and in working to achieve renewal and revitalization of large cities and their public schools. With these goals as a starting point, Levine and Havighurst outline desegregation policies that particularly take into account the overwhelming need to halt and reverse the creeping "innercityization" that has been occurring in many metropolitan areas. Recognizing that the guidelines and conclusions set forth require considerable modification and revision to fit local situations, we hope that this volume will guide educators who share these goals.

13. Policy Requirements for Successful Big-City Desegregation

John A. Finger, Jr.

During the last few years there has been rising opposition to the use of busing in an effort to achieve school integration, and advocates of busing have been placed in the position of defending the initiation and continuation of the system. Historical injustices against blacks and other minorities are widely acknowledged, but much of the public is unaware of, or unconcerned about, present injustices and official acts of discrimination. If injustices of racial isolation, segregation, and unequal opportunity are not to be perpetuated, desegregation is a necessity. The issue is not whether or not to bus, but whether or not to integrate, and it would appear that there is no way to achieve integration except by busing.

Equally important, however, are the questions of how to integrate and how to bus. Desegregation plans, particularly their busing components, need not tear cities apart and drive those who can leave to the suburbs. If we are to avoid these results, however, we need policies and procedures that deal with the issues and problems involved. This chapter examines some of the problems faced and the procedures used in several cities and suggests why some desegregation plans have been successful and why some have not.[1]

PERSPECTIVE ON ADVOCACY

Many people who seem willing to accept integration as a goal are unwilling to accept busing as a means of achieving it. The only way busing will ever be accepted is if the goal of integrated schools were to become so desirable that the inconvenience of busing would seem negligible in comparison. There are many laws and regulations that impinge on individual freedom or beliefs, and there are varying degrees of opposition to such laws, including taxation, compulsory school attendance, conscription, and the fifty-five-mile-per-hour speed limit. In spite of the fact that people are inconvenienced, most citizens recognize the need for taxes, school attendance requirements, military service, and speed limits. It is the purpose that gains them wide acceptance. People will undergo hardships and adversity if they recognize why it is necessary. There are also causes, such as abortion, that rouse equally ardent opposition and support. Busing, even as a means of achieving integration, seems, however, to lack strong advocates.

There are many members of Congress, for example, who realize that terminating busing will lead toward separatism and that consigning children to blighted neighborhoods will stunt their development, for antibusing legislation has encountered considerable opposition in Congress. Speaking openly in favor of integration by busing is not, however, expedient. The most that generally can be obtained in support of integration is silence or lack of opposition.

There is also a balance between how strongly people believe in the desirability of desegregation and the adversity they will tolerate in order to achieve it. An increase in the commitment to integration is much needed, but, even if that were not achieved, the balance could be more favorable if some of the hardships that accompany busing and desegregation were alleviated.

Students should never be required to walk excessive distances, especially if there is a school nearer to their residence than the one to which they are assigned. If busing is required, the transportation system should be well managed: buses should operate on time, routes should be efficiently planned, adequate but not excessive discipline should be enforced, seating should be comfortable, transportation should be available for activities after school hours and for emergencies.

As for the desegregation aspect, there are both long-term and short-term effects. Desegregation plans in some cities have suffered because more attention was paid to the shorter-term effects. These are the ones that occur when students are reassigned to a different school, when graduating seniors are moved to another school, or when athletic teams are separated. With effective planning and management, such difficulties can be resolved.

Long-term effects are different. Long walks or long bus rides do not go away; they persist year after year. Even if a student believes in the desirability of integration, the need to achieve that goal may not be strong enough to overcome the disadvantage of a long bus ride unless it is readily apparent that, by riding a bus, one can attend a better school. If reassigned students do not see a new school in a favorable light, compared with their previous assignment, if the integrated school ultimately proves to have segregated classrooms, ineffective teachers and programs, poor discipline, or excessive racial hostility, then the long ride simply is not worth the effort. Students in integrated schools continuously compare the outcomes being achieved with the inconvenience involved in achieving them. Attention needs to be directed toward reassuring every student who must take a school bus that the inconvenience is kept to a minimum and that it is justified by the result.

SUCCESSFUL DESEGREGATION PLANS

The desegregation plan devised for Charlotte, North Carolina, has been used as a model for other cities. The schools of North Carolina are organized by county, which has meant that the desegregation plan involves the entire county of Mecklenberg. The county is approximately forty miles long and twenty miles wide, and Charlotte is centrally located within the county. Individuals cannot easily work in Charlotte and live outside the school district. This made white flight difficult. Another circumstance that contributed to the success of integration in Charlotte was the corrective action taken by the court as soon as one area changed in its population. The desegregation plan there had built-in safeguards to encourage residential stability. There were walk-in schools in integrated neighborhoods, which made them the places to live in order to avoid busing.

During a session held to work out the Charlotte plan, one participant facetiously suggested that people buy trailers and locate them after school assignments were made. Another humorous solution to the problem was offered: make all the schools portable and relocate them as the population moved. During the planning for desegregation in Charlotte it soon became clear that the major problems in developing any desegregation plan, once the court gives its directive of what must be done, are how to prevent white flight and how to provide stability in housing. The grade assignment plan for elementary schools in Charlotte located the fifth and sixth grades in black neighborhoods and the first four grades in white neighborhoods. This encouraged residential stability because, except for families residing in integrated neighborhoods, *all* white elementary-level children were bused for two years. There was no place to move to avoid busing except to an integrated neighborhood or outside the county. Although each black child was bused four years while his white counterpart was bused only two and black children of primary school age were bused while white children were not bused until they were older, equal numbers of black and white elementary children were bused. The plan could not, however, easily evolve so that the artificiality of schools serving just grades five and six would disappear.

Subsequently, in three cities—Waco and Austin, Texas,[2] and Boston, Massachusetts—I proposed a plan in which the school organization would be 4-4-4 or 5-3-4. In those plans there were middle schools located in black or minority neighborhoods. Such a plan still had inequities because young black children were bused while young white children were not. A plan of this type might, however, make busing purposeful if black children felt that attending integrated elementary school was worthwhile and if white children considered the programs and facilities of the middle school to be good. Complete equity may be less important than feelings of satisfaction and acceptability by children and parents, improved educational experiences, and stabilized city populations. No city has adopted such a plan, probably because too much school plant alteration and construction is required, although high costs would seem a small price to pay for successful school desegregation.[3]

Cities differ, however, and a plan suited to one city may be quite inappropriate for another. In Denver, for example, anyone who has the financial means can avoid busing by moving to an outlying area. This is possible because, as in Detroit, the central city is bordered by smaller urban areas. The Supreme Court ruled that, in Detroit, except under certain circumstances the suburbs could not be included in a desegregation plan. The Denver plan does, however, have many features that provide residential stability. Denver, like Charlotte, has walk-in schools in integrated neighborhoods and integrates as many schools as possible when integration can be accomplished with a short bus ride. In the part of the city most distant from minority neighborhoods and possibly most prone to white flight, white students are bused at the junior or senior high school level but not at the elementary level. Instead, they attend elementary schools that receive minority children who have long bus rides for six years. The minority children are selected because they live within walking distance of both the junior and senior high schools they will attend.

As originally designed, Denver had a unique pairing feature whereby some ten thousand of Denver's forty thousand elementary pupils attended schools that were paired part-time. A child who went to his neighborhood school for half of the day and was not in an integrated classroom would spend the other half of the day in an integrated class, either in his own school or in one to which he was bused. Every child attended two schools and had two teachers and two sets of classmates, one integrated and one not. Children in the paired schools were rotated so that for one semester a child would remain in the neighborhood school and then for another semester he would be bused.[4] This feature of the Denver plan meant that students were actually members of two schools (one majority, one minority). Many children wore T-shirts with the names of both schools printed on them. Membership in two schools seemed to me to be a desirable feature in a desegregation plan. Part-time pairing probably lessened some of the apprehensions about desegregation, and this may well have accounted for the fact that the integration in Denver has, for the most part, been carried out peacefully and successfully. The success of this plan also undoubtedly owes much to the diligent efforts of the school administration, principals, and teachers, and to the effective work of the Community Education Council that the court appointed to monitor the desegregation program.

The Denver plan has been at least somewhat successful in meeting a goal that should be an important part of every desegregation plan: a prospective purchaser of a home or a prospective renter finds that the desegregation plan has little influence on the choice of location within the city, except insofar as there has been an attempt to maintain integrated neighborhoods. Meeting this criterion does more than prevent within-city movement. It assures citizens that the procedure is as fair as it can be. Parents do not discover that some friend has been lucky and avoided busing or that political influence has been used to obtain a preferred assignment. After preparing the Denver plan, I realized that there was a new type of pairing.

My plan for Dayton included the pairing of schools, with each school enrolling grades K-8 or 1-8, so that each child would attend a school near home for one-half of the year and a school away from home for the other half. Each class would, however, retain its students for the entire year, simply changing buildings at midyear. To avoid changing teachers at midyear, the teacher would change buildings with the students. The Dayton Board of Education requested that the district court allow rotation of students on a full-year rather than a half-year basis, and the court did so. In my opinion, however, then as well as now, the original plan would have done more to reduce the apprehension of white parents about their children attending schools in minority neighborhoods and would have provided more community involvement and concern toward assuring that each pair of schools functioned as a single unit.

Again, cities differ. What may be appropriate in Charlotte, Dayton, or Denver, may be completely inapplicable in Boston with its discrete ethnic groups, or in Detroit with a school population now 73 percent black, following a trend showing a regular increase of 2 percent in black population over the past fifteen years.

UNSUCCESSFUL DESEGREGATION PLANS

Some desegregation plans, it seems, were destined to fail. In Dade County, Florida (Miami), elementary children have been reassigned, and, even though large groups of children reside only a short distance from one school, many are required to walk as much as two miles to a different school. Requiring students to walk a long distance creates resentment among parents and children, a resentment that grows because the long walks continue.

Then there is Atlanta, another city that has become resegregated. The procedures there were such that resegregation was inevitable, as it was in Dallas under its initial desegregation efforts where similar procedures have produced similar results. In both cities the children in a neighborhood or area in which whites reside are assigned to a black school simply because the area is nearer a black school; other areas of the city remain untouched. Busing is generally avoided, but the affected areas lose most of their school-age children and the white population disappears. People with children do not rent or buy in the area, and those who can afford to do so move elsewhere. Even when families do not move out of the area, children are sometimes listed as living with relatives, or parents simply give false addresses.

The Charlotte model is used in Oklahoma City, but, since the plan has been implemented, new housing tracts have been developed. They are in areas annexed to the city, but they are incorporated as separate school districts before annexation. Oklahoma City could lose much of its white population to those areas if they are not made part of the Oklahoma City school district. If so, the city schools will become increasingly black.

In Raleigh, North Carolina, the school board submitted a preliminary plan using grade assignments similar to those used in Charlotte, but children from some areas of the city were not bused. Before the plan could even be considered by the court, real estate advertisements appeared that indicated which housing was in areas where there would be no busing.

The Boston plan is also residentially unstable. Boston faces many problems that probably result from the tediously slow process by which full desegregation has finally been required, a process that has allowed opposition to busing to become fully and completely organized and the animosities and ill will to become intensified and hardened. Should Boston survive those problems, it is doubtful that the consequences of its present pupil assignment procedures, which create preferential home locations and residential instability, can be surmounted.

Some desegregation planners have attempted to minimize the inconvenience associated with busing. A computer program that assigns students to schools and provides transportation routes would seem to be desirable because it could simultaneously minimize the number of students to be bused, travel time, and the number of buses required. This also, however, has some undesirable outcomes. A preliminary computer plan prepared for Denver was rejected. My attempt to use a computer program in Stamford, Connecticut, was unsuccessful. All the computer programs that I know of create residential instability. If, for example, students are selected on the basis of race and proximity to school, students residing in integrated neighborhoods are sometimes assigned to black schools if they are white and white schools if they are black. Sending black and white students in already integrated neighborhoods to schools elsewhere is generally not desirable since this eliminates an opportunity to make integrated neighborhoods more attractive than segregated ones.

This problem could be avoided by an alternative procedure whereby all students in a city block or some other geographic aggregate are assigned to a school, but this procedure also creates residential instability. Some children of the same race are bused all twelve years, and others are not bused at all. The residents of some areas of the city will be bused and residents of other areas will not be bused. Residential instability could even be exacerbated if influential people applied pressure to keep their residential area free of busing.

It is the courts that are carrying out desegregation procedures because the President of the United States and Congress do not have the courage to rectify the constitutional offenses identified by the courts. Many political leaders are well aware of the problems of blighted cities, problems that include poverty, crime, and violence. It is deplorable that they often do not direct their support toward remedies that would help to eradicate the sources of difficulty, including the integration of schools.

The courts may not be the most effective agency for carrying out such broad social remedies as desegregation, for courts do not have administrative capabilities built into their structure. Courts generally do not even have extensive research capabilities and must rely upon lawyers and the advocacy system to bring the facts, the law, and the precedents before them. A judge's task is to determine whether the facts in a case bear sufficient similarity to previous cases to justify relying upon precedent. Characteristics of cities are so different that a judge providing remedial procedures consistent with what has been approved by higher courts may have difficulty selecting procedures that are both appropriate and equitable.

Judges are human, too. Because of public sentiment against busing, a judge may adopt undesirable practices or fail to take steps known to be needed, desirable, or just. For example, too few buses may be ordered, inadequate school facilities may be tolerated, students may be reassigned from a school with excellent facilities to a substandard school, or some students may be bused many years and others not at all. A court, even while enforcing the equal protection clause of the Constitution, may violate the spirit of that very section by not assuring that students are accorded every possible convenience to compensate for the inconvenience of reassignment or busing. There is no way to achieve desegregation except by busing. Those who oppose busing, but favor integrated schools, advocate the unattainable. Their cozy platitudes of "Integration, yes! Busing, no!" could bring this nation to racial isolation and separatism.

Notes

1. This chapter is based on my article, "Why Busing Plans Work," which appeared originally in *School Review* 84 (May 1976): 364–372, and it is used here with the permission of the University of Chicago Press.

2. On May 15, 1976, the Fifth Circuit Court of Appeals ordered the District Court to implement my plan for Austin, Texas (*Overton* v. *Texas Education Agency*, Civil Action No. 73-3301), but the Supreme Court has returned the entire matter to the District Court for further findings of fact.

3. In June 1976 a plan based on these characteristics was prepared and submitted for plaintiffs in Buffalo, New York. Buffalo is a city in which such a plan seems especially workable and feasible.

4. The part-time feature of the Denver plan was later overturned by the higher courts. The plan was designed, however, in anticipation of this possibility, so that no major additional realignment of paired schools was required.

14. Jesse Jackson's PUSH Program for Excellence in Big-City Schools

Eugene E. Eubanks and *Daniel U. Levine*

Most of the other chapters in this book are concerned in one way or another with various issues involving the desegregation of big-city schools. They consider whether desegregation is likely to accelerate with withdrawal of white or middle-class students and whether the magnet school movement may help to halt or reverse trends toward racial and socioeconomic isolation in big-city schools. They seek to identify policies that can help to bring about successful desegregation and describe what has occurred in connection with desegregation plans in several large cities.

The present chapter, by way of contrast, examines an important new development concerned with the quality of big-city schools irrespective of present or probable desegregation status. This development is the emergence in a number of big cities of a significant effort aimed at improving conditions in the public schools, particularly those in the inner city. The movement is being led by the Reverend Jesse L. Jackson and the rapidly growing organization named PUSH (People United to Save Humanity), which he founded in December 1971.

As a disciple of the late Martin Luther King, Jr., Jesse Jackson certainly is interested in integration; he would scarcely oppose it or

218

support a separatist view. (PUSH seeks to enroll members from all backgrounds, minority and nonminority, rich and poor.) What he does recognize, however, is that efforts to improve big-city schools cannot wait for integration plans that have all too often proved chimerical and illusionary. He believes that much can be done, indeed must be done, to improve the effectiveness of big-city schools whether they are integrated or segregated. Speaking at commencement ceremonies at Southern University in Baton Rouge, Louisiana, on May 21, 1976, he made the following point:

Integrated education or association represents an opportunity for expansion, but does not represent an automatic change. You must put forth an effort. Whether the teacher is well-trained or not, has a Ph.D. or no "d," if the student is not willing to learn under either condition, will he learn? . . . The schools presuppose that there must be a will to learn and an urge for excellence.[1]

During the 1975–76 academic year, Jackson and PUSH made education their main priority and became active participants in efforts to reform public schools in big cities all over the country. Jackson traveled to Washington, D.C., Detroit, Los Angeles, New Orleans, Hartford, and other cities to speak with students, educators, and parents and to lay the groundwork for a PUSH for excellence in the public schools. Nationally prominent and respected educators—among them, the Hartford superintendent of schools, Edythe Gaines; the Atlanta school board president, Benjamin E. Mays; a Harvard professor, Alvin Pouissant; the superintendent of instruction in California, Wilson C. Riles—already are among PUSH's educational advisers, and school officials in several large cities have allocated funds to help the program. This intense round of activity climaxed in August 1976 at the annual PUSH convention in Washington, D.C. Further plans were developed to establish a PUSH Program for Excellence in Education on a nationwide basis in whatever cities it proved feasible to bring together citizens and educators who would work vigorously for reform in big-city education.

In Chicago, PUSH developed plans for working with ten high schools during the 1976–77 academic year and initiated plans for a massive parade to support improvement in the public schools. Plans were also worked out in cooperation with public school officials for stadium-sized rallies in Hartford and Los Angeles so that students, educators, and interested citizens could come together to dedicate themselves to the cause of transforming inner-city schools and neighborhoods.

A movement with this much impact in its early stages clearly is a phenomenon that is worth the attention of educators everywhere, if only because teachers and administrators all over the country would play a considerable part in it. But the PUSH program is much more than a highly visible ground swell of activity likely to impinge on the professional activities of many educators in big-city school districts. PUSH is now an important national organization that is attempting to improve conditions in inner-city neighborhoods through a concerted effort to root out or overcome forces that have made the inner city a difficult place in which to live and raise or teach children. PUSH leaders are developing programs in education and other areas that could, by significantly improving the inner-city environment, make it possible not just for the schools but also for other social institutions to function more effectively. If their efforts are successful, this may signal the beginning of a historic reversal of patterns of deterioration and disorganization ever more visible in large cities throughout the United States over the past few decades.

IDEOLOGY

The PUSH program is intended to bring the weight and resources of parents and other community residents, pedagogues, preachers and other community leaders, principals and other school administrators, and pupils together in an attack on the abysmal failure of schools in most large cities. The central concept in working to bring about this massive effort, called "total involvement," is initially aimed at changing attitudes and motivations of most pupils and other constituents through parental, peer, and other local community influences. The "key to success," Jackson has said, "is the forming of new educational team relationships between parents, preachers, principals, pupils and teachers, with each performing their respective roles."[2] The program hinges on a renewal of spirit, as Jackson has pointed out:

We contend that more fundamental than any material deficiencies in our schools are our spiritual deficiencies. We may need more money spent on education. We probably do need more efficient administration. We welcome new teaching techniques which will make teaching and learning more effective. However, more fundamental than any of these material needs, is the need to renew our spirits—to renew our hope in the future, our faith in ourselves, our resolve and determination to overcome, and the restoration of the will to learn. With a renewed and positive attitude, effort and action will follow.[3]

The PUSH program further calls for a return to basic courtesies and respect for authority and authority figures by students and a most intense directive influence by parents and other community leaders. Jackson considers one of the major causes of trouble in schools to be the massive dropout of parents and calls for parents to reassert their authority as parents. He advocates the institution of city-wide study hours from 7:00 to 9:00 p.m., during which time children would not be allowed on the streets, and there would be a total blackout of radio and TV.[4] Commenting on achievement in reading, he made the following statement:

We keep saying that Johnny can't read because he's deprived, because he's hungry, because he's discriminated against. We say that Johnny can't read because his daddy is not in the home. Well, Johnny learns to play basketball without daddy. We do best what we do most, and for many of our children, that is playing ball. One of the reasons Johnny does not read well is that Johnny doesn't practice reading.[5]

Jackson solicits the support of educators, politicians, the press, disc jockeys, and other people who might influence children and youth in working to bring about and maintain better academic performance among low-achieving students in towns and cities: "We want the black oriented media to find ways to publicly reward achievers. We want the black disc jockeys, who reach more black kids than the principals, to inform and inspire as well as entertain."[6]

According to the position of PUSH, children need adult supervision that provides motivation, a sense of caring, discipline, and sometimes even chastisement. These components are all part of love, and Jackson wants three institutions to enclose the child in a love triangle (see Figure 14-1). Reminiscing on how his own parents worked closely with his teachers and minister to give him the guidance he needed in the North Caro-

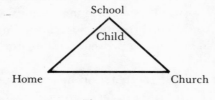

Figure 14-1

A love triangle

lina town in which he grew up, Jackson maintains that all three institutions must demand respect, achievement, and excellence from the child and demonstrate (as appropriate) the facets of love described above in order to mandate or secure the desired outcomes.[7]

Jackson goes on to state, "Children cannot be allowed to play the game of teach me if you can catch me. Children must be taught that they have a responsibility to learn as well as a right to education. Busing is absolutely necessary, but without a will to learn, busing is irrelevant."[8]

EDUCATIONAL PROGRAM

PUSH proposes the following strategies to bring about more positive influences relating to climate and atmosphere for learning in the school:

1. Establishment of "teams" of students whose skill and expertise is academic excellence.
2. Establishment of peace "Brothers" and "Sisters" to monitor and supervise in classrooms, the cafeteria, the auditorium, the hallways, and on the playgrounds.
3. Promotion of self-discipline and a sense of order among students — a sense of what is expected of one and what one expects of oneself.
4. Full participation in a city-wide council of students who will provide leadership to support discipline and academic excellence and to resist drugs, violence, and racism.
5. Establishment at the secondary level of a system of peer justice whereby many cases of misconduct would be judged and dealt with by students themselves on the relatively simple premise that people near or at the voting age, and thus presumed competent to judge issues of war and peace among nations, are competent to judge a case of spitball-throwing. Such a system, involving a civic function, would not only improve discipline but also have an educational value.

Jackson has summarized the reaction he encounters in arguing for these positions as: "Each time I suggest [to students] a program of self development they respond with overwhelming enthusiasm. Black teen-agers — some of the roughest, most street wise dudes you will ever meet — respond to that appeal."[9]

The challenge to the schools is as mighty and encompassing as the one to parents and students and calls for specific action on the part of the schools and teachers with notions of:

1. Formal opening and closing convocations in schools to enhance the meaning of institutionalized education.
2. Careful and constant explanations of the benefits of a good education addressed to the community in order to help develop a self-confident sense of where we are going and how far we already have come thanks largely to education.
3. All reasonable efforts to bring the parent to school to pick up report cards to ensure formal dialogue and contact between school and parent.
4. Creation of specific incentives for students and teachers to achieve excellence in the classroom. On this point, Jackson asks: "Why have we stopped pursuing excellence in the classroom? . . . We still pursue it on the football field, on the basketball court. High school coaches practice their athletic teams three and four hours a day after school. But are there any reading, writing, and counting teams in our schools?"[10]
5. Establishment of rigorous rules of behavior in the halls, and new dress codes reflecting modesty and dignity.
6. Removal of graffiti of despair as well as trash from and around schools.
7. Removal of violent weapons of all kinds from school grounds, even if electronic equipment similar to that used to detect arms at airports must be installed at school doors.
8. Requirements that the parent and teacher meet personally and converse at least once a year, even if this necessitates the teacher visiting the home of the student.

Another important aspect of the PUSH concept of total involvement is the role of the church. Jackson foresees a most active role for the church in the resurgence of education in schools serving low-status populations, particularly low-income minorities, and he calls for a reinstitution of a belief in "God-consciousness as part of the Cosmic Hierarchy . . . . The death of ethics is the sabotage of excellence,"[11] regular communications and cooperation between religious leaders and school faculties, provisions of platforms and scholarships in religious institutions for recognition of excellence in education, use of church facilities for studying and tutoring after school and on week-ends, and incorporation of educational progress and excellence as part of the responsibilities of the religious institution.

Jackson's charge to the community can be paraphrased as: "Racism knocked you down, racism keeps you down and profits from you being down, so obviously it will not pick you up. The community must initiate the action to get up from the knockdown." He urges the community to accept the challenge and be willing to do much more than is required by law or rules — to sacrifice certain rights voluntarily; to be willing to accept "service" as a general standard to be valued and acted upon both by children and adults; to cease general rebellion against all authorities; to set standards of excellence for all endeavors; to hold "State of the Community" meetings for mass audiences in big cities. These responses should be funded upon moral authority and ethics that complement academic and mental development.

ISSUES IN CARRYING OUT THE PROGRAM

An educational and social program as ambitious and encompassing as the one PUSH is now undertaking inevitably raises many important issues connected with definition and implementation. Delineating all these issues and analyzing them at length would require more space than is available here, but some of the most important among them should be acknowledged if only in a preliminary and summary fashion. In our opinion the most important ones involving the nature and potential of the PUSH Program for Excellence in Education are:

1. Can the program succeed if it is so highly dependent on the leadership of its charismatic leader? Jesse Jackson is not PUSH, and PUSH is much more than Jesse Jackson. Nevertheless, there is little doubt that much of its initial growth can be attributed to Jackson's dynamic and charismatic leadership. Most of the proposals being put forward by PUSH have been advocated before by parents, teachers, and others who have tried to generate motivation for academic learning among socioeconomically disadvantaged youth, though not in a form as comprehensive and easy to understand as the ideology and program of PUSH. As Jackson himself admitted in an interview on August 7, 1976, "I'm saying something that mom and dad say all the time, but it sounds different coming from Jackson." This, of course, is one reason why PUSH efforts in specific school districts include assemblies and meetings at which Jackson speaks with students and parents on their

home turf. The PUSH leadership is well aware of the dangers of having their efforts too dependent on one person. Jackson has acknowledged the problem himself: "Our movement needs a combination of the charismatic and the systematic."[12] PUSH is attempting to institutionalize its program and its leaders are struggling to obtain resources to employ personnel to work on a day-by-day basis. So far these efforts are being rewarded in the form of growing support for the program, but whether they will succeed at a grass-roots level where Jackson is not present to provide inspiration and leadership must be considered an open question at this time.

2. Can participants in the PUSH program be effective in carrying out their distinctive roles both cooperatively and individually? Related to the issue of dependence on inspirational leadership is an important question concerning the degree to which actors in the PUSH movement can each make their special contribution in a cooperative effort to improve social and physical conditions in the inner city. As mentioned earlier, one of Jackson's main tasks is to articulate what others are not in a position to say persuasively or even to say at all. For example, he was able to persuade more than thirty unemployed residents of one inner-city neighborhood in Chicago to volunteer their time to help provide security and supervision around an elementary school that had become dangerous to attend. Since these individuals were unemployed, he argued, why not use their time to make a contribution to their community and the welfare of its young people? This suggestion coming from educators probably would have been mostly ineffectual, and political leaders probably would have been most hesitant to offer it at all.

By the same token, PUSH leaders recognize that they are dependent on educators for technical expertise in improving instruction once classroom conditions have become more conducive to teaching and learning. At some point in the change process community pressure will have to be brought to bear on faculties that lack the leadership, skill, or motivation to take advantage of this opportunity, and at that time major clashes may well occur with teachers' unions, administrative groups, and other professional associations. In many neighborhoods it might even prove necessary to force confrontations in order to generate support from inner-city residents who may be disinclined to play any part in community affairs and to bring together people in the community whose most immediate problem is just surviving.

Jackson and his organization are not trying to force such confrontations; indeed, they tend to view this strategy as an obsolete relic of the 1960s. Instead, they insist that the most important deficiency in compensatory education in large cities has been lack of full cooperation as equal partners on the part of all interested parties. Academic reform will come about, Jackson tells us, "in proportion to the emergence of active participation of the missing elements,"[13] that is, parents, students, community leaders. Nevertheless, it is only realistic to expect that at some point PUSH will face the kind of crunch that may tear apart the coalition of partners it is trying to put together to bring about improvement in big-city schools.

3. Will the PUSH program be perceived as "blaming the victim"? In the past, a number of programs in education and other areas that have attempted to help improve conditions in inner-city neighborhoods have failed, largely perhaps because they were perceived by their potential clients as "blaming the victims" for their own troubles. Any program designed to help powerless people help themselves may fail for this reason, because people will not generally participate vigorously in an effort that they think maligns and stigmatizes them. Jackson and other PUSH leaders are well aware of this problem; they are, after all, on the firing line and encounter it firsthand. About all that Jackson or anyone else can do about it is to make his position unmistakably clear at all times, frequently reiterating the truth that self-help need not be either logically or practically equivalent to blaming the victim. With his outstanding oratory and his great gift for synthesizing many important themes and for communicating them to the people he is trying to reach, Jackson seems so far to be succeeding in getting the distinction across more successfully than others generally have been able to do: "I'm not saying we should blame the victim. But I am saying we have to stop victimizing ourselves."[14]

4. Will "practicing" academic subjects yield anything like the same gains that practice can accomplish in sports and physical exercise? One of the main emphases in the PUSH program is on "practicing" in academic subjects like reading in much the same way that some youngsters develop their skills in basketball, baseball, and other physical activities. Undoubtedly, improvements in academic performance among socioeconomically disadvantaged students depend on their spending more time, both inside and outside of class, in an effort to master academic subject matter. Recent research tends to verify the

commonsense notion that simply spending more time in school and, particularly, the amount of time actually involved in learning activities are significantly correlated with the amount of learning students demonstrate in the classroom. Unfortunately, however, it is uncertain whether more practice and study by themselves would accomplish a great deal in improving the performance of students in big-city schools. Improved instructional approaches are needed to diagnose and overcome the learning difficulties of disadvantaged students, and methods of instruction must be modified so that students are not mainly repeating their mistakes, which appears to have happened in many after-school or other "add-on" programs under Title I. Jackson and other PUSH leaders recognize that practice in academics is only a part of the solution to achievement problems in big-city schools. They have seized upon the practice-and-study idea because it is easier for parents, students, and others to understand and because it represents something concrete that inner-city residents perhaps can begin to work on immediately. There are dangers in oversimplifying the learning problem in big-city schools to this degree, a danger comparable to the traps some teachers have fallen into when arguing that students "can't learn because they are hungry" or some parents have fallen into with statements like, "If kids aren't learning it must be because teachers aren't teaching." In particular, practice may even prove dysfunctional if it turns out that the wrong habits are being repeated or if students perceive little improvement after practice and become still more alienated. In addition, overemphasis on this approach makes PUSH highly dependent on the expertness of teachers now in the schools, who presumably will provide appropriate guidance in telling pupils what and how to study.

5. Is religion too much commingled with the public schools in PUSH's approach to educational reform? If only on constitutional grounds, there are serious questions concerning the central role that PUSH advocates for religion and the churches in seeking to reestablish the "moral authority" its leaders believe is required for substantial academic improvement in big-city schools. PUSH leaders can point out that their program does not require membership in a church or attendance at church services, but the program is built explicitly on commitment to religious principles, and it sometimes is expressed — as at school assemblies — in terms closely resembling Christian fundamentalist ones. This may make the PUSH effort at school reform not

only vulnerable in terms of possible legal suits but also repugnant to many potential supporters it seeks to include in the "total involvement" concepts. The issue we are raising here is really much larger. We live in a scientifically oriented society in which religion plays a lesser part in shaping attitudes and behaviors than it did in previous eras. In this sense our society has become much more "rational" and complex than it was generations ago; indeed, it is partly the complexity of contemporary society that has made big cities almost unmanageable by utilizing established political and social institutions and policies. As conditions in big cities, particularly the inner city, have deteriorated, we have produced a plethora of "scientific" analyses and reports delineating detailed "systems" approaches to solve the problems that exist there. We need more science and technology, these reports implicitly tell us, to solve the problems that some would attribute to science and technology in the first place. It is precisely at this point that Jackson argues that commitment and love are more basic than science and rationalism in solving educational and other problems that confront us in big cities. It is not that PUSH leaders reject technology and professional expertise; they firmly assert that this must be supplied by the technicians and the professionals. They do insist, however, that a sense of community, moral authority, and motivation based on emotional commitment must precede the development of solutions based on science and rationality. Who is to say they are wrong?

6. Can the PUSH program succeed in the face of urban conditions that strongly work against the success of any organized effort to help the poor and the powerless? Perhaps this question is too obvious to be worth asking, but the preceding analysis suggests that it may be worth addressing briefly in order to place PUSH in an appropriate historical and social context. PUSH is attempting to bring about what amounts to a revolution in the way inner-city populations and institutions interact and function, explicitly recognizing that anything short of such a revolution probably will fail in the same manner as many programs in the 1950s and 1960s failed. As much as anyone, PUSH leaders are aware that the obstacles they face are nearly insuperable, that they are placing a lot of faith on possibly weak reeds (for example, active cooperation on the part of entrenched bureaucracies), and that they may be expanding their program too fast and spreading themselves too thin in launching a concerted attack on the forces that have created deterioration and despair in large cities. On this point they argue,

with much justification, that big-city problems in education, social welfare, employment, and so forth are national rather than local in origins and scope and that only a comprehensive national effort reaching directly to the grass-roots levels of the family and the peer group has much chance to succeed in local neighborhoods. One may well quarrel with the diagnosis and the program, but hardly with the fortitude and dedication required to undertake so enormous an effort. In assessing their chances, we can do no better than offer the following quote from a *Washington Post* article by William Raspberry:

> That sense of entrapment in love may have been a good deal easier to achieve in tiny Greenville, N. C. (pop: about 12,000 when Mr. Jackson was born there in 1941) than in the teeming cities where uprootedness and unconnectedness combine to produce the very anomie Mr. Jackson is trying to attack.
>
> To a significant degree, what he is proposing is the establishment of small towns in the city, a series of caring communities in which every adult is parent to every child.
>
> Jesse Jackson is, in short, proposing a miracle. And yet, with a little luck and a lot of focused commitment, it could take hold. Not that thugs would suddenly become young gentlemen and hall-rovers instant scholars.
>
> But it just may be possible to reestablish in the classrooms a situation where serious scholarship, mutual respect and discipline are the norm, and where peer pressure serves to reinforce that norm.
>
> It certainly is worth trying.[15]

COMMENTS AND CONCLUSIONS

The PUSH Program for Excellence in Education is built on a solid foundation of socialization theory. It begins with the premise that socialization is most successful when the forces that shape a child's attitudes and behaviors operate in a consistent and unified manner to communicate beliefs and understandings essential for success in the society of which he is a part. It emphasizes that parents, neighbors, peers, teachers, church officials, and other adults in the local community who interact personally with children must work together to develop motivation and habits that can enable the child to succeed in the society's major institutions. Community control of schools, Jackson tells us, would not contribute much to the improvement of public schools unless it started with "the community controlling the child."

PUSH further emphasizes—more explicitly and perhaps pragmatically than has heretofore been the case—that inner-city youth have been particularly victimized by socialization forces that work at cross purposes: school versus street, parents versus peers. The importance of the mass media, particularly disc jockeys, and of political institutions also is explicitly emphasized in PUSH's diagnosis of the problems that parents, educators, and other socializing agents face in raising children successfully in a modern, big-city environment. The PUSH program thus embodies an excellent sociological analysis translated convincingly into language meaningful and understandable to those who are not social scientists.

PUSH's educational program also represents excellent social psychology. It acknowledges that attitudes and behaviors do not change overnight, but it insists that change must begin somewhere. It also recognizes that such changes are not likely to be firmly rooted and pervasive with respect to institutions as central as the school unless they have deep emotional wellsprings and involve the formulation, acceptance, and acting out of specific roles in the institution.

Similarly, PUSH leaders clearly are aware that ritual and ceremony can be important or even necessary elements in the design and operation of an institution that needs to win greater commitment and loyalty from people who participate in it. These characteristics are among the most important elements that social psychologists have identified as being necessary for a true "conversion" experience that mark substantial changes in the ways people believe and behave in society. PUSH is trying to provide a conversion experience powerful enough to generate a different environment in which big-city schools, particularly those in the inner city, can function more effectively than they have in the past.

Most aspects of the PUSH argument have an internal logic that is difficult to challenge. As regards PUSH's insistence that low-status and minority citizens must accept responsibility for their own success or failure as well as for changing conditions within their communities, for example, Jackson and his staff vigorously assert that self-help need not and should not be equated with compromise of basic rights and principles. They are determined to avoid the pitfalls that Booker T. Washington eventually encountered when he argued in the 1890s that black Americans would have to lift themselves by their own bootstraps.

With equal concern for the logic of their position and the changes that will have to occur if their vision is to become reality, PUSH leaders insist that inner-city citizens somehow will have to establish cooperative relationships with the police and other governmental agencies.

Jackson, for example, asserted that crime probably will not be reduced much in the inner city unless something can be done to prove to the community that the police are "an extension rather than an occupation."[16] The Reverend Frank Watkins (PUSH communications officer) similarly argues that inner-city residents have to work and take more responsibility for bringing about improvements in local conditions with respect to recreation, jobs, social welfare services, and other elements that go into "building a society" in which children can grow and prosper; otherwise, the inner city will remain as anomic as it is today.[17]

All these arguments seem not only impeccable in their logic but exceptional in their awareness of the range of reform needed in big-city institutions and of the traps that lie in wait for reformers whose arguments are simplistic or one sided.

The weakest element in the PUSH Plan for Excellence in Education probably involves its relatively slight emphasis on the problems likely to arise in improving curriculum and instruction once big-city schools have been made better places in which to teach and to learn. We are not as skeptical, in other words, about PUSH's overall strategy and the societal analysis on which it is based as we are about its pedagogy.

When PUSH addresses issues of social control and student behavior, its platform is relatively specific, much more so than many other groups that plead for order and discipline in the schools. PUSH proposals for dress codes, periodic community-school assemblies, required homework and study hours, close cooperation with the mass media, and parent participation requirements are refreshing in their specificity and promising in their occasional divergence from "conventional wisdom" about what can or should be done in the public schools. With regard to proposals for change in curriculum and instruction, however, or to analysis of reforms needed in school organization and administration, PUSH is mostly silent. Perhaps this is what one should expect given the fact that its leaders are laymen who realize they will have to cooperate with teachers and administrators if real change is to occur in big-city schools.

From this point of view the PUSH program poses an enormous challenge to teachers and administrators in big-city schools. Jackson told us that he believes teachers do know how to teach if students are attentive and motivated; after all, most teachers have had considerable preparation and experience. "I am confident," he said, "that educators have the technology," and he also expressed the belief that many administrators have the "presence," the expertise, and the determination to organize their schools for more effective instruction if parents demand and support such changes.[18]

We wish we shared this confidence. Some public school administrators with whom we have talked disagreed with Jackson's general assessment of the capabilities of teachers and administrators in big-city schools. They pointed out that most teachers have neither the preparation nor the experience needed to work with promising instructional systems that might improve academic performance in inner-city schools. Even if students and parents cooperate fully with previously harried teachers and administrators, there is some doubt as to whether educators in the inner city could effectively implement improved programs of instruction.

Our own experience in big-city schools tends to support this latter perspective. We have seen some inner-city schools where students and parents had excellent relationships with teachers and administrators, yet little or nothing was done to make instruction more effective than in other schools where relationships were poor. It is partly for this reason that we are not particularly sanguine about the prospects for lasting improvement in inner-city schools unless efforts such as the PUSH program incorporate specific and systematic school-wide plans for change in curriculum and instruction.

Elsewhere we have described some of the major elements in a serious effort toward big-city school reform as:

— Outstanding administrative leadership at every level — principal, middle management, and the superintendency . . . .
— Staff development efforts . . . much larger than . . . in the past, . . . carried out intensively on a school-by-school basis with far greater input from teachers and the community.
— . . . a thorough reorganization of traditional school practices, including scheduling, student/teacher relationships, the grouping of pupils, evaluation practices, and the utilization of instructional methods and materials. . . .
— . . . [more provisions for] different educational environments for students who cannot function well in regular schools. . . .
— Community resources . . . joined to school resources in order to ensure that both are fully utilized. . . .[19]

The PUSH Program for Excellence in Education may well signify a tremendous step forward with respect to several of these elements.

Clearly, it embodies an unusually vigorous and promising attempt to join community and school resources in the service of big-city school reform. Its leaders are painfully aware of the urgent imperative to bring about improvements in the selection and performance of administrators at all levels. They appeared abstractly aware that pervasive and systemic change is required with respect to staff development, curriculum, instruction, and other aspects of educational programming, but as laymen they reserve such matters for professional educators. If it worries them greatly that professional educators have been ineffective for many years, they choose not to emphasize this belief publicly. They assert instead, that community participation will increase their effectiveness.

Thus, PUSH has joined the issue. For well over a decade teachers and administrators have been complaining that inner-city students and parents have not been receptive to pleas for cooperation to improve the schools and that negative forces in the inner-city environment have stood in the way of success in the school. Jackson and other PUSH leaders agree, and express determination to bring about change in inner-city communities that will make it easier for teachers to work in the classroom. "We don't know how well teachers can teach," Jackson has said, "until we provide a conducive atmosphere for learning. The present atmosphere is like sending Hank Aaron to bat with a popsicle stick, or sending Muhammed Ali to fight with one arm tied behind his back."[20]

If PUSH succeeds in this effort alone, that is no mean accomplishment. If educators find that organizations like PUSH indeed have made the inner city a better learning environment but then fail to improve academic performance among inner-city students, that will be a rare opportunity missed and a great tragedy.

Notes

1. Jesse L. Jackson, "Moral Crisis in Education," commencement speech at Southern University, Baton Rouge, La., May 21, 1976.

2. Jesse L. Jackson, presidential address at the fifth annual PUSH National Convention, Washington, D.C., July 21, 1976.

3. Jesse L. Jackson, "PUSH for Excellence in Education: A Tentative Position Paper," mimeo, unpaged paper for PUSH, Chicago, May 3, 1976.

4. Quoted in Chet Fuller, "Govern Thyself," *Atlanta Journal*, March 22, 1976.

5. Quoted in William Raspberry, "Racism and Victims," *Washington Post*, March 8, 1976.

6. Jesse L. Jackson, "Give the People a Vision," *New York Times Magazine*, April 18, 1976.

7. Personal interview, August 7, 1976.

8. Jackson, "Give the People a Vision."

9. *Ibid.*

10. Quoted in Fuller, "Govern Thyself."

11. Jackson, "Moral Crisis in Education."

12. Richard H. Weiss, "Jesse Jackson," *St. Louis Post-Dispatch*, September 19, 1976.

13. Personal interview, August 7, 1976.

14. Quoted in Raspberry, "Racism and Victims."

15. William Raspberry, "The Discipline Revival," *Washington Post*, February 2, 1976.

16. Personal interview, August 7, 1976.

17. *Ibid.*, August 8, 1976.

18. *Ibid.*, August 7, 1976.

19. Eugene E. Eubanks and Daniel U. Levine, "Big-City Desegregation since Detroit," *Phi Delta Kappan* 56 (April 1975): 521–522, 550.

20. Jackson, "Moral Crisis in Education."

15. Instructional Improvement in Inner-City Schools

Robert J. Havighurst and *Daniel U. Levine*

Magnet programs that make big-city schools more attractive, policies designed to promote stable desegregation, and partnerships between inner-city residents and educators — all may contribute to improved achievement of students in the schools. But such improvement will also depend greatly upon the development of approaches to instruction that will bolster the academic skills of inner-city students, for they constitute a large proportion of the enrollment in the schools. Some recent efforts appear to yield promising results in improving the academic skills of economically disadvantaged students in the inner city.[1] We believe that the following generalizations, based on reports of those efforts, should be taken into account in working toward the improvement of public schools in large cities.

1. Achievement in reading, mathematics, and other basic skills declined for many years in most large cities as the public schools experienced a sizable influx of economically disadvantaged students who attended schools in low-income areas. This increased the proportion of economically disadvantaged students in those schools, as well as schools throughout the city.

2. As this influx slowed or stopped and special compensatory education programs were introduced in the later 1960s, the decline in

235

achievement scores also slowed or stopped, except where there was an exodus of middle-status students or where there were special problems, such as prolonged teachers' strikes.

3. The influence of early childhood programs such as Head Start or Follow Through helped to improve the academic achievement of preprimary and primary students in many inner-city schools. Some cities reported gains in achievement through the second or third grades. Primary grade achievement at or near national norms began to be reported for Kansas City, Missouri, in 1973, and for District Ten of the Chicago public schools in 1974.[2]

4. Even for inner-city schools where such gains were reported, however, academic achievement in the middle grades and above was generally about as low as it had been before compensatory education was widely tried, which is to say that the average achievement in reading and other basic skills remained one or more years below grade level by the time students reached the sixth grade and two or more years below national norms by the time they reached the ninth grade. At these levels of achievement, a substantial proportion of pupils was not performing well enough to function satisfactorily in a complex industrial society.

One can speculate about why compensatory education in inner-city schools appears to reach a plateau in effectiveness, even where it has achieved some success in the preschool and primary grades. Perhaps efforts toward staff improvement and curriculum development have been less extensive or effective in the middle grades than in the lower grades. Perhaps the curriculum becomes more abstract in the middle grades, so that lack of appropriate early childhood experience to prepare children for abstract intellectual tasks becomes more salient at that point than in the lower grades. Perhaps peer group and neighborhood influences that do not support the goal of academic achievement become more important in the middle grades than they are in the first few years of school. Systematic research is needed to pinpoint the important causes of the general ineffectiveness of schooling for inner-city children in the middle grades. Even without such research, however, it is clear that new instructional approaches are needed if academic gains reported for preschool and primary programs in inner-city schools are to be extended to later grades.

Until recently, about all that could be said with assurance was that significant gains in the middle and secondary grades would require early intervention[3] and greater cooperation between parents and school.[4] It is also clear that chances for success are highly dependent on factors that are known to be important to make any educational innovation work well—outstanding administrative leadership, large-scale programs for staff development, changes in organizational arrangements to support the innovation, competent planning and evaluation.

PROMISING INSTRUCTIONAL APPROACHES FOR INNER-CITY SCHOOLS

Recent reports of improvements in achievement in the primary and lower-middle grades of inner-city schools at a few locations have emphasized the development of instructional practices sufficiently different from previous approaches to warrant the designation "new instructional systems."

Follow Through

The Follow Through program was initiated by Congress in 1967 to improve the achievement of economically disadvantaged students in the primary grades after national evaluation of Head Start programs suggested that academic gains for the latter approach were not being maintained after kindergarten and first grade. Follow Through has been organized on a "planned variation" basis, with a number of different programs being tried in a variety of locations and with unusually thorough evaluations to try to determine which alternatives are most effective.

The evaluation of Follow Through, like the program itself, has been expensive and controversial. By 1974, an estimated $300 million already had been made available for the program, more than $23 million had been contracted for the national evaluation,[5] and difficulties encountered in evaluating a program of such magnitude and complexity were exceeded only by the difficulties of administering the program initially. On the basis of a special study including data on the 1973–74 school year (the seventh year of Follow Through) the Comptroller General of the United States concluded that "problems . . . in both the initial design and implementation of the experiment will limit the Office of Education's ability to reach statistically reliable overall conclusions on the success or lack of success of the approaches for teaching young disadvantaged children."[6] The federal government did not learn nearly as much as it wanted to know about which alternatives work best and which settings are most conducive to success.

Evaluations of Follow Through have, nevertheless, yielded some knowledge about instructional approaches that improve the performance of economically disadvantaged students. The most salient report for our purpose is the study conducted by Jane Stallings and others at the Stanford Research Institute. After examining data on first- and third-grade classrooms in thirty-six cities and towns, the researchers concluded that at both grade levels the highest reading scores were:

obtained in classrooms using systematic instructional patterns where the teacher provides information and asks a question about the information. The child responds and the teacher immediately lets the child know whether the response is right or wrong. If he is wrong, the child is guided to the correct answer. If he is correct, he receives praise, a token, or some form of acknowledgement.[7]

Likewise in mathematics, the report continued, children had higher scores:

where teachers used systematic instructional approaches. . . . In classrooms where textbooks and programmed workbooks were used frequently, the test scores on math were especially high. In addition, the use of instructional materials such as programmed materials, Cuisenaire rods, or Montessori materials contributed to higher math scores.[8]

Although this report did not deal with children above the third grade or provide separate information on students from inner-city neighborhoods, it did suggest some instructional features that may have accounted for the improved achievement of a sample of students in locations that included a number of big cities. After examining reports by Stallings and other researchers who have studied programs in reading and mathematics at the primary level for students of low socioeconomic status, Barak Rosenshine observed that "a drill pattern consisting of questions that the students could answer, followed by feedback and subsequent questions," and "a pattern of direct instruction, consisting of small steps at the student's level and a great deal of work mediated by either the teacher or workbooks, all of which is directed by the teacher," appeared to be most functional for such students.[9]

DISTAR in Chicago

The DISTAR (Direct Instructional Systems in Training for Arithmetic and Reading) program is used in many school districts, including a number of inner-city schools. Characteristics of the program, which extends through the second grade, include highly structured lessons with emphasis on demonstration and drill, on immediate rewards for appropriate behavior, on "take home" lessons in which parents learn to help children develop independent study skills, and on the adult-centered verbal bombardment approach developed by Carl Bereiter and Siegfried Engelmann.[10] In reading, the emphasis is on word attack skills.

DISTAR has been successfully used in Chicago's District Ten, which contains twenty schools in West Side neighborhoods where the median family income was approximately $4,700 in 1970. Under the leadership of District Superintendent Joseph Rosen and his staff, the program was introduced in all elementary classrooms through the second grade, and it has been made the focal point for all district planning efforts at that level, including staff selection, in-service training, discretionary budgeting, and further curriculum development. The keynote of the program developed in District Ten is mastery:

The grouping of children close to the teacher so that feedback from the pupils is heard at once, and the constant striving for total pupil involvement ascertains that mastery will develop. In addition, mastery tests are administered after each fifth lesson, and these tests are built into the program.[11]

The results to date have been impressive. In 1975, 1,470 second graders attending some of the most difficult inner-city schools in Chicago obtained an average reading score of 2.7, just slightly below the national average of 2.8.[12] Administrators in District Ten, concerned about extending these gains into the middle grades, have concluded that pupils require much broader and more intensive experiences inside and outside the classroom if they are to develop the reasoning and thinking skills required for further gains.[13] The staff in District Ten is now trying to provide such experiences while maintaining a coordinated program stressing the sequential mastery of basic academic skills.

Child-Parent Centers

One of the most promising approaches to improving instruction in inner-city schools is that initiated in Chicago in 1967 by the Child-

Parent Center. This program, which has been expanded over the
years, included approximately 3,300 students at nineteen centers by
1976. Students are enrolled for two years of preschool education before kindergarten and continue in the program through the third
grade. Evaluators of the program have described the principles upon
which it is based as:

1. direct parent involvement in the center program and in activities designed to
   meet parent needs;
2. elimination of factors such as social and health problems that may interfere with
   successful learning experiences;
3. use of learning materials which incorporate a specific learning approach with a
   strong language orientation;
4. structured readiness and reading programs so that frequent feedback is available; and
5. a structured, consistent, long-term approach.[14]

The programs at the centers all "aim at developing greater facility in
the use of language. . . . To further this aim and to strengthen pupil
self-identity, all programs also emphasize the use of rewards and
praise for pupils when they successfully complete a learning task."[15]

As early as 1973 third-grade scores on the Metropolitan Achievement Test were at or above national norms in reading and mathematics. Since that time, data on some of the elementary schools attended
by children who have been in the program show fifth- and sixth-grade
reading scores at or above national norms and far above average for
Chicago or for surrounding elementary schools.[16] A study conducted
by the Research and Evaluation Division of the Chicago Public
Schools indicated, however, that gains among center graduates were
being maintained only among students who were kept together as "intact cohorts" after the third grade, thus strongly suggesting that
"graduates from successful compensatory programs should be moved
from grade to grade as a group for as long as practicable."[17] This conclusion in turn suggests that such programs should be implemented as
much as possible at the school and neighborhood levels in order to develop classroom environments in which the gains of early childhood
programs can be sustained into the middle and upper grades.

Elementary Reading in Philadelphia

Achievement in elementary reading in the Philadelphia public
schools has improved since 1970 when a systematic program was initi-

ated to raise levels of reading performance throughout the district. Researchers in Philadelphia report that, after much searching and several false starts, some success has been attained in tailoring behavioral objectives to teacher-selected instructional materials and that both are now more specific and fewer in number.[18] A uniform statement of goals has been developed for city-wide use, reflecting a move toward emphasis on mastery of specific skills in decoding, comprehension, and literature.[19] Because of the need to provide continuity for children from poverty areas, who frequently transfer from school to school within the system, greater uniformity has been mandated in instructional materials. Reading is emphasized throughout the language arts program.[20]

The Philadelphia approach has also stressed staff development and the provision of monitoring and evaluation services at the building and classroom levels in order to make sure that classroom instruction focuses on the identification and remediation of specific learning problems of individual children. As a result of these efforts the median for district-wide reading scores among second and sixth graders increased to the 59th and 33rd percentiles, respectively. In the late 1960s these scores generally were 5 to 15 percentile points lower.[21] These figures represent substantial district-wide improvement in reading performance at both grade levels. Since Philadelphia has a high proportion of inner-city schools, it seems reasonable to conclude that appreciable gains have been recorded in the middle grades in many of those schools.

Mastery Learning

The mastery learning approach, which is being tested in many types of schools at many educational levels, is based on principles outlined by Benjamin S. Bloom.[22] The central argument underlying mastery learning is that 95 percent of students can "master" what the schools have to teach at practically the same level of mastery, with the slower 20 percent of the students needing 10 to 20 percent more time than the faster 20 percent. Although slower students require more time than others to achieve mastery, they can do so if their knowledge level is accurately diagnosed and if instructional materials and methods of teaching appropriate to their level of knowledge are used in a proper sequential manner.

Many students have difficulty keeping up with their regular class because they come with a variety of "entry skills" or "entry knowledge." Bloom says that in such a situation the teacher's task is to find out who the "slower" learners are and where they stand with respect to the knowledge and skills expected of students at their grade level. The teacher then proceeds to teach them systematically from the base of their level of entry skills and knowledge. The most important considerations, he argues, are:

(1) that the student's ability to learn as indicated by the time and effort required to learn a particular set of tasks is highly alterable and (2) that under ideal conditions there will be little variation in students' ability to learn when judged in terms of time and effort required to learn one or more learning tasks for which the students are adequately prepared and motivated and for which instruction is appropriate to the learners. . . . Variations in learning and the level of learning of students are determined by the students' learning history and the quality of instruction they receive.[23]

In mastery learning attention is focused on a unit smaller than an entire course. An entire course, such as fifth-grade reading or the entire reading curriculum of a school, is too complex to be studied all at once with the detailed attention that is needed. Accordingly, the basic unit for mastery learning is defined as a "learning task" that comprises what is "usually referred to as a learning unit in a course, a chapter in a textbook, or a topic in a course or curriculum." Such a task might require from one to ten hours of student time. Bloom and his students have conducted studies indicating that the learning tasks of a school subject can be defined objectively by experienced teachers. Thus a program of mastery learning can be set up with learning tasks defined. Such a program can be studied in a research project and eventually refined and published for teachers to use.

Bloom and his associates believe that quality of instruction should be defined in terms of the cues or directions provided to the learner, the participation of the learner in learning activities, the reinforcement that the learner secures, and the feedback or corrective system that is instituted for overcoming problems arising in the learning process. Bloom cites numerous studies that show substantial gains in achievement by classes where these procedures have been used as compared with conventional classes.

It would appear that mastery learning theory and practice offer particular promise in inner-city schools where achievement levels are generally very low, where students progress slowly, and where the instruction they receive is probably less appropriate than in most other schools. Schools in large cities, and particularly those in the inner city, can provide a good test for the mastery learning approach.

Researchers in the Chicago public schools have been putting together a Chicago Mastery Reading Package consisting of four elements: skill units, comprehension units, enrichment activities, and basal readers. The package was tested for classroom implementation with encouraging results. In an experiment using the first three skills units, each of which included two or three word attack skills and one study skill, tests given after remediation showed impressive pupil gains over initial tests.[24] By September 1975, the package was available for use in all Chicago public schools.

It is equally important that much is being learned about how to implement mastery learning in a real school setting as opposed to highly controlled situations such as those in which Bloom and his associates have carried on their studies. Jeffrey Smith and John Wick report the following conclusions regarding classroom implementation of mastery learning procedures:

1. It is unreasonable to expect a teacher to be able to monitor more than three instructional activities at the same time (even if *all* the teacher is doing is monitoring). . . .
2. Many pupils fail to master skills because they are absent (either physically or mentally) when instruction was initially given. Often these students merely need the instruction to be presented to them in order to reach mastery.
3. Pupils who fail to master after initial instruction often can be brought to mastery quite rapidly if their particular problems with a skill can be specifically identified.
4. Components of a task unrelated to the skill being taught can make the critical difference in student perseverance on a task until the skill is mastered. For example, if a student can cut out cards, work with crayons, or play an instructional game, he may stay with the task longer.[25]

In 1976 Lorin Anderson, Corinne Scott, and Nicholas Hutlock reported the results of an experiment in the Lorain, Ohio, public schools in which students in a mastery learning school learned "an equal or a greater amount of mathematics" and also retained more material and became more homogeneous with respect to mathematics skills than did students in a comparable nonmastery school.[26] Students in the mastery learning school, which included grades one through six, also had more positive attitudes toward mathematics and had more confidence in their mathematical ability than did students in the nonmastery school.[27] The mastery learning school apparently was an inner-city one. The results of the experiment supported mastery learning theory regarding both achievement and attitudes of students taught a specific set of materials with appropriate methods of instruction.

While it is clear from the above that inner-city schools in some cities have shown improved achievement in basic skills in the primary grades, it is also clear that reports of gains in achievement in the middle grades are fragmentary and not well documented. It is still far from certain that such gains can be sustained in even the "best" inner-city schools, much less extended to the majority of such schools located in poverty areas of the large cities.

We do believe that gains in academic performance may be attainable if appropriate approaches are developed for use with educationally and economically disadvantaged students in inner-city schools. We believe that such approaches should at least be characterized by such features as:

1. Early and sustained intervention in the form of sequenced compensatory education that begins at preschool ages and continues through the middle and upper grades. Some evidence also suggests that inner-city students who participate in early intervention programs should remain together in later grades to avoid "washing out" their academic gains in those grades.

2. Carefully structured curricula and instructional methods that emphasize mastery of fundamental skills on a sequential basis, continuous diagnosis and remediation of specific individual learning problems, and reinforcement of success at every stage of the learning process.

3. Constant attention to the ingredients needed to make any major instructional innovation effective: outstanding administrative leadership, close cooperation between parents and the school, continuous staff development related to the goals of the innovation, and built-in monitoring and evaluation as an integral part of program planning and development.

Finally, it should be recognized that the detrimental effects of living and going to school in an inner-city environment may continue to make marked academic gains in the middle and secondary grades difficult or even impossible for many students no matter how much curriculum and instruction improve in inner-city schools. It is possible that community development efforts on the scale of the PUSH Program for Excellence in Education and the elimination of social isolation are also required if academic performance among inner-city students is to continue to improve.

And some improvement in instructional systems is needed whether or not inner-city students attend segregated schools. If they were to continue to attend economically and often racially isolated schools in the inner city, the chances for improving academic achievement would depend largely on systematic efforts to deliver instructional services more effectively. Even if they were enabled to attend schools with meaningful socioeconomic and racial representation and greater progress could thereby be made, major efforts to improve instruction would still be required.

Notes

1. We are well aware that the assessment of compensatory education programs for inner-city students is very difficult. State and national reports, such as Title I surveys, generally do not provide separate evaluations on the performance of inner-city students as compared with economically disadvantaged students in general. Technical problems encountered in the assessment of the impact of compensatory educational programs are so horrendous that some researchers have recommended throwing out the results of most evaluations. (See B. Karsten Tallmadge and Donald P. Horst, *A Procedural Guide for Validating Achievement Gains in Educational Projects* [Washington, D.C.: U.S. Government Printing Office, 1976.]) Even where acceptable evaluations have been conducted with inner-city schools, specific implications for future programming have been difficult to draw because data from "successful" schools are frequently embedded in data from a much larger group of "unsuccessful" schools, with little information available to distinguish the former from the latter.

2. Robert L. Carroll, "Model Cities Money Gone; Blight, Decay Stay," *Kansas City Times,* October 14, 1976, 8D; J. S. Fuerst, "Education and the Ghetto School: II," *Public Interest,* No. 43 (Spring 1976): 60.

3. Urie Bronfenbrenner, "Is Early Intervention Effective?" *Teachers College Record* 76 (December 1974): 279-303.

4. Fred C. Niedermeyer, "Parent-Assisted Learning in the Inner City," *Urban Education* 8 (October 1973): 239-248.

5. Comptroller General of the United States, *Follow Through: Lessons Learned from Its Evaluation and Need to Improve Its Administration* (Washington, D.C.: U.S. Government Printing Office, 1975), 24-25.

6. *Ibid.,* 25.

7. Jane Stallings, "Relationship between Classroom Instructional Practices and Child Development," paper presented at the annual meeting of the American Educational Research Association, San Francisco, Calif., April 1976, 7.

8. *Ibid*.

9. Barak Rosenshine, "Classroom Instruction," in *The Psychology of Teaching Methods*, Seventy-fifth Yearbook of the National Society for the Study of Education, Part 1, ed. N. L. Gage (Chicago: University of Chicago Press, 1976), 368.

10. Carl Bereiter and Siegfried Engelmann, *Teaching Disadvantaged Children in the Preschool* (Englewood Cliffs, N. J.: Prentice-Hall, 1966).

11. District Ten Reading Staff, *Relationship between the DISTAR Instructional System for Teaching Reading and Language and the Continuous Progress Program of the Board of Education of the City of Chicago* (Chicago: District Ten Reading Staff, Chicago Board of Education, 1974, mimeo), 6.

12. Fuerst, "Education and the Ghetto School," 60.

13. District Ten Reading Staff, *Field Experiences to Enhance Reading* (Chicago: District Ten Reading Staff, Chicago Board of Education, 1976, mimeo).

14. A. Jackson Stenner and Siegfried G. Mueller, "A Successful Compensatory Education Model," *Phi Delta Kappan* 55 (December 1973): 246.

15. *Ibid*.

16. Fuerst, "Education and the Ghetto School," 64.

17. Siegfried G. Mueller and Jeanelle Jennings, "The Chicago Child-Parent Center Revisited," *Phi Delta Kappan* 56 (September 1974): 50.

18. Marciene S. Mattleman and Michael H. Kean, "An Urban Pilgrim's Progress: A Retrospective Analysis of a Five-year Reading Plan," paper presented at the annual meeting of the American Educational Research Association, San Francisco, Calif., April 1976.

19. *Ibid*., 4.

20. *Ibid*., 5.

21. *Ibid*., 12.

22. Benjamin S. Bloom, *Human Characteristics and School Learning* (New York: McGraw-Hill Book Co., 1976).

23. *Ibid*., 15-16.

24. Jeffrey K. Smith and John W. Wick, "Practical Problems of Attempting to Implement a Mastery Learning Program in a Large City School System," paper presented at the annual meeting of the American Educational Research Association, San Francisco, Calif., April 1976, 13.

25. *Ibid*., 11-12.

26. Lorin W. Anderson, Corinne C. Scott, and Nicholas Hutlock, "The Effects of a Mastery Learning Program on Selected Cognitive, Affective, and Ecological Variables in Grades 1 through 6," paper presented at the annual meeting of the American Educational Research Association, San Francisco, Calif., April 1976.

27. *Ibid*.

16. Developing and Implementing Big-City Magnet School Programs

Daniel U. Levine and *Connie Campbell*

Five years ago the term "magnet school" was virtually unknown. Today it is widely used to refer to an important movement for the improvement of public schools, particularly in big cities. Senator John Glenn and other members of Congress have been working to provide substantial funding for the development of magnet school programs. A national conference on magnet schools attracted hundreds of representatives of school districts to Houston, Texas, in the spring of 1976. Magnet programs have already been established in Boston, Cincinnati, Houston, Milwaukee, Minneapolis, St. Paul, and St. Louis. Planning groups for magnet programs have been organized in other big cities throughout the country. Few other movements in American education have spread so quickly.

There appear to be at least four reasons for the growing interest in magnet schools. First, such schools are thought to have a potential for reducing racial isolation in large school districts that are confronted with legal pressures for desegregation. Boston, Milwaukee, and St. Louis are implementing magnet programs as part of court-ordered desegregation plans, while Cincinnati, Houston, and Minneapolis moved to establish magnet schools in advance of specific court orders. In either case, magnet schools are offering attractive programs that

will, it is to be hoped, persuade parents to send their children to desegregated schools. Second, most magnet programs offer a variety of options, usually including "open" educational environments as well as
"fundamental" schools that stress structure, rules, and basic academic
skills. Third, the improvement of instruction in big-city schools is a
major goal of magnet programs, Fourth, federal, state, and local funding
is potentially available to support the development of magnet schools.

Magnet schools have been operating in some cities for many years,
although they were not so designated until recently. New York has
long had specialized district-wide high schools in science and in the
arts. Boston's Latin School, which emphasizes academic achievements, has attracted top students from throughout the city for years.
Many cities have offered advanced vocational programs at district-
wide schools similar to some of the high schools now being established
as part of magnet programs.

It is appropriate to ask whether there is anything new about the
magnet school movement. We believe that the present movement is
distinctive. First, it aims to serve a much larger clientele than the selective magnet schools of the past in that it includes programs for av-
erage-achieving students and for students whose special talents were
generally ignored until the recent developments in diversified magnet
programming. Second, it clearly incorporates social goals involving
desegregation and the future of the cities, whereas previously such
goals were seldom considered, much less made explicit. If carried out
successfully on a sufficiently large scale, the magnet school movement
may make an important contribution toward improving the quality of
life in our cities and metropolitan areas.

But expenditures for magnet schools will prove justified only if the
movement succeeds in accomplishing its goals. As with any innovation, there are many ways of mishandling development and implementation, and many problems will be encountered in working to
attain the goals of the program. Our purpose in this chapter is to call
attention to certain considerations that appear to be most important
in planning magnet programs.

ADMINISTRATIVE REQUIREMENTS

We turn first to the identification of administrative and organizational requirements for the successful development of magnet pro-

grams, drawing largely on our study of the program in Houston. The magnet school plan in Houston was prepared by an administrative team of school district personnel. Having been released from other duties, several members of this team were able to spend a considerable amount of time in working on the plan. Team members were knowledgeable about programs and individuals throughout the district and could determine whether magnet concepts might work well in a given school. Team members and other personnel from the central office of the school district were in a position to identify building administrators who could provide strong leadership. Experience has shown that the success of an innovative magnet program depends heavily upon such leadership. Principals must act vigorously to recruit students and faculty, to coordinate schedules, and to solve other problems associated with a new magnet program. It would be a serious mistake to underestimate the importance of choosing outstanding administrators for magnet schools.

What is equally important, the general superintendent, other top-level administrators, and area superintendents in Houston consistently demonstrated strong commitment to the project.[1] They helped especially in persuading big-city principals in the nonmagnet schools not to subvert the recruitment of students for magnet programs. They provided assistance in communicating with potential students. In Cincinnati and Minneapolis also, the superintendents and their key staff members have been closely identified with and strongly supportive of their magnet school programs. The importance of top-management support may seem self-evident, but we have seen many highly publicized and outwardly impressive urban education programs fail partly because the backing of top management consisted only of a formal endorsement followed by continuous neglect.

Resources for Magnet Schools

The development of a successful magnet school program can be expensive. In Houston, approximately $4 million was spent to initiate magnet programs at thirty-one campuses during the 1975–76 school year. In St. Louis, the magnet program was budgeted at approximately $7 million for a maximum of 3,820 students for 1976–77, roughly double the average per pupil expenditure in other public schools in that city.[2] In Boston, magnet school programs are being developed with much assistance from higher educational institutions and from business, at a cost that is very difficult to calculate in dollars. In Chicago, approximately $31 million was spent to build a highly specialized facility for the Whitney Young Magnet High School that is expected to enroll 2,000 students, excluding those in a special program for students with hearing impairments.

It should be noted, however, that much of the money for magnet school programs is used for initial rather than recurring expenditures in order to meet costs for planning and for facilities and equipment. A number of programs, particularly at the elementary level, do not require annual expenditures much in excess of normal costs per pupil.

Sufficient Planning Time

It may be tempting to initiate a magnet school program very quickly in order to alleviate pressures for desegregation and to move rapidly to reduce white or middle-class withdrawal from the public schools. Experience suggests, however, that ample time must be allowed for the development of magnet programs.

In Houston, approximately five months elapsed between the appointment of the administrative team and the opening of the magnet school program in the fall of 1975. Although the magnet schools constitute a small fraction of the schools there and only a few thousand students have changed schools, the plan calls for fundamental changes in instructional arrangements in some of the participating schools. The schools in Houston had already completed a major assessment of needs for each school, in which principals worked closely with communities to identify goals and programs for their schools. If this assessment had not been undertaken and if the plan had involved an integration effort directly affecting a majority of the district's pupils, five months would have allowed too little time for planning. Officials had already had considerable experience in arranging "majority-to-minority" transfers. Many of these transfers of students were incorporated into the arrangements for magnet school programs. Other students were transported by special magnet school vehicles. Had these arrangements not been possible, the number of students transferred to magnet schools might have been much smaller, and transportation would have been less efficient.[3]

A period of approximately six months was available for planning the magnet program in St. Louis, but final court approval was not forthcoming until June 1976, and so recruitment of students for the following fall was not completed until after that time. According to Samuel Miller, executive director of the program, this shortage of time for recruitment helped to explain why the magnet schools opened with an enrollment that was 70 percent black instead of the planned enrollment of 50 percent black and 50 percent white. "If we had done all of our student recruitment during the school year . . . our job would have been a lot easier."[4]

The length of time needed to plan a new instructional program, select and prepare teachers, recruit students, and establish relations with community institutions that can serve as resources will, of course, vary. We believe, however, that the planning of a magnet program for 3,000–4,000 students requires at least nine or ten months of intensive planning.

Publicity

In launching a magnet school program widespread publicity is needed in order to attract students from all over the city and to build confidence among middle-class families in the quality of instruction in such a school. Some cities have gone well beyond usual practices to provide the public with information. In Cincinnati, special packets containing application blanks and listing sources of additional information were sent home to parents. Hundreds of community meetings have been held, and community support groups have been working actively in Cincinnati to explain and seek support for the alternative school programs, partly because district officials have found that grass-roots communication is vital in convincing parents to send their children to schools outside their local neighborhoods. The Houston school district furnished transportation from the central office to magnet school sites for interested parents who wanted to visit one or more programs before enrolling their children. In Boston, material describing the magnet school program was printed in seven languages. In both Cincinnati and Houston, detailed newspaper accounts described magnet programs, and campaigns to recruit students were conducted on radio and television. Without such special efforts neither city would have come close to reaching its goals for recruiting students.

Security

Security of students is an important consideration when magnet programs are located in deteriorated neighborhoods, as has been the case in some cities. Many parents believe that it could be dangerous for their children to attend such schools. Steps may have to be taken to reassure parents that their children will be safe. This is especially true in cases where a select group of students in a magnet program constitutes only a small proportion of the total student body in the building where the program is housed. Magnet schools located in inner-city areas may have to provide supervised transportation if they hope to attract students from outlying parts of the city or from suburbs. St. Louis has established a policy providing for such arrangements: "Students attending the magnet schools will be picked up by specially chartered buses in their neighborhoods . . . and will be transported directly to the school. The buses will be supervised and the children will be dropped off at the school's doorway or within the schoolyard itself. They will be returned home with similar care."[5]

INSTRUCTIONAL ISSUES

The planning of instructional programs for magnet schools raises questions that need to be resolved. Four such questions will be discussed here: How different will the programs in magnet schools be from those available in conventional schools? Will students and magnet programs be properly matched? Will the use of external resources be an integral part of the magnet programs? Will magnet schools be organized so as to promote integration?

Planning for Programs That Are Different

Special purpose schools have existed in some cities for a long time. The Houston Technical Institute (part of the magnet program initiated in Houston in 1975) and the specialized vocational and technical schools in Chicago and other cities are examples. There could be a strong temptation in the future merely to attach the label "magnet" to such schools without making really significant changes that would justify the use of such a label. In other high schools, students could be provided with an additional hour each day for scientific subjects, and the schools could then be renamed "magnet" schools. They would not deserve the designation unless some genuinely innovative ideas were employed to give the science program new strength.

At the elementary level, meaningful efforts have been made in most cities to introduce individualized instructional procedures, but such changes sometimes amount to little more than fancy labels when there has been minimal or no change in practice. We are reminded of the "ungraded" schools and schools with "continuous progress" programs that we have seen in several cities where both staff and students continue to refer to the first, second, or sixth grade and where continuous progress means only that students are no longer retained in a grade because of academic failure. We also believe that some "fundamental" or "traditional" magnet schools publicize their disciplinary procedures to a greater degree than they have done in the past, but do little more than before to provide, as they claim to do, more structured guidance to help students master basic learning skills.

We are concerned, therefore, that attractive new magnet school programs may be designed merely to appeal to modish yearnings for either "free" or "disciplined" schooling on the part of different groups of parents. We fear also that some magnet programs will really not be characterized by the changes described in press releases about them from the central office. Under such circumstances, magnet school programs may generally disappear, as have other highly publicized programs that have preceded them, without having contributed much to the improvement of learning opportunities in big-city schools.

Matching Students and Programs

Big-city magnet programs with which we are familiar place little emphasis on determining whether students are selecting programs that are most suitable for them academically and intellectually. Instead, nearly the entire emphasis frequently appears to be on providing options — options that parents and students may elect to pursue, whether appropriate or inappropriate. The assumption seems to be that parents and students are the best judges of the available alternatives and should be left alone to make their choices. There is, of course, much to be said for enlarging options in schools and for regarding clients as capable of making their own decisions. We do not believe, however, that parents and students generally have been receiving sufficient information and guidance to make wise decisions. We fear, in particular, that too many choices are being made largely on ideological grounds with little attention to the problems and learning styles of individual students. This may be happening among middle-class parents who elect to send their children to relatively unstructured magnet schools of the open classroom type without considering whether the children can function independently in such a setting. It also may be happening among parents who feel that disciplinary practices in local schools are lacking and that enrolling their children in "fundamental" magnet schools will result in academic gains, regardless of how the child might function in this highly structured situation. For these reasons we are not optimistic about the degree to which various types of magnet schools are likely to benefit many of the students who choose to enroll in them.

Several researchers have worked out methods for diagnosing learning differences and for devising differentiated instructional treatments appropriate to such differences.[6] Administrators could draw upon these ideas as they work out their own methods for matching students to magnet programs. Some studies suggest that students of differing social backgrounds tend to learn best in environments specifically geared to their particular learning needs and stages of development. For example, David Hunt and his colleagues conducted studies in which it was found that students with "high" conceptual abilities learned more in relatively unstructured classroom settings than in structured ones. The opposite was true for students whose level of conceptual development was less complex.[7] A disproportionate number of students at the lower levels of conceptual development tended to come from economically disadvantaged families. The findings suggest that instructional programming should take into account the learning styles and cultural backgrounds of students before they are assigned to differentiated learning environments. Robert F. Peck has noted that these considerations are also important across cultures:

There are important differences in the dynamics of the learning process among students of different cultures. No single style of teaching works equally well with all of them . . . . In a ten-year, eight-country study of coping style and achievement, the most outstanding finding was not one of national, sex, or age differences, but the large, systematic deficit in educational achievement of . . . working-class youth in all countries. What is more, the working-class youth showed many parallel deficits in coping skills and in self-esteem in most of the countries. As might be expected, numerous interacting effects were observable with age, sex, and social class.[8]

The magnet school movement recognizes that students differ in learning needs, and magnet schools attempt to provide diversified instructional environments in which these differences can be addressed. Parents should be adequately apprised of the characteristics of the program that may be most suitable for their children. Also, magnet schools should emphasize the development of more individualized programs within each school, such as Individually Guided Education (IGE), Program for Learning in Accordance with Needs (PLAN*), and other instructional systems that may make it possible to select appropriately differentiated learning activities for students.[9]

Utilization of External Resources

One of the important goals of most magnet school programs is to utilize resources outside the school to enhance the interest of students and to improve the appropriateness of instruction. Magnet schools in Boston draw on the resources of higher education and business more systematically than has been done heretofore in large cities. In St. Louis, business has been similarly involved in carrying out several magnet programs. At the High School for Mathematics and Science several firms (Emerson Electric Company, Mallinckrodt Incorporated, and the Monsanto Company), in collaboration with the Washington University Medical Center, are helping to develop and teach new curricula. Numerous cultural organizations, including the St. Louis Symphony, the Art Museum, and the Municipal Opera, are also providing services that help make the two magnet schools for the visual and performing arts more attractive to potential students.[10]

Utilization of prestigious outside resources undoubtedly aids in attracting clients and can improve the quality of instruction in schools. It is relatively easy to assert that a relationship has been established with an outside institution or to send students and staff into the field to learn. It is more difficult, however, to work out cooperative relationships that make these external resources an integral part of a major school program. To do so often requires changes in practices for grouping students, in school scheduling patterns, and in budgeting or accounting regulations, not to mention changes in traditions of school governance and in the attitudes of all participants.

Magnet Schools and Integration

There is reason to believe that decisions about the structure and organization of magnet schools will determine to a great extent the patterns of interaction among pupils. These patterns reveal whether the goals of integration are being pursued intelligently or are being defeated in practice by instructional arrangements that make them difficult or impossible to achieve. If students are grouped homogeneously within a magnet school on the basis of academic test scores and if that grouping separates students of different racial backgrounds for most or all of the school day, it is difficult to see how integration is being promoted. In a similar way, if students in a magnet program are spending most of the school day in a separate wing of the school, the degree of integration in the school as a whole may be minimal. As Elizabeth G. Cohen has pointed out in a review of the research on the effects of public school desegregation on race relations, "knowledge that a school has 20 percent black students tells us nothing about the critical conditions in that organization favoring one type of social interaction over another. The school must be analyzed in its organizational context as an institution which strongly structures the nature of the contact between the races."[11]

Cohen's own research on desegregation among students has been based on the widely accepted premise that intergroup activities are most likely to have positive results when they are based on "equal status" contact. Schools should be examined, she points out, "not so much in terms of racial composition, but in terms of the conditions necessary for 'equal status contact.'"[12] Cohen has conducted a series of laboratory-type studies that examine the behaviors and performance of students in interracial groups. Her results suggest that "expensive and radical changes in the social structure of the school and its curriculum content may be necessary"[13] if the goals of integration are to be accomplished in the schools.

A recent study of a magnet-type middle school illustrates how organizational and instructional arrangements in a magnet school can affect the goals of integration. In that school, organization facilitated integration in the sixth and seventh grades. (In the eighth grade, however, an accelerated academic track was comprised largely of white students, while a regular track was comprised largely of black students.) Some of the administrative and organizational characteristics that contributed to positive interracial contact in this school were described as follows:

School authorities clearly endorse positive intergroup relations and support an extensive program of activities designed to help students get to know one another. The fact that Wexler's students come from 26 different feeder schools is also conducive to the formation of new interaction networks since many children have none of their previous classmates in their new classes. The fact that the school is new has greatly increased the opportunities for students to be cooperatively involved in working for shared goals. For example, large numbers of students participated in the formation of new special-interest organizations and in a variety of fund-raising activities. . . .

Wexler's commitment to fostering equal status contact is illustrated by its staffing. The top four administrative posts are evenly divided between blacks and whites. Similarly, each grade has two counselors, one white and one black. . . . Equal formal status for white and black students is supported by the policy adopted in the sixth and seventh grades of distributing black and white students into individual classes roughly in proportion to their numbers in that grade. [14]

SOCIAL GOALS

Magnet schools are often seen as an integral part of an urban educational program directed toward the attainment of social goals relating to racial and socioeconomic balance in the public schools, to the improvement of educational opportunities for inner-city students, and to the long-range development of the central city and the metropolitan area.

Racial Balance

One of the foremost goals of many magnet school programs is to eliminate or reduce the number of schools where one race predominates. No universally accepted standards exist to define such schools or to determine when a school is no longer racially segregated. For this reason, school officials sometimes have considerable leeway in planning to meet goals of racial balance through magnet school programs and in deciding whether these programs are moving far enough and fast enough in the direction of desegregation to satisfy those goals.

There is, presently, room for debate regarding the impact of existing magnet programs on desegregation, as well as the potential of these programs for reducing segregation in the future. Desegregation goals necessarily vary from district to district because they reflect each district's unique demographic situation and its external pressures for desegregation. It is difficult, therefore, to discuss desegregation in magnet schools in general terms.

In Houston, the magnet school program was initiated voluntarily following the failure of court-ordered arrangements for the pairing of schools — arrangements that clearly had been increasing rather than reducing segregation. In Cincinnati, school officials initiated a large-scale magnet alternative program while a desegregation suit was firmly mired at various levels of the court system. In Milwaukee and St. Louis, by way of contrast, magnet school programs are being developed more directly in response to court cases involving desegregation. One obvious implication is that school officials interested in achieving desegregation through magnet schools should initiate such a program

well in advance of external pressure from the courts and the federal
government. Otherwise, they may lack the time needed for careful
development of such a program.

An examination of the data on the racial composition of enrollments in magnet programs in Houston and Cincinnati can provide
some preliminary indication of the effects of these programs on integration. As Houston officials are the first to point out, the magnet
school program there was not a plan for the racial integration of the
district as a whole. The major desegregation goal, to be achieved by
1977, was to reduce by thirteen the number of schools that had minority or nonminority populations of 90 percent or more.[15] (In 1976, 109
of Houston's 234 schools were predominantly one-race schools by this
definition.) During the school year 1975–76 thirty-four magnet school
programs were established, and, by 1977, 5,000 students were to be
transferred into those programs.

Even though Houston's goal is limited, experience there suggests
that the magnet school approach can help to achieve some movement
toward stable integration in a big-city district. During the 1975–76
school year, 587 minority students (black and brown) and 670 white
students transferred into magnet schools with enrollments between 25
and 75 percent minority during the previous year. Altogether, approximately 4,600 students from a total district enrollment of about
213,000 had transferred into magnet programs as of August 1976, a
figure that was only 400 short of the district goal of 5,000.[16] While
some of these transfers probably are attributable to white withdrawal
from low-status minority schools, they nevertheless represent gains in
integration as compared with the situation that developed in the original plan for paired schools. Only four schools, however, became less
than 90 percent minority or nonminority in 1975–76 as a direct result
of the magnet program—less than half the number Houston officials
had hoped to achieve through the program.

It should be noted also that many of the magnet programs being developed in Houston provide for only limited contact between pupils of
differing racial and ethnic backgrounds. At the elementary level, for
example, students in the cluster magnet schools join students of different racial and ethnic backgrounds for only one week a year; thus the
opportunity for a meaningful reduction in racial isolation is limited.

The pattern in Cincinnati appears to be somewhat similar to that in
Houston. Many of the magnet programs have a good balance of

minority and nonminority students, often approaching a 50-50 ratio, and many of the students in these programs previously were in schools that were either predominantly white or predominantly minority. As shown in Figure 16-1, white enrollment declined at a slightly slower rate in 1975 and 1976, after the alternative program in Cincinnati was initiated on a sizable scale, than in the preceding three years. What is even more encouraging, the Taueber segregation index, which indicates the percentage of students of one race who would have to transfer in order to achieve a racial balance in each school reflecting the district racial balance as a whole, has declined substantially since the alternative program was announced in 1974. As shown in Figure 16-2, the index for 1976–77 was lower than it has been since 1963.

On the other hand, as shown in Table 6-2, in only three of fifty-two schools with a black population of 50 percent or more in 1974–75 was there a reduction of 5 percent or more in enrollment of black pupils in 1975–76 when the alternative programs were initiated. Thus, Cincinnati, like Houston, still has a long way to go in reducing racial isolation and in overcoming trends that have resulted in resegregation of big-city schools during the past two decades.

It must be kept in mind that both Houston and Cincinnati, like many other big-city districts, had been experiencing a serious continuing decline in white enrollment during the late 1960s and early 1970s. Houston Superintendent Billy Reagan believes that the magnet programs can help to stop this decline by offering attractive learning opportunities and by allaying fears that the district would be ordered into forced busing.[17] In Cincinnati, the magnet programs have been credited with drawing 1,076 students back from private schools for the 1975–76 school year, leading Donald R. Waldrip, former superintendent, to observe that investment in the magnet alternatives there "will continue to yield benefits, while an even greater investment in forced busing would lead only to massive flight."[18] The results achieved in Houston and Cincinnati provide encouraging evidence that magnet school programs can help to increase racial integration.

Socioeconomic Balance

To our knowledge, no systematic information is available on the socioeconomic composition of the enrollment in magnet schools in Houston, Cincinnati, or other cities that are developing fairly large-scale magnet programs. Where magnet programs are selective, as

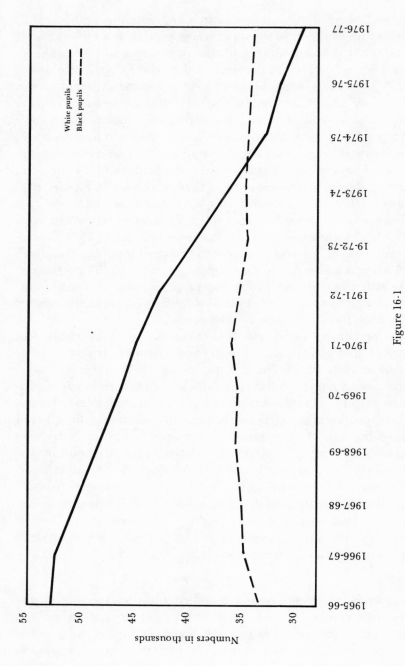

Figure 16-1

Enrollment in the Cincinnati public schools by race and year, 1965–66 to 1976–77 (*Source:* Cincinnati Public Schools)

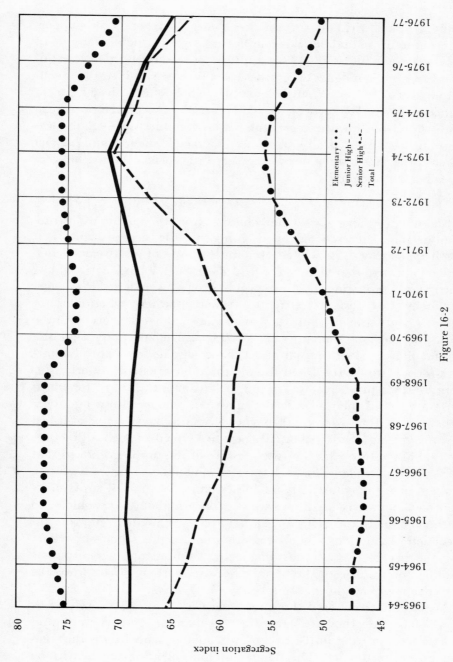

Figure 16-2

Taeuber segregation index for the Cincinnati public schools by level and year, 1963–64 to 1976–77
(*Source*: Cincinnati Public Schools)

many are, it is virtually certain that a large percentage of students come either from middle-class families or upwardly mobile families of low socioeconomic status. This appears to be the case regardless of whether or not a magnet program is racially segregated. At the racially integrated Whitney Young Magnet High School in Chicago, for instance, only a limited proportion of black students accepted for admission come from low-income families whose children are eligible for free lunches. As is true with respect to racial integration, magnet school programs may be providing very little socioeconomic integration on a city-wide basis.

Effect of Magnet Schools in Inner-City Schools

Magnet programs may actually detract from the quality of instruction in inner-city schools by draining off the best students and teachers, leaving those schools even more devoid of positive academic leadership than they were in the first place. Such a tendency could be particularly pronounced with respect to programs designed to encourage inner-city transfers to attractive schools elsewhere, whether or not those schools are officially designated as magnet schools. Monroe Swan, the only black member of the Wisconsin Senate, voted against a law facilitating city-suburban transfers because he felt that the suburban schools would try to enroll only the most talented minority students of the central city — to "rip off the cream of the crop," for which the state would then provide the suburban schools with a bounty.[19] School officials in cities where magnet programs have been established seem cognizant of the potentially negative effects of such a practice. Several officials in Houston, while aware of the problem, hoped that the loss of top students through transfer would allow new leadership to emerge in regular inner-city schools.[20] James W. Jacobs, superintendent in Cincinnati, has also expressed concern about the problem. In both Cincinnati and Houston, efforts are being made to improve instruction in inner-city schools and other nonmagnet schools by reducing the size of classes, providing better equipment, increasing the number of teachers' aides, and otherwise working to improve the effectiveness of neighborhood schools.

We are not convinced, however, that such efforts are likely to be successful unless they are part of a systematic and far-reaching program for improving instruction on a school-by-school basis throughout an entire district. The danger in concentrating too heavily on magnet schools, which are probably the most flashy and salable component of a program for instructional improvement, is that massive physical and human resources will be used for them while other components of such a program will get little attention. If this is allowed to happen, inner-city schools will continue to be undesirable places for learning, and the educational opportunities for young people in the big city will not be markedly better in the future than they are today.

Urban Redevelopment

It is possible that magnet schools may play a vital role in the redevelopment of the inner city and in the conservation of racially and economically mixed neighborhoods by offering the superior opportunities for schooling needed to retain middle-class families in the central city. In Houston, school officials believe that their magnet program has helped encourage movement of young middle-class families into several deteriorated neighborhoods where older but structurally sound houses are now being restored. In Cincinnati, the magnet programs may be contributing to stability in attractive renewal neighborhoods such as the Walnut Hill neighborhood and the Mt. Adams area, which is close to already redeveloped parts of the central business district. Our description in Chapter 9 gives some indication of what the Whitney Young Magnet High School might contribute to the overall renewal of Chicago. But the generalization that magnet schools may play a major part in city planning cannot be viewed as an established fact in any city. Indeed, this generalization can never be much more than a hypothesis until school and other government officials in some city do more to break down the walls that have traditionally separated public school planning from most municipal planning efforts.

CONCLUSION

We have tried to identify some of the key considerations in developing and implementing a big-city magnet school program that not only might enroll a significant number of students, but also might appreciably improve educational opportunities and contribute to improving the overall quality of life throughout a city. On the basis of this analysis, one might construct a continuum for characterizing the seriousness, utility, and comprehensiveness of big-city magnet school programs. The two poles of the continuum could be described as follows.

The Magnet School Hustle

Largely an attempt to satisfy the actual or probable desegregation requirements of a federal court, the magnet school plan is hastily thrown together, and a few hundred middle-class or upwardly mobile low-status students are induced to enroll in it. Much of the program consists of established components given glamorous new labels, and use of these labels makes it politically feasible to divert more resources to schools enrolling a substantial proportion of middle-class students or to schools in which middle-class students are taught separately in a magnet class. A limited number of middle-class families are thereby persuaded to keep their children in the public schools for a few more years, often at substantial costs for transportation and instructional programming.

Meanwhile, a large proportion of students in the central city continue to attend predominantly one-race schools; some of the best students and teachers from dysfunctional, predominantly low-status schools transfer to the magnet schools; and, although a few superficial advantages such as slightly reduced class size may accrue on paper to some of the inner-city schools, the central city as a whole and its school district remain for the most part racially and socioeconomically segregated and continue to evolve still further in this direction at a slightly slower rate.

Magnetization for City Renewal

Before a court order for district-wide desegregation is imminent, school officials begin to develop a magnet school program designed to improve educational opportunity for a few thousand students, to contribute to the redevelopment of the inner city, and to help maintain high-quality neighborhoods in the central city and the metropolitan areas as a whole. Following a year of careful planning, a substantial program is aimed initially at improving the match between the learning styles of students and the public school opportunities currently available to them and at maintaining and increasing racial and socioeconomic balance in schools and neighborhoods. In the following few years the program is painstakingly expanded to include as much as 40 percent of the public school students in the central-city schools.

At the same time, care is taken not to deprive predominantly low-status schools of their best students and faculty, substantial resources are made available and used to support efforts at systematic reform in these inner-city schools, and an overall plan for improving the quality of instruction available to all students in the district is worked out and implemented. Civic and business leaders and other interested citizens are enlisted to support all these activities as well as efforts, where appropriate and possible, to expand the magnet school program to include suburban school districts around the central city. School planners begin to work closely with municipal and metropolitan planning agencies to establish magnet school facilities in present or potential neighborhoods designated for urban renewal or community conservation. By the end of a ten- or fifteen-year period, attractive public school opportunities are available throughout the central city and the metropolitan area, and socioeconomic and racial isolation have been substantially reduced.

This admittedly visionary description of what magnet schools might help to accomplish is far from realization in any big city at the present time. It cannot be achieved, furthermore, unless magnet school programming is explicitly worked out in conjunction with other aspects of educational policy and planning that are mentioned elsewhere in this book, particularly in Chapter 17. Magnet school programs will not by themselves contribute much to the solution of major problems in our large cities, but the degree to which magnet schools are coordinated with educational and community planning will have a major bearing on whether or not the neighborhoods in which they are located will continue to deteriorate or will, instead, constitute magnetic nuclei for city renewal.

Notes

1. A Project Management Committee consisted of the Superintendent for Instruction, the Executive Deputy Superintendent for Instruction, the Deputy Superintendent for General Instructional Services, the Deputy Superintendent for Administration, and the Deputy Superintendent for Occupational and Continuing Education.

2. Martha Shirk, "Board Reviewing City 'Magnet School' Plan," *St. Louis Post-Dispatch*, February 10, 1970, 3A.

3. Daniel U. Levine and Connie Moore (Campbell), *The Magnet School Program in Houston, Texas: A Description and Commentary* (Kansas City, Mo.: Center for the Study of Metropolitan Problems in Education, School of Education, University of Missouri-Kansas City, 1976, mimeo); *id.*, "Magnet Schools in a Big City Desegregation Plan," *Phi Delta Kappan* 57 (April 1976): 507–509.

4. Jeff Gelles, "Selling the Magnet Schools to Parents," *St. Louis Post-Dispatch*, September 1, 1976, 3A.

5. *Ibid.*

6. Herbert Thelen, *Classroom Grouping for Teachability* (New York: John Wiley & Sons, 1967); Bruce R. Joyce and Marsha Weil, *Models of Teaching* (Englewood Cliffs, N.J.: Prentice-Hall, 1972); David E. Hunt, "Person-Environment Interaction: A Challenge Found Wanting before It Was Tried," *Review of Educational Research* 45 (Spring 1975): 209-230.

7. Peter D. Tomlinson and David E. Hunt, "The Differential Teaching Effectiveness of Three Teaching Strategies for Students of High and Low Conceptual Level," paper presented at the annual meeting of the American Educational Research Association, Minneapolis, Minn., March 1970.

8. Robert F. Peck. "Needed R and D in Teaching," *Journal of Teacher Education* 27 (Spring 1976): 19.

9. For descriptions of the most prominent of these types of approaches, see *Systems of Individualized Education*, ed. Harriet Talmage (Berkeley, Calif.: McCutchan Publishing Corp., 1975).

10. Linda Lockhart Jones, "First-day Attendance Off at Magnet Schools, " *St. Louis Post-Dispatch*, September 8, 1976, 1-6E.

11. Elizabeth G. Cohen, "The Effects of Desegregation on Race Relations," *Law and Contemporary Problems* 32 (Spring 1975): 271-299.

12. *Ibid.*, 289.

13. *Ibid.*, 297.

14. Janet W. Schofield and Andrew Sagar, "Interracial Interaction in a New 'Magnet' Desegregated School," paper presented at the annual meeting of the American Psychological Association, Washington, D.C., August 1976, 5-6. See also Janet W. Schofield, "Ethnographic Study of a 'Nearly Integrated' Urban Middle School," Phase 1 Project Report, NIE Contract No. 400-76-0011 (Pittsburgh, Pa.: University of Pittsburgh, 1976, mimeo).

15. "Magnet Schools Short of Goals," *New York Times*, July 25, 1976, 23.

16. *Ibid.*

17. *Ibid.*

18. "Chronicle of Race, Sex, and Schools," *Integrateducation* 14 (May-June 1976): 54.

19. Quoted *ibid.* (July-August 1976): 35.

20. Personal interview, January 22, 1976.

17. Desegregation Policy, Urban Development, and the Future of Big-City Schools

Daniel U. Levine and *Robert J. Havighurst*

During the past three decades the inner core of many big cities has, in socioeconomic terms, become largely low status. In some cities much of the remaining area has also experienced such a change. Racial and economic segregation have become characteristic of the school systems, with a large proportion of pupils attending inner-city schools to which white and black middle-class families are increasingly unwilling to send their children. Where desegregation has been attempted, it frequently has succeeded only in reducing the commitment of middle-class families to the central city and to its institutions. If present trends continue, the population of many of our large cities will become predominantly black and Hispanic as well as low status socioeconomically. Chapter 1 documents fully the process by which these changes are taking place.

Projections of past and current trends, especially changes in population, can be unreliable because the assumptions upon which they are based may turn out to be wrong. Yet studies of the central cities and suburbs that comprise our major metropolitan areas leave little doubt that, unless major economic and educational policies are initiated to arrest or reverse them, the population trends now affecting those areas will continue in the immediate future.

A recent article by Arthur M. Louis cites the "vital statistics" for the fifty largest American cities.[1] A variety of indexes were used to give a composite rating to each city. The best ratings were given to the following cities, which were ranked in this order: Seattle, Tulsa, San Diego, San Jose, Honolulu, Portland (Oregon), Denver, Minneapolis, Oklahoma City, and Omaha. Examining this list, one can see that these "better" cities are all well under a million in population. Louis notes that several of them have expanded their boundaries by annexing suburbs, while others originally included an extensive area of open land that later became suburban in character. He says, "By absorbing suburbs, with their lower crime rates, greater affluence, and better health and housing conditions, a city can dramatically improve its vital statistics."[2]

Moving up from the bottom of the list, the order of the cities is as follows: Newark, St. Louis, Chicago, Detroit, Baltimore, Birmingham, Jacksonville, Cleveland, Norfolk, and San Antonio. These cities received low ratings because of deteriorated housing, high crime rates, inadequate transportation, poor health conditions, inferior education, substandard income, and other characteristics associated primarily with the low socioeconomic status of the population in the inner city. It seems clear, therefore, that the key to correcting conditions in these "worst" cities lies in an attack on the problems of the inner city.

Leaders in city government, business, and education are working to improve the inner city, as are leaders of minority groups. For example, the Reverend Jesse Jackson, the black leader of PUSH (People United to Save Humanity), has called on blacks to take more responsibility for bettering conditions in the big cities, especially for improving the schools. Referring particularly, but in our interpretation not exclusively, to inner-city schools that are predominantly black, he wrote: "It is time, I think, for us to stand up, admit our failures and weaknesses and begin to strengthen ourselves . . . . What we must do for our young people is challenge them to put hope in their brains rather than dope in their veins . . . . Violence against students and teachers, perpetrated by students, is steadily and dangerously increasing . . . . Discipline has broken down. We need to change this because it is necessary for our development [to do so]."[3]

The inner core of the city, with its downtown offices, central library, museums, department stores, theaters, and universities, cannot function effectively unless it is integrated racially and economically. And these facilities, with few exceptions, cannot be dispersed among the suburbs. To prevent the spread of undesirable phenomena associated with life in the inner city over a still larger area, the inner city must be renewed and brought back to full vigor.

Our discussion in this chapter applies primarily to city school districts that have 25,000 or more pupils, including a high percentage of minority students, and that are surrounded by higher-status and largely white suburban school districts. As pointed out by several authors in this book, these central-city districts have experienced a decline in middle-class and white enrollment that appears to be associated with actual or imminent desegregation. Schools in these districts are already composed largely of lower-status students, or will soon become so if desegregation plans are not carefully drawn. The future of the school districts and the cities in which they are located will be dismal indeed unless comprehensive efforts are made to reverse trends that have resulted in segregation by both race and economic status.

Plans for school desegregation in smaller cities and in cities with few low-status or minority students appear to be working quite satisfactorily, but desegregation plans in large cities have not been successful. In this chapter we shall examine some possibilities for redevelopment of the central city so as to achieve stabilized integrated communities, and for metropolitan approaches to planning in order to bring about a better socioeconomic and racial balance than now exists in these areas.

NEEDED CHANGES IN CITIES

Establishing Middle-Income Housing in Inner Cities

In the 1950s, funds were allocated for the building of high-rise apartment blocks in areas with badly deteriorated housing. Such construction was a mistake, we feel, since these buildings, often located in segregated areas, were all rented to low-income families. The policy created racially segregated, low-income ghettos and contributed substantially to the spread of decay in the inner city.

New and well-maintained middle-income housing is essential for a stable community. There are often stretches of vacant land near the downtown area of large cities, some of it formerly railway freight yards, some of it the result of the demolition of deteriorated housing. Several cities are now encouraging private capital to build middle-income housing on such land. If rents are not too high, these areas could provide attractive housing for middle-income families, including families with children. Public transportation would be readily available to downtown areas, thus relieving families of dependence upon automobiles, which are increasingly expensive to operate. A number of other forces, such as rising costs of middle-class developments far out in the suburbs, are supportive of redevelopment of the inner city as a socioeconomically mixed area,[4] where middle-income families may see advantages of living near the central business district that outweigh potential disadvantages.

Stabilizing Middle-Income and Mixed-Income Neighborhoods

During the past twenty years in some large cities a number of residential areas have been populated by black or Hispanic minorities in the low- to middle-status range. Mixed-income groups still remain in traditionally ethnic neighborhoods in the central city. Most big cities also still have at least some residential areas with a substantial middle-class Anglo population, or with a good balance of socioeconomic levels and sometimes of racial and ethnic groups as well.

These middle- and mixed-income residential areas can be expanded by city planning and by investment of private capital so as to increase the stable low- to middle-income population. They may even replace some low-income slum areas, which can happen without undue pressure on the present occupants of these areas because their numbers have already begun to decrease in many cities. A middle- and mixed-income area of this sort may not, however, supply a sufficient number of students of high school age to support a secondary school. Parents must then send their children to high schools that are perceived as having a student body of predominantly low socioeconomic status. Such families are inclined to move elsewhere and are not likely to be replaced by other middle-income families. To counteract such movement, something must be done to make certain that secondary school programs of high quality are available. One of the most promising possibilities is the establishment of attractive magnet schools to which students can be transported without charge. According to James N. Jacobs, superintendent of schools in Cincinnati, the potential market for magnet schools is 20 to 40 percent of the student population of a school district. A magnet program serving that many students could be an important element in helping to maintain socioeconomically and racially mixed neighborhoods in big cities and at the same time help to renew the inner city.

Encouraging Residence in Integrated Neighborhoods

As John Finger notes in Chapter 13, desegregation plans should encourage rather than discourage residence in integrated neighborhoods. Plans based simply on the principle of distributing minority pupils to each school roughly in accordance with the proportion of minority population in a school district tend to discourage neighborhood integration. They require some parents to send their children from "naturally" integrated schools to schools that may be predominantly minority. Such plans, moreover, mean that children in integrated neighborhoods are frequently required to attend schools where the student body is largely of low socioeconomic status or are so perceived. These plans actually undermine the chances for stable integration by encouraging withdrawal from integrated neighborhoods and schools and by discouraging the in-migration of families who might help to stabilize racial and socioeconomic integration.

In contrast are plans that enhance the attractiveness of an integrated neighborhood by assigning students living there to their local schools and that diminish the problems of segregated neighborhoods by transporting the students—white or black, rich or poor—living there to schools elsewhere. If properly designed, a plan based on this approach can help generate wider support for integration in additional neighborhoods and schools. Residents of neighborhoods that are in the present or probable path of growth of the inner city might vigorously support such a policy. Yet virtually nothing has been done in most cities to capitalize on this potential source of support.

Toward the Stable Integration of Schools

Plans for school desegregation can be designed so as to undermine local commitment to schools and neighborhoods, or they can do the opposite. They can ignore common-sense arrangements concerning the assignment of pupils and transportation, or they can minimize the distance a student must walk or be transported to school. They can be implemented precipitously, or they can be phased so as to allow for relocating school facilities, for switching from traditional school buses to minibuses, for establishing new patterns of grade organization, and for other major changes that will make the desegregation plan feasible and even attractive. Care in the development and implementation of plans for desegregation can build confidence in school authorities, while arbitrary decisions aimed only at the achievement of a racial balance in each school approximately equal to that of the district as a whole can destroy such confidence.

The establishment of subdistricts within large cities can provide some of the flexibility needed to move toward more stable integration.[5] In Boston, for example, the goal of racial balance for each subdistrict took into account the fact that it is harder in some neighborhoods than in others to achieve a racial balance in schools that is proportional to that of the district as a whole. In Detroit, where minority students constituted 75 percent of the population when desegregation was implemented in 1975, three subdistricts were left predominantly black in order to allow for a more stable racial balance in the remaining subdistricts. (That arrangement was later ruled unacceptable by the Sixth Circuit Court of Appeals.) In both cities, the involvement of parents and community groups at the subdistrict level probably contributed to a more acceptable desegregation effort than would otherwise have been the case.

It is clear that stable integration of schools cannot occur without formal commitment by local school boards to that long-range goal and without actions demonstrating the strength of that commitment. If there are no such a commitment and no such actions appropriate to it, the public will have little confidence that trends toward segregation will really be reversed, and middle-class families will continue to withdraw their children from public schools perceived as having too high a proportion of students of low socioeconomic status. Among the actions a school board could take would be the establishment of magnet schools and magnet programs that would play an important role in contributing to the stability of integrated neighborhoods, particularly if such schools are part of a larger urban renewal effort.[6]

None of these efforts, however, is likely to prove effective over a long period of time unless the courts are willing to consider both socioeconomic and racial factors in cases involving school desegregation and unless desegregation plans are drawn up on a regional or metropolitan basis. The later sections of this chapter discuss the attitude of the courts on these matters and the need for planning on a metropolitan-wide basis.

The Importance of Socioeconomic Balance

We believe that racial and socioeconomic balance can be achieved and maintained in many big-city schools and neighborhoods. We also think that many families are willing to live in neighborhoods that are integrated socioeconomically and racially and to send their children to schools in those neighborhoods, if they have confidence that a good balance will be maintained in local institutions. That confidence now seems to be lacking.

Socioeconomic balance appears, nevertheless, to be a prerequisite for the successful operation of many big-city social institutions, including the public schools. Major national studies on academic achievement indicate that socioeconomic integration is more important than racial integration in affecting achievement levels,[7] and yet desegregation plans have historically given little attention to maintaining, much less achieving, a favorable socioeconomic mixture. Perhaps this is one reason that research does not consistently show that desegregation is associated with gains in achievement by minority students.

There is reason to believe that big-city schools do not function successfully once they have reached a "threshold" point characterized by concentrated urban poverty and disorganization, perhaps because they are then overloaded with problems that interfere with the accomplishment of their primary purposes.[8] Such considerations seldom have been regarded seriously in planning for urban development in general or for school desegregation in particular. But they are taken into account by parents who see academic standards and performance levels declining in local schools whose student bodies are becoming largely low status.

THE COURTS AND DESEGREGATION

If the above analysis is correct, then socioeconomic balance is more important than mere desegregation of each school so that the composition of its student body reflects district-wide racial percentages. While some scholars have reached this conclusion,[9] the courts as well as school and other governmental officials seldom have been willing to weigh socioeconomic balance in drawing up plans for desegregation in the public schools.

The courts have not considered socioeconomic factors because the Constitution does not address itself directly to prohibiting discrimination on the grounds of social class. In addition, judicial opinion in school desegregation cases has focused on the elimination of vestiges of past practices that denied minority children the chance to attend schools with white children. Case law on this issue seems to have evolved to the point where minority students have equal educational opportunity in constitutional terms so long as they can attend schools that are not more than 90 percent minority in racial composition. It is immaterial that many such schools are largely ineffective partly because they have a preponderance of students of low socioeconomic status or that big-city desegregation plans that have been found acceptable by the courts and federal executive agencies frequently tend to generate a still larger increase in the proportion of students attending predominantly low-status and minority schools. The Constitution has been "satisfied" by a legalistic effort to reassign and transport pupils in such a way as to allow attendance at schools with a small (and frequently temporary) reduction in the proportion of minority students. We believe that the requirements for socioeconomic balance must be introduced in plans for school desegregation if long-range integration is to be achieved in the nation's large metropolitan areas. To do so, however, would require a change in the legal theories used heretofore to decide major school desegregation cases.

One of the few times that socioeconomic balance has been considered as a primary element in planning for desegregation in a big city was in Norfolk in 1968 and 1970. Norfolk school officials had proposed to eliminate as many inner-city schools as possible while desegregating their school system. The plan was challenged on the grounds that it retained some predominantly black schools. Following testimony concerning racial and socioeconomic balance from such witnesses as Thomas Pettigrew, the Fourth Circuit Court of Appeals rejected the school board plan, partly because it retained some predominantly black schools and did not eliminate all inner-city schools.[10] In a subsequent case *(Brunson v. Clarendon County, South Carolina)* Judge Sobeloff referred to Pettigrew's testimony as follows:

[Pettigrew's thesis] is that the value of a school depends on the characteristics of a majority of its students and superiority is related to whiteness, inferiority to blackness. Although the theory is couched in terms of "socioeconomic class" and the necessity for the creation of a "middle-class milieu," nevertheless, at bottom, it rests on the generalization that, educationally speaking, white pupils are somehow better or more desirable than black pupils. This premise leads to the next proposition, that association with white pupils helps the blacks and so long as whites predominate does not harm the black children.

. . . The inventors and proponents of this theory grossly misapprehend the philosophical basis for desegregation. It is not founded upon the concept that white children are a precious resource which should be fairly apportioned. It is not, as Pettigrew suggests, because black children will be improved by association with their betters . . . . School segregation is forbidden simply because its perpetuation is a living insult to the black children and immeasurably taints the education they receive.[11]

The arguments in these decisions should be reconsidered. It is not some inherent superiority among white students that makes segregation in big-city schools so undesirable. It is, rather, the existence of inner-city schools and neighborhoods in which conditions are detrimental to growing up and raising a family. And it is not socioeconomic theory that makes inner-city schools inferior places in which to teach and learn, but rather the piling up of problems inside and outside the schools that educators, parents, and others have generally not been able to solve.

Pursuing this argument a little further, one sees that the courts, not the socioeconomic theorists, have been operating on the pernicious principle that whiteness is somehow superior to blackness by assuming that whites are required—even if only in very small numbers and whatever their social class—somehow to mitigate a stigma alleged to characterize black schools.[12] The courts thus emphasize the principle of classification by race alone, ignoring what actually happens to minority as well as nonminority children in inner-city schools. When applied to big-city schools with a high percentage of socioeconomically disadvantaged students, the argument results in adding injury to insult by moving low-status students from one low-status school to another, neither of which is likely to offer adequate educational opportunity.

The implicit argument, in our opinion, is similar to Marie Antoinette's recommendation to substitute cake for bread. That is to say, if inner-city schools cannot be eliminated, let the minorities have the satisfaction of attending ineffective schools as long as whites also attend. The basic problem, as Michael Novak has pointed out in an essay on busing, is that legal theory does not sufficiently recognize the relationships existing among social class, race, school achievement, and the growth of inner-city poverty and decay:

. . . In the older cities of the northeast, the courts have moved out still further into difficult empirical terrain. In cities like Boston, Buffalo, Cleveland, Providence, and so
forth, it is quite easy to discern relatively segregated ethnic neighborhoods for virtually every ethnic migration into these cities during their long history. In such cities, it is
difficult to show empirically that blacks are more segregated than whites of the same
social class; or that in funding, administration, or quality of teaching, predominantly
black schools are inferior to those of whites . . . . If the courts command busing only
because of the disadvantage of blacks, but do nothing to help working class whites
overcome disadvantage, race seems to have become a decisive reason for judicial discrimination. The social structure of the northern cities has for decades meant relative
educational deprivation, by class and ethnicity . . . . The class structure is built into
the very fiber of the educational structure; the one is almost defined by the other.[13]

Similar arguments can and should be made with respect to racial
balance and the issue of white flight. As Wegmann, Orfield, and
others point out elsewhere in this book, the underlying factor that is
sapping the vitality and threatening the viability of big cities is not so
much the flight of whites as the withdrawal of middle-class whites *and*
blacks from the public schools and other social institutions. In ignoring socioeconomic balance, courts and federal agencies that require
only racial balance have been contributing to the withdrawal of the
middle-class population from big cities and thereby to growth in the
proportion of inner-city schools and neighborhoods. This may avoid
"insulting" minority pupils in the minds of those who do not understand the roots of big-city school problems, but it also locks both
minority and white students of low socioeconomic status more firmly
in the unwholesome environment of the inner-city. The rationality
and desirability of such plans have been assessed by Robert E. Manley,
a respected desegregation attorney in Cincinnati:

The time has come to stop the judicial numbers game. A court that effectively orders
racial balance accomplishes nothing if the middle-class reaction to the coercion implemented by the court results in middle-class flight and leaves the judicially supervised school system occupied mostly by poor blacks and those whites not sufficiently
affluent to escape. The problem is much more complicated than the mere coercion of
racial balance in the school system. It involves very complicated problems of urban
planning and design which have not been adequately addressed by any judicial opinion.[14]

METROPOLITAN REMEDIES FOR SCHOOL DESEGREGATION

Implicit in the foregoing arguments has been the necessity for designing big-city desegregation plans on a metropolitan or regional
basis. Desegregation on a relatively limited basis within the central

city is not acceptable, for such plans leave many socioeconomically disadvantaged students in predominantly low-status schools and neighborhoods that provide inadequate educational and social opportunities.

If one defines elimination of schools that are 90 percent or more minority as the primary target in big-city desegregation plans, it is technically possible to achieve desegregation temporarily in every large city except Washington, D.C. If, however, the requirements of racial balance are set more realistically so as to encourage stable integration with a good mixture of white and black students, and if requirements of socioeconomic balance are added, it will be found that many big-city school districts have too few middle-status or white students to allow for attainment of these larger goals. In the area of Kansas City, Missouri, for instance, two-thirds of the pupils in the public school district are minority students, and approximately 80 to 90 percent of the elementary pupils are now attending inner-city schools. Such circumstances make it impossible to achieve anything but a simple-minded definition of desegregation within the central-city school district in Kansas City.

Metropolitan or regional remedies are crucial to the success of one of the major strategies we have recommended for achieving stable integration in the central city—making integrated neighborhoods more attractive than segregated ones. Manley has noted:

What courts have been doing with many of their orders for integration has been to create product differentiation in the minds of home buyers in regard to different segments of real estate in the metropolitan housing market. When a school system is placed under an order to engage in forced busing for racial balance in its schools, the white middle class and an increasing number of the black middle class differentiate the housing under the jurisdiction of the school system as being so undesirable that they withdraw from the market for that housing. Correspondingly, housing that is located under the jurisdiction of a school board in the same metropolitan community that is not under a court order to engage in forced busing for the purposes of integration suddenly is differentiated as being especially desirable.

. . . Courts will either have to discontinue orders to compel busing for integration in portions of metropolitan areas, or confine their action to those areas where the standards enumerated by the Supreme Court in the Detroit case permit a metropolitan remedy. The economic impact on the housing market of a metropolitan remedy, instead of intensifying product differentiation in the housing market, actually reduces it below the level at which it has traditionally existed prior to *Brown* . . . . This will eliminate a major imperfection in the housing market that existed long before the courts got in the business of integrating schools. It will facilitate the population involution that should lead substantial numbers of affluent families to reclaim the underutilized ring around the center of core cities, and thereby lead to a recycling of cities.[15]

Metropolitan or regional remedies also are desirable from other points of view. For example:

1. Regional remedies can help to minimize inconveniences by reducing the time and distance students would have to travel. A desegregation plan that allows interchange between the outer part of the central-city district and an adjoining suburban district may involve less inconvenience for students and parents than one that transports students from opposite ends of the city district.

2. Regional remedies can allow for the inclusion of integrated or resegregated suburban neighborhoods, thus helping to maintain neighborhoods that have potential for achieving stable integration.

3. Regional remedies provide a larger base from which to attract students and faculty to magnet schools and other special purpose schools, as well as a larger base from which to obtain resources for such schools.

4. Regional remedies may enable central-city school districts in financial difficulties to obtain a more equitable share of funds to bolster local school programs.

5. Regional remedies can reduce the likelihood of overt conflict that often attends desegregation efforts in big cities by bringing more middle-class suburban communities into a plan, thereby reducing the tendency for low-status white groups in the city to feel that the "burden" of desegregation falls primarily on their communities.

Metropolitan remedies appeared unlikely after the Supreme Court's decision in the Detroit case of 1974, but events since that time have shown that such remedies are not out of the question in most metropolitan areas provided that cases concerning them are properly argued in court. One of the key decisions in the Detroit case reads as follows: "Before the boundaries of separate and autonomous school districts may be set aside by consolidating the separate units for remedial purposes or by imposing a cross-district remedy it must first *be shown* that there has been a constitutional violation within one district that produces a significant segregative effect in another district, . . . that racially discriminatory acts of the state or local school districts have been a substantial cause of interdistrict segregation [italics added]."[16]

The Supreme Court has since approved decisions requiring regional remedies in the metropolitan areas of Louisville, Kentucky, and Wilmington, Delaware. Plaintiffs presented evidence in both cases that action by the state had been an important cause of school desegregation in these two areas. One critical element in the case concerning Louisville involved the fact that, prior to 1954, black students from Jefferson County schools outside Louisville were required to attend schools inside the city. The courts reasoned that boundaries of the school district could be considered no more sacrosanct for purposes of hindering desegregation in 1975 than they had been permeable for purposes of enforcing segregation before 1954. Like Louisville, other large cities in the seventeen southern and border states had bused students across school district lines to enforce segregation prior to 1954. Hence a real possibility exists for attaining regional remedies in many of those cities.

The case regarding Wilmington has great relevance for northern and western cities in terms of establishing a precedent for regional remedies. Arguments in that case hinged to a great extent on the issue of housing. The major ruling in 1975 by a panel of federal judges, later affirmed by the Supreme Court, emphasized the fact that state action related to housing had helped to bring about segregation in the city's schools:

The growth of identifiably black schools mirrored population shifts in New Castle County. To a significant extent these demographic changes . . . resulted not exclusively from individual residential choice and economics, but also from assistance, encouragement, and authorization by governmental policies . . . . Prior to passage of federal and state open housing legislation in 1968 . . . racial discrimination in the sale or rental of private housing in New Castle County was widespread, was tolerated or encouraged by the real estate industry, and was sanctioned by state officials.[17]

Since similar discrimination in housing was encouraged by state officials in metropolitan areas all over the United States, effectively argued cases presenting evidence of this duplicity may well win regional remedies in many metropolitan areas in the North and West. In February 1977 the Supreme Court remanded a decision ordering a regional remedy for segregation in the Indianapolis public schools back to the Seventh Circuit Court of Appeals because plaintiffs in the case had failed to prove that segregation resulting from the actions of school officials, governmental housing authorities, and other state agencies had been created intentionally. Future cases will have to present much evidence indicating intent to segregate in housing and school policies if regional remedies are to be ordered by the courts.

We have argued that the central city can be revitalized as a socio-economically and racially balanced area if a high priority is attached to this goal and if it receives central consideration in the development and implementation of plans for school desegregation. The goal may not be attainable, however, unless it is considered in a metropolitan context by both public and private institutions. Schools constitute only one of the factors involved in middle-class withdrawal from the central city, and often only a minor factor. As Wegmann has pointed out in Chapter 1, governmental intervention to desegregate schools has in some instances precipitated white withdrawal. It is equally true that lack of positive governmental intervention in changing neighborhoods surrounding the inner city has been responsible for continuous resegregation.

Governmental action to disperse minority and low-income families into suburban communities is particularly important in connection with efforts to renew the central city. As Manley points out, movement in this direction will "serve as a reminder to the affluent whites that their retreat to suburbs no longer provides the security they sought [and] also will expand the amount of land in the underutilized ring around the center of the core city [that would be] available for redevelopment and rehabilitation to meet the needs and tastes of families with higher incomes."[18]

Public education and housing are two of the most important aspects of urban living with which such planning must be concerned. Inevitably, however, the financing of governmental activities in metropolitan areas will need to be reviewed in order to provide support for the improvement of education and the rehabilitation of housing. State and federal assistance will also be necessary. For example, the state government of Wisconsin is paying the costs of transportation for students who transfer from school to school or who cross school district boundaries to reduce racial imbalance in the Milwaukee metropolitan area. State government has contributed substantially to meet transportation costs in the Houston magnet school program, and special state funds helped bring about improvements in instruction associated with desegregation in Boston.

GUIDELINES FOR DESEGREGATION PLANS

The factors considered in the foregoing pages lead us to recommend the following policy guidelines for developing and implementing school desegregation plans in large cities:

1. Desegregation plans should give equal attention to achieving and maintaining socioeconomic balance and racial balance.

2. Desegregation plans should be developed and implemented on a metropolitan or regional basis and should include at least the first tier of school districts surrounding the central city.

3. Desegregation plans should be part of larger, comprehensive, and long-range programs of metropolitan development involving all levels of government as well as the private sector.

4. Local, state, and federal funding should be provided to support policies required to achieve racial and socioeconomic balance in schools and in housing in the metropolitan area and especially to assist with the renewal of the inner city.

5. School boards should make formal commitments to maintain a good racial and socioeconomic mixture in school populations and to strengthen the quality of instruction available in all schools.

6. Desegregation plans should provide students with maximum convenience in transportation.

7. One aim of desegregation plans should be to make integrated neighborhoods more attractive than segregated ones, by maintaining current enrollments in schools already having a well-balanced student population and by providing magnet school programs and other special services for schools located in integrated neighborhoods.

The broad strategy suggested by these guidelines is based on the assumption that municipal government, public school officials, and civic leaders can and will work together in developing concerted plans to make the city more attractive to people at the middle-income level. It also assumes a substantial effort to bring the central city and its suburbs into close collaboration. Such an effort could take the form of a coalescence of central city and suburbs into a single area-wide or county-wide governmental unit, or it may be limited to closer coordination of the activities of existing governments.

Bold efforts are needed to achieve the kinds of desegregation policies outlined here. The success of these efforts will make possible the survival of big cities and the improvement of the quality of life within them. Failure, on the other hand, can only lead to further decline of large cities and ultimately of the metropolitan areas of which they are a part.

Notes

1. Arthur M. Louis, "The Worst American City," *Harpers* 250 (January 1975): 67–71.

2. *Ibid.*, 17.

3. Jesse L. Jackson, "Give the People a Vision," *New York Times Magazine*, April 18, 1976, 72–73.

4. Robert E. Manley, "Metropolitan Interaction between Housing Markets and School Integration Policies," paper presented at the annual meeting of the National School Boards Association Council of School Attorneys, Miami, Florida, April 1975, 21–22.

5. Desegregation plans based on subdistricts may, however, reduce rather than increase flexibility if they are not properly designed and implemented. It could happen, for example, that pupils near the boundary of one subdistrict would be discouraged from attending a school in another subdistrict where their presence might contribute to stable, long-term desegregation.

6. An example of federal action that would help promote stable integration of schools is the proposal that special tax incentives be provided for families willing to locate in neighborhoods where they would be a racial or ethnic minority. See U.S. Commission on Civil Rights, *Fulfilling the Letter and Spirit of the Law: Desegregation of the Nation's Public Schools* (Washington, D.C.: U.S. Government Printing Office, 1976).

7. James S. Coleman *et al.*, *Equality of Educational Opportunity* (Washington, D.C.: U.S. Government Printing Office, 1966).

8. Daniel U. Levine, Jeanie K. Meyer, Chris Kukuk, Burke O'Hara Fort, Kenneth R. Mares, and Robert S. Stephenson, "Concentrated Poverty and Reading Achievement in Five Big Cities" (Kansas City, Mo.: Center for the Study of Metropolitan Problems in Education, 1976, mimeo).

9. For example, see Willis D. Hawley and Ray C. Rist, "On the Future Implementation of School Desegregation: Some Considerations," *Law and Contemporary Problems* 39 (Spring 1975): 412–426; Alan B. Wilson, *The Consequences of Segregation* (Berkeley, Calif.: Glendessary, 1971).

10. *Brewer* v. *Norfolk City School Board*, 434 F. 2d 408 (1970).

11. *Brunson* v. *Board of Trustees of School District No. 1 of Clarendon County, South Carolina*, 429 F. 2d 820, 824, 826 (1970).

12. It is true that some judges have been relatively clear in basing their conclusions on the argument that de jure black schools reflected inferior status in society and hence had to be at least temporarily eliminated for this indication of historic discrimination to be legally rooted out. Stated this way, the argument is not based directly on the premise that predominantly black schools are necessarily or always inferior or unconstitutional.

13. Michael Novak, "Busing: The Four Regions," *EMPAC!* No. 8 (July 1976): 3–4.

14. Manley, "Metropolitan Interaction between Housing Markets and School Integration Policies," 12.

15. *Ibid.*, 33–34.

16. *Milliken et al.* v. *Bradley et al.*, 94 Sup. Ct. 1069 (1974).

17. *Evans et al.* v. *Buchanan et al.*, C. A. No. 1816–1824 (U.S.D.C. Del., March 27, 1975).

18. Manley, "Metropolitan Interaction between Housing Markets and School Integration Policies," 31–32.